The Practice
of
Communicative Theology

THE PRACTICE
of
COMMUNICATIVE THEOLOGY

Introduction to a
New Theological Culture

MATTHIAS SCHARER

BERND JOCHEN HILBERATH

The Crossroad Publishing Company
New York

The Crossroad Publishing Company
16 Penn Plaza — 481 Eighth Avenue, Suite 1550
New York, NY 10001

Printed in the United States of America

The text of this book is set in 11/13 Adobe Garamond.
The display faces are Adobe Garamond and Optima.

Library of Congress Cataloging-in-Publication Data is available

ISBN 10: 0-8245-2560-4
ISBN 13: 978-0-8245-2560 6

Contents

Foreword

This first English language book on communicative theology owes thanks to many persons. This specific style of doing theology has found its way into the English-speaking world thanks to our American colleagues Bradford Hinze (Fordham University, New York) and Mary Ann Hinsdale (Boston College), who are members of the Research Group on Communicative Theology. They have made substantial contributions to the preparation and carrying through of the two Congresses on Communicative Theology (2002 and 2005) and have energetically promoted the present publication. Bradford Hinze is co-editor with us of the series Communicative Theology—Interdisciplinary Studies in the Lit-Verlag. For the present book, originally published as the first volume of the series Communicative Theology in the Grünewald-Verlag, he has written an extensive introduction addressing the American theological scene. Thus in the first place we extend our thanks to our American colleagues and friends.

The present book is a translation and partial revision of the second edition of the foundational publication *Kommunikative Theologie*. Its translation was the work of several persons. A first draft was done by Cristian Mocanu. This draft was reworked by Anne Kathleen Schaeffer-Dürlinger (chapters 2 and 8) and Thomas Riplinger (chapter 3-7). Our gratitude goes to these translators for their excellent work. The translation was further edited by Teresa Peter and Doris Mairhofer to whom we also express our gratitude. The entire translation was subsequently worked through by Mary Ann Hinsdale and Bradford Hinze, for which we also wish to thank them.

Gwendolin Herder of Crossroad Publishing gladly took up the idea of publishing a translation of this foundational text on communicative theology, and John Jones has attentively and helpfully accompanied the project as editor. To them we extend our hearty gratitude. We hope that our ideas will find an interested reception in the Anglo-American language area.

Bernd Jochen Hilberath
Matthias Scharer

Introduction

Bradford Hinze

The publication of the English translation *The Practice of Communicative Theology* provides an opportunity to introduce the co-authors, Bernd Jochen Hilberath and Matthias Scharer, and to situate their contribution, which has largely focused on Western Europe, in the context of comparable discussions in North America.

Origins of Communicative Theology

To begin, let me say a word about the two authors and their collaboration. Bernd Jochen Hilberath is professor of dogmatic theology and the history of dogma at the University of Tübingen and is director of the Institute for Ecumenical Research. With a background in theological hermeneutics, he has used his teachings and writings to explore trinitarian theology and pneumatology and their significance for communion ecclesiology and ecumenical theology. Hilberath has been actively involved in ecumenical and interreligious dialogues, and his main research project concerns the concrete, personal, and practical significance of *communio* in relation to communication and ecclesial cooperation.[1]

Matthias Scharer is a professor of practical theology in the fields of catechetics and religious education at the University of Innsbruck, where he leads a research team working on communicative theology; this team also works closely with another research team devoted to "Religion-Violence-Communication-World Order." Scharer's approach to religious education is influenced by his research into many forms of pedagogy, group process, and adult faith-formation, especially Theme-Centered Interaction (TCI), as developed by Ruth C. Cohn. He has lectured widely in Western and Eastern Europe, Latin America, Africa, and Asia on this process and has conducted seminars employing TCI. His own approach to religious formation and education has been influenced by the time he has spent in Latin America in base Christian communities.[2]

The collaboration of Scharer and Hilberath began in the 1990s when they came together under the auspices of the Pastoral Theological Institute in the diocese of Mainz, Germany, to discuss the interconnection of dogmatic theology and pastoral theology. Scharer had developed a Theme-Centered-

1

Interaction model of communication and learning in his own approach to practical theology, while Hilberath had long cultivated a personal and pastoral approach to dogmatic theology, reflecting his studies with the theologian Theodor Schneider and his longstanding work on the theology of Karl Rahner.

Scharer's and Hilberath's initial exchanges were positive, and over the next decade they collaborated in the design of workshops that would bring together lay pastoral ministers, priests, and theologians. Their aim has been to address themes of abiding theological relevance and pastoral urgency by integrating pedagogical methods and group processes. Their theology has been guided by their audiences; they work with them to discover what the diverse people in their groups desired and needed as they wrestled with theological issues in their everyday personal lives and in their pastoral ecclesial and pedagogical ministries. For Scharer and Hilberath, the goal of learning theology is not about acquiring information but about exploring the deeper connections of experience and deeply held convictions as these bear on everyday life and practices.

Their teamwork in preparing these workshops provided the context for them to develop the material for this book and to cultivate communicative practices—and thereby to advance a new theological culture. Scharer's great skills at working with smaller and larger gatherings of people enabled groups to create a space for an individual to express his or her identity and struggles and to bring the diversity of opinions to the surface; this provoked discussion and crystallized important issues. These groups likewise fostered deeper relationships and the formation of a group identity and, at times, a collective pastoral mission. Hilberath invited participants to explore their deepest personal convictions and the pastoral implications of Christian beliefs, biblical and creedal traditions, and liturgical practices. In particular, he fostered engagement with the personal and practical implications and interconnections of basic Christian convictions about the Triune God, the human person, the community, and the world.

During the 1990s Scharer and Hilberath developed a series of five-day seminars for persons working in ecclesial communities and in schools. Recurring themes in these workshops include such topics as the importance of relationships explored in light of the profession of faith in the Triune God, how to discern the traces of the Holy Spirit in life and community, exploration of the reasons why young people leave the church, and the place of the Eucharist in the life of the Christian community.[3] The specific design of these week-long seminars stimulated adult learning. The group process is constructed as the week unfolds by a leadership team that is continually responsive to the ongoing suggestions of the entire group and the difficulties it faces. Each day is built around interrelated themes, group communication processes, learning to express one's own position, and learning from others, as well as attending to group dynamics, the role of passionate engagement on issues, and conflict in groups. Participative leadership is given special attention.[4]

The German edition of this book, *Kommunikative Theologie: Eine Grundlegung*, was published in 2002 (2nd edition 2003). Since its publication there have been two conferences on communicative theology. The first addressed the theme "Truth in Relation: The Triune God as Source and Orientation of Human Communication"[5] and was held from February 27 to March 1, 2003 at the University of Innsbruck. The second conference took place in November 2005 in Stuttgart and addressed topics pertaining to communicative theology, *communio* ecclesiology, and ecumenical and interreligious dialogue.

In their respective university settings, Hilberath and Scharer have continued to encourage collaboration among theologians in different disciplines and have offered courses and developed programs aimed at promoting cooperation between systematic theology and practical theology.[6] At Innsbruck, Scharer especially is working with an interdisciplinary group of researchers, primarily theologians with diverse expertise, on a project exploring the potential of TCI to address situations of conflict in order to reduce violence and to explore the deeper theological issues involved. This project draws on a postconciliar theology of the traditional theological *loci* (the *loci proprii,* such as Scripture and tradition),[7] and their relation to the insights and methods of nonviolent peace initiatives, which can be understood also as *loci—loci alieni.* The core question being raised in this project concerns how salvation takes a concrete social shape.

Communicative Orientations in North American Catholic Theology

What is the contribution that Scharer and Hilberath's book makes to theology and pastoral ministry? What is distinctive about their proposals? In order to answer these questions it will be helpful to situate their collaborative effort against the backdrop of the influential approaches to modes of communication in theology in North America. Four orientations to communication can be identified—dialogical, hermeneutical, contextual, and technological, or, more fully: dialogical personalism in the life of faith; a hermeneutics of discourse in the church, academy, and society; communication in the construction of local theologies; and the new Areopagus established by modern communication technologies.

Dialogical

In North America, one influential trajectory in Catholic theology is associated with the tradition of personalism. Here we give special attention to the role of interpersonal dialogue in the internal communication in the church. Personalist philosophers such as Martin Buber and Gabriel Marcel have offered analyses of the role and significance of dialogue, particularly one-on-one dialogue, in the formation of personal and social identity. Various theologians in the second half of the twentieth century began to examine interpersonal dialogue in the individual's life of faith and in the life of the church, as well as in the interaction that takes place in the narrative settings of the Scriptures. This was particularly pronounced in the Protestant neo-Orthodox theology of Karl Barth in his analysis of the place of Jesus Christ in salvation history as witnessed in the Scriptures. Dialogical personalism has likewise been espoused and developed by Catholic theologians in Europe, North America, and around the world across a wide spectrum of viewpoints.[8]

One of the most influential approaches in Europe and in North America is associated with the Catholic *ressourcement* theology of Hans Urs von Balthasar, who combined a personalist approach to dialogue in the life of faith and in the Scriptures with his own appreciation of aesthetic and dramatic modes of communication as reflected in the liturgy and the Scriptures.[9] Likewise, Joseph Ratzinger, now Pope Benedict XVI, has drawn on the personalist insights into dialogue in Catholic theology, which he has traced back to the influence of Plato and Augustine. In his official teaching, Pope John Paul II, influenced by his own background in philosophical personalism, fashioned a distinctive combination of these philosophical and theological traditions, including a personalist approach to the contribution of Thomas Aquinas, which carried on Pope Paul VI's attention to dialogue.[10] In North America, the work of Avery Cardinal Dulles affirmed the dialogical personalism associated with the theologies of Balthasar, Ratzinger, and John Paul II, while combining his own special attention to the symbolic and sacramental modes of communication in Catholic practice.[11]

These personal approaches to dialogue in the life of faith, in the scriptural witness, and in liturgical practices have an abiding significance; and as we will see, they are prominent in a distinctive way in the work of Scharer and Hilberath.

Hermeneutical

The importance of conversation and other modes of communication, especially open, public discussion and debate, among people in various sectors of the church, the academy, and society at large has been accentuated by a group of theologians associated with a second trajectory of Catholic theology that has hermeneutics as its focus. This approach is broadly associated with twentieth-century interpreters of Thomas Aquinas—Karl Rahner, Edward Schillebeeckx, and Bernard Lonergan—who have engaged transcendental philosophy, phenomenology, existentialism, and hermeneutics. Drawing on a transcendental approach to anthropology, these theologians aimed at promoting a deeper understanding of the complex, and at times critical and creative, interaction of texts and traditions by individuals and historical communities.

Lonergan was particularly alert to the issues of communication as he developed an understanding of method in theology in terms of various functional specialties. Stressing the communicative nature of all human meaning and the decisive importance of communication within the historical heritage of Christianity, Lonergan underscored the hermeneutical character of all efforts to gather data, to interpret data, and to judge the meaning and truth of texts and traditions, as well as the decisions and actions elicited by these carriers of tradition. Consistent with the Thomistic structure of disputed questions, discussion, and debate, Lonergan emphasized the need for forthright discussion and debate in theology in order to foster deeper intellectual, moral, and religious conversion and the expansion of horizons in the process of reaching sound judgments and decisions about matters of belief and action. Lonergan identified communication as one of eight functional specialties that constitute the theological enterprise within the church: "Through communication there is constituted community and, conversely, community constitutes and perfects itself through communication."[12]

David Tracy is credited with advancing, in a multifaceted theoretical manner, the importance of conversation and debate in theology and the church, and the importance of theological topics in the wider academy and in society. Here, while continuing the legacy of Lonergan, he moved far beyond it by making extensive use of the conversational approach to texts and traditions developed in the hermeneutical philosophy of Hans Georg Gadamer. Drawing from Paul Ricoeur's philosophy and various theological resources, Tracy posited that conversations regularly break down and are interrupted, so that there arises a need for debate and explanatory theories to address these issues. In his theoretical explorations, Tracy was among the first to give special attention in North American Catholic theology to Jürgen Habermas's theory of communicative competence,[13] while also invoking the earlier Anglo-American tradition of Charles Sanders Peirce, George Herbert Mead, and Josiah Royce, even as he continued to explore a wide range of postmodern theorists such as Jacques Derrida, François Lyotard, and Emmanuel Lévinas.[14]

Contextual

Reflecting the achievements of liberation theologians in Latin America and inculturation theologians in Africa and Asia, Robert Schreiter advanced a pioneering analysis of the concrete practices of communication in the development of local theologies.[15] This contextual approach represents a third trajectory. The singular contribution of Schreiter has been his combined attention to contextual issues of local evangelization and the promotion of justice and reconciliation in situations of conflict employing a semiotic approach to culture. He promoted a fuller understanding of the interactive communicative role of the entire believing community, small groups, and individual theologians, prophets, and poets in the construction of local theologies. His semiotic approach to culture showed appreciation for various interrelated levels of communication: *syntactics*—the grammar-like rules that function in the relation of signs; *semantics*—the content or meaning of the message, and *pragmatics*—rules that govern communication in the range of meanings. Schreiter has been especially alert to the dynamic interaction at the boundaries of cultures and to the introduction and transmission of religious traditions as bearers of communal identity and as agents of communal change.

The interest in the development of local or contextual theologies, which marks this third orientation, is shared by a wide range of thinkers who have diverse governing theological commitments and draw on various allied disciplines and theories. Stephen Bevans's work has been particularly helpful in identifying various models of contextual theology around the world and in North America.[16] Analyzing the contextual character of theologies includes for him not only a treatment of culture but also personal and collective experiences, social location, and social change. These contextual matters are explored in relation to experiences of the past reflected in Scripture and tradition.

Contextual theologies have taken on numerous concrete forms in North America, reflecting the experience of distinctive cultural groups. Black Catholics have called for remedial communication with the descendents of Africa in response to the aftermath of the slave trade and ongoing practices of racism in the church and in society.[17] Hispanic immigrants from Latin America have wrestled with basic questions about the power of language, and local cultures and traditions of popular religiosity as a source of memory and identity and as ingredients in an unfolding living tradition.[18] Besides facing prejudice and economic hardship, newer immigrants from Asia have been keenly aware of the influence of diverse religious traditions, such as Islam, Buddhism, and Hinduism, on their own identity and on the dynamics of ecclesial, economic, and political life.[19]

In their own way, each of these groups, joined by other new immigrants from the Caribbean, the Middle East, and Eastern Europe, has raised major concerns in contextual theologies about the problems of "misunderstanding" in intercultural communication.[20] For dialogical personalism, the problem of misunderstanding is about overcoming obstacles and limits in knowing another individual and oneself. For the hermeneutical approach, individuals and groups must face recurring misunderstandings of texts and traditions. For these particular forms of contextual theology—Black, Hispanic, Asian, among others—misunderstanding is a question of prejudice against linguistic, cultural, and religious traditions, which contributes to economic and social hardship, and all too frequently results in conflict and violence. These various groups have sought to answer this question: How can the challenges of intercultural communication be faced so that what can be the source of enmity and conflict may be recognized and received as gift and blessing?

Consistent with the efforts of those concerned with constructing local theologies is the work on religious education espoused by Thomas H. Groome, among many others. Drawing on Jürgen Habermas's earlier work on the relation of theory and practice, and on Paulo Freire's praxis-based pedagogy, Groome advanced what he called a "shared Christian praxis" approach to religious education and pastoral ministry.[21] Dialogue among members of a community is the basic communicative context for his approach. The dialogical engagement of community members is concerned with the praxis of everyday life. People must be invited to share with members in community their own personal stories and vision, to discuss the Christian narratives and visions, and to enter into collective discernment and decision making as one's personal stories and visions are interpreted in light of the Christian stories and visions.

Technological

In addition to these three main trajectories of theology in North America, there have been various efforts by people with diverse expertise to address the issues related to communication, the church, and theology.[22] Paul A. Soukup has offered an analysis of the research done on communication and theology based on six aspects of the communicative process: "as language, that is, a structured system of conveying meaning; as aesthetic experience; as creation of culture; as interpersonal dialogue; as sender-receiver or rhetorical communication (the broadcasting model); as theological analogue, that is, modeling human communication on the divine."[23] These various approaches are not integrated. In keeping with newer mediums of communication, what John Paul II has called the new Areopagus of the modern age,[24] Soukup has been particularly concerned about the church's practice of using new communication technologies (including radio, television, film, and Internet) without a theory or theology to evaluate the use of such means. "Little theological reflection on communication has sought a comprehensive understanding of communication; most has examined only aspects of communication, or examined communication from restricted ecclesiological stances."[25]

On what basis—according to which principles or orienting frameworks—should the various means of communication be guided or evaluated? Consider, for example, the problems raised by the fact that, given the open-access and democratic character of the Internet, a Web site or blog can easily present itself as an official or authoritative interpretation of church teaching when it is not. A poorly designed or out-of-date parish Web site can repel young people who are searching for a church, while certain Web sites and blogs are spending a great deal of energy and resources to appeal to young people. If we step back from these particular situations, we need to ask what does theology have to contribute to ongoing reflection on communication? Soukup specifies three specific goals. First, there is a need to "establish some theological touchstones for the churches to use in judging their use of the means of communication,"[26] mindful of the fact that there is a correlation between certain ecclesiologies and communicative practice. Second, there is a need for guidelines to evaluate the means and the content of the communication from a Christian ethical perspective. Third, there is a need to cultivate a more advanced understanding of the process of communication, the myriad facets in the world of communication, and the various technological modalities. At each level there is a need for theological rigor and an honest appraisal of the process and instruments of communication. What is ultimately required, Soukup argues, are methods for studying communication and theology.

The consideration of these four trajectories could be enlarged, if space permitted, to include the distinctive contributions made by Africans, Asians, and Latin Americans, which have also had a profound impact on North American theologies. In the cases of these contributions from the Southern Hemisphere, the deliberations of episcopal conferences and synods of bishops have worked in tandem with theologians in efforts to develop hybrid approaches combining the first three orientations—dialogical, hermeneutical, and contextual—suited to their own settings, but also with far-ranging implications for developing the communicative competence of the church universal.[27]

Distinctive Agenda of Communicative Theology

Hilberath's and Scharer's communicative theology shares certain convictions about communication with these four trajectories in Catholic theology in North America: with the first, the importance of interpersonal dialogue in the church; with the second, the role of the wider conversations, disputed issues, and debates in theology and in the wider academy and society; and with the third, the urgent need to advance communal processes of developing local, contextual theology. In conjunction with the fourth trajectory, they acknowledge and are concerned about the wide range of communicative means and methods and media in the church—both information-based and nonverbal — as they accentuate the importance of group processes.

The self-communication of God and the relational understanding of God's identity and mission in the world, and communicative character of the human person and God provide the crucial anthropological and theological framework for their work, especially as these present the battleground for false individualistic views of the human and the false isolating gods of the marketplace. The human person and God offer the context for their argument about the communicative character of God's revelation in history and in the church as a communion. This theological vision makes available a framework and justification for their approach to the process of communication in the church in terms of Theme-Centered Interaction (TCI). It is their distinctive development of this TCI approach, which they have initially developed from the psychoanalyst and social-education theorist Ruth C. Cohn, that most strongly differentiates their method from others.

What I believe is most important about the work of Scharer and Hilberath, and with them the Communicative Theology Research Group, is that they are experimenting with and reflecting on group processes that promote personal and collective discernment and decision making in the church.[28] Their main achievement is that they have developed a theologically integrated approach to group communicative practices. The reason this work is so important and timely is that it speaks out of the word and the spirit of the Second Vatican Council. Moreover, communicative theology embodies some of the most important insights derived from the practices of Base Christian Communities and Small Christian Communities that are developing all over the world and that provide the basic building blocks for any church renewal and reform and engagement with pressing social and political issues. What may be the most promising contribution of communicative theology is that it sheds light on what should be some of the basic ingredients involved in conciliar and synodical forms of discernment and decision making in the church—about its identity and mission in parishes and dioceses, as well as nationally and internationally.

CHAPTER 1

Theology as Process

Communicative theology is theology done in and from a living process of communication. In the present chapter, the arguments for doing theology in this way will be developed by exploring the notions of *theology* and *communication*.

I. "Communicative Theology" Not Just a Tautology

To call theology "communicative" may seem just a restating of the obvious. Paul Watzlawick's statement that "humans cannot *not* communicate" is true also for theology; in other words, theology *must* be communicated. Of course, traditionally theology has had a great deal to do with books (to the point that the length of a bibliography and the number of footnotes are sometimes taken as indicators of a book's seriousness). Thus, writing and reading appear to be the two communicative actions of theological science. Here, to be sure, something important for theology comes to the fore, and it ought to be made public. Indeed, the title *professor* is derived from the Latin verb for "speaking publicly" or "proclaiming a belief."

At the same time, however, while writing and reading are important, they basically represent secondary communicative acts. The primary act of theological communication often refers to public speaking. (In fact, the German term for lecture, *Vorlesung*, refers both to reading and hearing because *Vorlesung* literally means reading before an audience.) Thus, the primary act of theology may seem asymmetrical in principle—with one person reading out and the others receiving as listeners in an auditorium. This asymmetrical relationship has deeply influenced many people who do theology either as students or professionally. In one of our classes, an articulate and experienced grammar school religious education teacher said: "I would never have dared to formulate a theological position on my own. Whenever I tried, I would remember my professors and all the theological books I read. I was trained to go there for the information."

In light of this example, we need to ask whether lecturing is a relevant practice. As an institution, lecturing comes from a time when there were few books. In an electronic age when information can be obtained in so many ways, one wonders whether we should give big public lectures anymore.

From the viewpoint of a communicative theology, we are not primarily concerned with increasing the efficiency of theological lectures, nor do we want to do away with them and find another more effective form of this communication. More important than questioning the methods and means of mediating theology, our fundamental concern is the connection between the way theology is mediated and its subject matter[1]—questions that show up, among other places, when one moves beyond the principal distinction between lecturers and listeners. Our main concern is to give a new definition of the subject of theology in whose framework a lecture can again be given its proper place.

So doing communicative theology does not mean changing the lecture hall into a chat room nor reversing the relationship between teachers and students on an ideological basis of egalitarianism. It is much more a question of taking into account the fact that teachers are also learners and that learners provide the teachers with something to teach. This means more than the frequent advice teachers are given to "meet people where they are." Such advice still regards people as passive learners. When those who "know it all" come to meet people "where they are," then the latter are at best in the position of subjects receiving knowledge. In this model of communication, teachers still appear as experts in the teaching and learning situation with prepackaged courses that they need only to unpack, lay out, and explain.

Again and again, in talking with teachers and pastoral ministers, one hears the phrase "forget all that academic theology you learned." This statement is not just false, it is also unfair if it is understood one-sidedly as meaning the complete inadequacy of theological education. On the basis of our own experience, we believe the statement is unfounded, although we certainly do not want to pass over the problem in silence. If a student's experience is really that one's theological education is inadequate and this becomes an overall prejudice, then one might also question the quality of the modes of communication in theological education as well as the attitudes of teachers and students. Take, for example, persons who want to become qualified as quickly as possible for teaching or pastoral work. For them, theology is a necessary evil, and the phrase "you can forget all that academic theology" becomes an excuse to avoid dealing with issues concerning theology and communication. On the other hand, research into the efficiency of theological-education institutions warns us of the need for some self-critical reflection. It is neither a question of "meeting people where they are" nor of simply asking people to do what fits in smoothly with their experience, the traditions they have inherited, or the patchwork religious world they have created for themselves. For communicative theology, in the lecture hall and elsewhere, it is a matter of taking seriously the fact that people are involved in reciprocal relationships and have distinctive though not firmly fixed roles.

The adjective "communicative" therefore highlights something that is actually already contained in the word theology. So again, is the term "communicative theology" redundant? Our answer is that it is worthwhile to avoid the mistaken impression that we are only stressing that the findings of theology need to be communicated, that is, passed on. In fact, communicative theology, rightly understood, is directed precisely against the distinction between content and its application. Here two points should be borne in mind: on the one hand, the application, at least in qualified communicative forms, is already part of the content, and, on the other hand, the content itself cannot be constituted without a communicative act. This means a completely new and specific definition of the relationship between theory and practice, between theology and a life of faith. Since this is something to which people are not accustomed, misunderstandings are unavoidable. The task of this book is as far as possible to make people aware of these misunderstandings from the start.

To express it formally: theology is not "some thing" that then is to be communicated; rather, *communication* is the central content of theology. So communication is neither a thing added or applied to theology nor a substitute for what theology should really be. Theology is itself a communicative event, and when it no longer is this it stops being theology. This thesis, certainly unusual and perhaps jarring to many, presupposes a particular understanding of communication on the one hand and of theology on the other.

II. Then What Does Theology Mean?

When we ask "Then what does theology mean?" the most important word is "then." Our task here cannot be to propound a theory of theological science. It is much more a question of broadly indicating what is meant by the concept of communicative theology in the light of the presuppositions already introduced in the first section.

The very fact that we frequently ask "What is theology?" shows how far from self-evident the nature of this endeavor is, this "word" about "God" (*theos* + *logos*). There are many possible answers to this question. In the sphere of Western culture the particularity of Christian theology can be broadly indicated if we contrast the Greek and the biblical understanding of theology and the understanding of God and truth on which they are founded.

Looking at the world of Greek spirituality, we can distinguish three stages in theology. Analogous to the spirituality of ancient Rome, these three stages followed on one another over time in well-defined forms and existed alongside one another as mythical, philosophical, and political theology. Essentially, philosophical theology develops out of a critique of mythical theology. The overly anthropomorphic tendency in mythical theology leads to the desire for a "purified" understanding of God. The philosophical theology that results has its place in spiritual as well as social history since it emerges from the context of the *polis*. This social aspect appears even more strongly in the so-called political theology of antiquity since, to put it simply, it constitutes the ideology of the *polis*, the city-state, and the (Roman) empire.

For the sake of our argument, the most interesting stage is that of philosophical theology insofar as it presents itself, despite its specific historical context, as more independent than the forms of theology that arose in biblical places and in biblical times.

The timeless, though certainly not absolute, character of Greek philosophical theology is essentially related to the so-called Hellenistic concept of truth. While we should avoid abstract contrasts between Hebrew and Greek thought, it is true that history is not a locus of the divine in Greek philosophy; rather the divine is characterized as absolutely transcendent, simple, and unchangeable, as well as free from passion and suffering. Much the same is true of the divine's independence of place. No philosophical theology became a theology of the *polis*, or of a group inside the *polis*, to the extent that it has in Christian communities or in the church.

The Bible highlights a vastly different understanding of God. In general terms, it may be said that Yahweh as the God who will be with us—and "with us" precisely in God's absolute transcendence—wishes to be, and can be, a God involved in human history. The theology of the Trinity, clothed as it is in homiletical and catechetical language, is precisely the product of the biblical and Christian opposition to Hellenistic thought. Unfortunately, it often appears to people as a kind of higher mathematics. Specifically, trinitarian theology thinks simultaneously in terms of transcending time and being powerful in time, of transcending history and being powerful in history, and articulates eternity as the fulfillment of time and of humanity, not as the disempowerment of the divine. God can enter history without ceasing to be God; humans do not become less but more human the nearer they come to God. Thus, Christians are able to see the trinitarian concept of God as consistent with monotheism because for Christian thought the relativity that is necessarily part of history becomes a category of existence rather than simply the accidents of chance and their consequences. To be sure, this Christian understanding of God, endorsed by the Council of Nicaea in 325 C.E., was often obscured in the succeeding centuries by an overly vigorous adoption of Hellenistic categories of thought. Fundamentally, Nicaea marked the "Copernican revolution" in the understanding of reality insofar as the Christian understanding implies a relational ontology, that is to say, a perception of reality (of "that which is") in a perspective of relationships.

The biblical God's power in time corresponds to God's power on earth. So the earthbound character of Christian theology is founded in the fact that the Christian God is a God who wills to become human, who wants to come among the human race. This attachment to place thus means that Christian theology exists because a believing community exists. Theology springs from the consciousness of and the reflection on one's own lived faith (consciousness and reflection that turn out to be necessary from the beginning) in the interest both of internal clarity and of making this faith plausible to others.

If people nowadays sometimes get the impression that theology looms threateningly over lived faith, then the relationship we have just described becomes severed or at least interrupted. In denouncing this status quo, theology needs to demonstrate to itself that what is at stake here is not only something that affects the mere application of theology—this too must be taken into consideration, of course—but something that goes to its very heart: Christian theology fails itself if it does not remain oriented to the lived faith of the church as the community of believing subjects.

Theology is reflection—reflection on the lived faith of the church in its many dimensions. From its origin it has been determined by communicative relationships, and it is unthinkable without them. Theology is not merely a duplication of what happens in God's kingdom in the form of witness (*martyria*), service (*diakonia*), and worship (*liturgia*), and in the practice of individual parishes and in the wider church. On the contrary, it is reflecting, thinking critically, testing, investigating, making plausible, explicitating and, one hopes, inspiring this communicative practice of faith.

Questions for Reflection

- How have you "learned" theology?
- What image of theology influences your thinking and action?
- Where and how do you experience theology as a communicative event? Where and how do you not experience it this way?
- In which events, encounters, and experiences were you patronized theologically? And in which were you recognized as a person?
- Are there traumatic (or liberating) experiences in your theological biography? If so what are they?
- How do you see and experience the connection between theology and the lived faith in parish or church?

III. The Specific Character of Communicative Theology

The practice of faith as the point of departure is the permanent reference and ultimate goal. But why should we call this practice of faith a *communicative* practice?[2]

In discussions in parishes and at the local level, and among theologians, the different uses of the word "practice" repeatedly lead to misunderstandings. Some see all theory as fundamentally inimical to practice while others fear that the discussion of "practical matters" will undermine a scholarly approach to theological theory. We seem, therefore, to face a hard choice between lived reality and theory.

The alternative, however, is skewed. In the aftermath of the Second Vatican Council, people would typically discuss questions that presupposed certain alternatives. One characteristic question was: Do the laity have a share merely in the church's service to the world, or do they also have a share in its work of salvation? According to the Second Vatican Council, we have to say that everything that Christians do because of their faith is a work of salvation. When it proceeds from faith, service to the world is a work of salvation. So, with regard to this study, we may hold fast to the fact that by the word "practice" we understand everything relevant to faith that is done by Christians or, indeed, by any human person. We therefore start from a concept of practice that embraces the relevant experiences of human beings, particularly those of members of the church and of theologians.

Theology is frequently referred to as "the science of faith." This expression can be misleading, however, because it is often understood as an exercise in cognitive knowledge in a highly restricted sense. In this case, faith is understood exclusively as the intellectual assent to propositions. Faith in the comprehensive sense is what we have just explained as practice: the life and actions of Christians as believers. In fact, theology could be designated the science of the practice of faith. The expression "communicative theology" recommends itself as a way of avoiding, on the one hand, misunderstandings of the expression "science of faith," and, on the other hand, the cumbersome expression "science of the practice of faith."

At this point, we must begin to explain what "communicative" means in this context. In chapter 2 we offer a preliminary description of the meaning of communication in the context of society and the church today. At this point, let us begin with a distinction drawn by the philosopher Jürgen Habermas. Habermas, who has increasingly been exploring the significance of religion (its modes of expression, not its truth content) for human practice, makes a distinction between instrumental and strategic action, on the one hand, and communicative action, on the other.[3] They are distinguished from each other by the type of rationality and the goal to which each lays claim: in the first case, it is a matter of instrumental *decree*; in the second, of communicative *understanding*. There is a wide array of forms of communicative action. The decisive criterion for a Christian *communio* is its orientation toward both verbal and nonverbal communication as this shows itself in a concrete *communio*.[4] This means that no possible action is ruled out as irrelevant from the start; rather, the criterion of the quality of an action is its relation to communication inside the community.

Of course, from this perspective it is clear again that communication cannot be reduced to verbal expressions. Everything that works toward establishing, maintaining, and perfecting the faith community is to be described as communicative action. (This broad definition already suggests that from the perspective of the *communio* of believers, there are also communicative actions whose subjects need not or cannot be human beings.)

A classification of communicative acts in the faith community in their order of importance cannot be undertaken by individual human subjects in the community. (It is part of the self-understanding of this faith community that those communicative actions that have God as their author must be clearly distinguished.) The importance of a particular action depends not on who performs it but what end it serves. In this sense one can distinguish communicative actions of a special kind in the field of communicative praxis. In a particular comment on the use of speech as we have just described it, Peter Hünermann speaks of communicative acts that every social group needs for its own preservation. As he puts it:

> Communicative actions differentiate themselves from other actions by the fact that they are directed towards other people and involve them in their historical freedom in action. Among the many kinds of communicative actions are a few that are constitutive for a particular group. In and through the performance of these actions the group comes into being and preserves itself. Without these communicative actions there would be no group. These constitutive actions become metaphors of living together. It is only through these metaphors that such a form of life can come into being. Only in an ever-renewed acting out of this metaphor of life does it continue to exist.[5]

It is not surprising that Peter Hünermann chooses this anthropological approach to elucidate what we understand as sacrament. Sacraments are specific communicative actions that are constitutive for the faith community. That is to say, a faith community that no longer meets for prayer and the celebration of the sacraments is undermining itself from within. But the sacraments in particular make clear again that constitutive actions are actions that serve the building up of the faith community in an all-inclusive, holistic way. Through communicative actions, people help one another to become truly human.

We are calling our particular way of doing theology "communicative theology." Since there is communication in all theology, "communicative theology" embraces everything that relates to theology in any way. But not every theology is directed toward the communicative faith practice of the people of God; not every theology explicitly makes this process of communication the benchmark for its thinking. While it is true that the concept of communicative theology embraces all areas of theology, it does not replace other approaches such as liberation or feminist theologies. The reason for this lies in the *perspectives* that these other theologies bring into the whole of theology.

Thus, for example, in liberation theology a certain perspective is opened on the task of theology, and a communicative theology certainly does not rule this out when it considers the matters that come up for discussion in relation to the God who sets us free. In fact, liberation theology makes tangible something written by Thomas Aquinas (who was again recommended as a master of theology by the most recent Vatican Council)[6]: Theology should treat all things as *sub ratione Dei*, in the light of God. Theology as the *logos* of *theos*, as "talk" about "God," does not speak only about God, but in the truest sense of the word, about God and the world—about the world, but from God's perspective. Liberation theology does this in the perspective of a liberating God; feminist theology above all in the perspective of women's experience of God. At times there are historically conditioned situations that have the effect of steering the work of theologians in a particular direction. Karl Rahner's transcendental theology was an attempt to surmount neoscholastic theology, which had become sterile, by asking what are the conditions of the possibility for humans to believe.[7] *Transcendental* is the technical term for these reflections on the conditions of the possibility: what can move the human being, in his or her experience of the self and self-fulfillment, to credit a belief that God has become human?

Another important form of theology in the twentieth century was dialectical theology, principally founded by Karl Barth.[8] Following the breakdown of cultural Protestantism and liberal theology, and the consequent collapse of particular expressions of Western culture after the First World War, Barth put the stress on the radical difference between God and the human race, on humankind being radically at the mercy of God. He called the tensions between God's "yes" and the human race's "no" "dialectical." At least in the early phase of dialectical theology, Barth saw in religions the futile and, what is more, sinful endeavor of people to reach up and come close to God. God's revelation says a radical no to every human religion, and this is why Barth thought for so long that he must state that there is no point of contact between human beings and God's revelation. Later he had to revise his viewpoint, for God's revelation naturally needs to be addressed to someone, the person to whom God reveals God's self. So human beings at least must be constituted as recipients of the message. The reason for our brief excursion into the history of theology is that here, too, we see how indispensable it is that the concept of communication be understood as a connection between subjects if we are to understand theology and what happens in theology.

Communicative theology is, accordingly, theology that the communicative practice of the *communio* of believers reflects. Such a theology must itself be understood as a communicative event. This does not exclude the fact that hard work at one's desk, in the library, or in the archives is just as necessary. But when one takes an overall view of theology, all individual pieces of work combine in the communicative acts such as meeting, discussing, and debating.

Questions for Reflection

- In your opinion, how do the various theologies differ?
- With which theologies were/are you confronted in your studies and practice?
- What insights are opened for you by the distinction between communicative theology and other theologies?
- To what extent has your theology always been "communicative"?

IV. How Does Communicative Theology Work?
A Preliminary Observation

As we have seen, theology as "speaking of God" is, in the Christian sense, always also speaking of human beings. It is speaking of human communicative actions in relation to the God who has revealed God's self in many ways and finally in Jesus Christ. We can also put it like this: the subject matter of theology is the activity of communication that derives from belief in the one and Triune God, who in essence is relationship and who communicates God's self. This remains true even if the Christian perspective of hope can only implicitly inhabit human communication, or if the actions of Christian faith fall short of their inherent communicative potential. In this sense, one can describe theology as a way of understanding and explaining what is worthy or unworthy of God and humankind by means of human communication, and what power of communication is indeed given in Christian belief.

The question of *how* Christian theologians arrive at their "communicative" knowledge, that is to say, at their theology, is inseparably bound up with the object of their knowledge: with the God who became human in Jesus Christ, who reveals the divine self to women and men, who dwells within them as primal source of life and enables them for comprehensive acts of communication.

In His goodness and wisdom God chose to reveal Himself and to make known to us the hidden purpose of His will (see Eph. 1:9) by which through Christ, the Word made flesh, man might in the Holy Spirit have access to the Father and come to share in the divine nature (see Eph. 2:18; 2 Peter 1:4). Through this revelation, therefore, the invisible God (see Col. 1:15, 1 Tim. 1:17) out of the abundance of His love speaks to men as friends (see Ex. 33:11; John 15:14-15) and lives among them (see Bar. 3:38), so that He may invite and take them into fellowship with Himself.[9]

The decisive foundation for a communicative theology is revelation—as God's self-disclosing "communication" with the human race, and as the endowment of humans with the capacity for comprehensive communication. When communication takes place between God and humans, what is passed on is not just some partial knowledge about the central meaning of life and the world, about their history and future; communication between God and human beings reveals "truth in relationship."

> It is incompatible with exclusion and expulsion, with deprivation and suppression. It makes itself felt in the restlessness of the spirit and the heart, which cannot stop comparing and bringing together the things that belong together, which remain on the trail of the Absolute and want to see it celebrated as the absoluteness of God—as the reign of God. . . . The Absolute remains a crucial challenge to widen the perspective and to resist an interest-driven limitation of perception, to avoid the mechanisms of tunnel vision and piece-meal analysis, and to surmount any obstacles to perception and the power of imagination.[10]

The search for "truth in relationship" characterizes theological inquiry as a communicative event, in which the contemporary contexts and experiences of people's lives are explored for those traces of God's Spirit that allow an impression of God's absolute devotion to humankind to become transparent. But how can those traces of God's Spirit be investigated when what is theologically meaningful ought to be recognized implicitly rather than explicitly? What does asking about "truth in relationship" mean for method in theology?

1. A Theological Method Where the Source of Its Assertions Can Be Identified

The history of the various arts and sciences and their contemporary situation make us aware that the methods used to research a particular subject cannot be represented as quasi-neutral. Scholarly procedures are conditioned by questions of meaning, orientation, and truth. This holds true for every area of knowledge, and particularly for a communicative theology.

With regard to communication, questions about the content of theological discourse and questions about scholarly method condition each other. In a communicative theology, God's perspective and the mode and manner of human inquiry stand in reciprocal, and reciprocally critical, relationship. Through the misunderstandings, disappointments, and conflicts experienced by the group in communication processes an impression of the "gifted" character of communication shines through. This may refer to the relationship with (but also to the otherness and strangeness of) One who grants understanding and reconciliation but who also makes difference and even strangeness possible.

The critical correlation between content and form in communicative theology is also relevant to the context in which theology comes into being. A theology developed in politically and economically marginalized Latin American countries or in an Indian or African context will come to its knowledge by another route, and also know something other than a theology that has arisen in northern countries. A theology "produced" at a desk in a lonely study reflects other methods of investigation and arrives at different conclusions than a theology developed in the living processes of a group or community.

2. Form, Medium, and Content of Communication Must Not Be Separated

According to a late modern understanding of communication, the observation that one can detect the origin of theological assertions in form, medium, or content is particularly challenging. Rather, a criterion for judging the effective working out of communicative theology must be employed. What does this imply for today's communication-based society, which is directed toward an indiscriminate and unlimited relaying of information? What are the consequences for theology when a clear choice is made for the inseparable interplay of the form, medium, and content of communication in theology? Doesn't the content of faith change considerably depending on whether it "comes across" in encounters between people or, to quote Habermas, is made accessible in "communicative acts"?[11] Or does it matter whether information relative to faith is passed on by means of technical media? Doesn't the Christian Word of God imply a living encounter with concrete people? Is this encounter not an offer of identification, combined with the freedom to refuse the identification?

Here we need to consider the alternatives between the ambiguity of interpersonal encounters and the living testimony of faith on the one hand, and the lack of ambiguity inherent in conceptual mediation on the other. Since it is easier to check the correctness of concepts than the "truth" in human encounters, churches often place more trust in correct concepts than in the authentic witness of the faith of living people. Trust in the sense of the faith that resides in the people of God is being undermined.

Whether the emphasis is more on the correct content of faith or on the truth of faith that reveals itself in relationships, it must be stressed that no communication arrangement can guarantee to make accessible the truths of Christian faith. Fundamental theological boundaries in the study of faith would be overstepped if the communicative approach were carried out in such a way that communication of the faith was thought to be guaranteed by a certain content, a particular method, or by the use of an unfailing medium.

Rather, it can only be a question of more or less correct conditions for the possibility of the communication of faith. The assent of faith must still be left to God's gift and to the free response of women and men to that gift.

3. Theology as Critical Reflection on and Understanding of the Communication Event

Theology's traditional concentration on a conceptual formulation of the truth of faith cannot do justice to the inseparable connection between theory and practice, between content and form in today's communication-based society. What is required is a discriminating theological hermeneutics of the entire communication event. There are good reasons why the churches (and the state as well) provide themselves with a theology. In an open society, theologians have the task of opening up the possibility for critical thought and action. This is made possible by the dialogue between Jewish-Christian and ecclesiastical tradition, seen in light of the social challenges of today, which is made available to everyone as an aid to decision making in concrete issues of communication. In other words, it is the difference between a business model, which draws on highly qualified staff for its strategic planning and decision making, and the church's theology, which builds on the tradition of faith and has the power to overthrow that logic of strategic planning and to offer healing and liberating impulses to a society, including even its non-Christian members, who are oblivious of its traditions.

4. Participating and Cooperating Theologians

At the same time, there is a danger that such a critical dialogue between theology and everyday practices in church and society might lead "experts" to create power structures whose binding injunctions practitioners of faith would have good reason to reject. We need to discuss "the power of knowledge"—and that includes theological knowledge. Is theological knowledge about being invested with a "power of interpretation," a superiority of judgment regarding every possible matter which also could be deployed strategically? Or is it a question of "communicative power" that risks participation in the "powerlessness" of existential contact? The essential characteristic of communicative "powerless power" is the ability to respond and be moved, combined with a high capacity for conflict.

What was said of the students in the lecture hall is thus particularly true of the relationship between theologians doing scholarly work and pastoral ministers working in parishes, schools, and religious education. Detached from an engaged and participatory communication, theology done in official quarters and imparted from the top down may be correct, but it will not alter practice. Only suitable communication procedures, by which we mean those that deny any inherent hierarchy between professional theologians and practitioners, will alter practice in the long run. These are processes of communication that draw on the skills of everyone, where expertise remote from real life has no place, but where people cooperate in striving to find a theological practice that answers the needs of the community. It is clear that such a claim challenges theology done in the academy. Some theologians, however, have already embraced this challenge.

We believe Gustavo Gutiérrez, for example, to be one of the most credible examples of an engaged and participatory theology.[12] As Matthias was able to witness personally in a *communidad* of the poor in the suburbs of Chiclayo, a thousand kilometers north of Lima, nearly every young person there knows this world-famous theologian from personal encounters. On the occasion of a large congress organized in Europe by the international journal *Communio,* which Gutiérrez was expected to attend, he astonished participants with the news that he would not come to Europe because he wanted to show his solidarity with women in Lima who were demonstrating against the lack of kerosene. A theology developed from participation with men and women engaged in local issues requires making hard choices.

Questions for Reflection

- Where and how has theology helped you so far to understand communication?
- What will change in your theology, your "God-talk," if it is conditioned not just by its content but also by the form and medium of communication used?
- What is your social location as a theologian or a student of theology in society and church? With whom do you express your solidarity? In what social practices do you participate?
- Which preferential option(s) have you made?
- Who or what are you excluding from your theology?

V. The "Gaze" of Communicative Theology

To summarize, communicative theology can be understood as a process that directs its "gaze"[13]—in the sense of a theological hermeneutics—toward the communication event. This gaze is not about distancing, in the sense of an "objective" hermeneutics, but is shared and participatory. It is a gaze that comes from being sensitive to the communicative event without becoming soft, weak, or diluting its identity. Communicative theology happens in the living tension between the "power" in communication and the "power in powerless." It will be experienced if theologians are receptive to the conflict-rich character of communication events and let go of the "power of theological interpretation" with which they seek to understand communication processes. Theologians must retain a balance between their involvement in the process and their ability to interpret the event so that leadership remains possible. What is foreign to communicative theology is the "strategic" power of interpretation that uses targeted hermeneutical knowledge in order to reach goals that have not been disclosed and are not transparent to all participants. The guidance of theological processes happens—in figurative terms—neither *in front of* nor *for* the persons concerned but *with* them. What hermeneutical model is available for this endeavor?

It cannot be only a matter of the hermeneutics of faith traditions, nor a model simply for understanding biographical, communal, and contextual faith experiences. The model must be able to offer a comprehensive vantage point on the whole faith-communicating event. In addition, we need a hermeneutics that facilitates participation in the communication event and simultaneously furthers the "understanding" of processes. Based on many years of theological work with and in groups, we will briefly introduce a communication model that will be developed in detail in chapters 6 and 7. Our approach in the communication model is one of Theme-Centered Interaction (TCI), as described by Ruth C. Cohn. This model applies to communication in groups and involves the essential components of a theology understood as a science of the practice of faith. It transforms an application-oriented hermeneutics by fostering participation in the event in light of the ecclesial practices of communication in society and at the same time remains capable

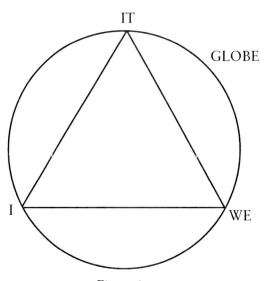

Figure 1

of offering guidance and interpretation. People train themselves in this model to sharpen their gaze on successive points of view involved in communicating the faith and understand how to hold various perspectives together in a differentiated discussion and in "dynamic balance." In this way they will be able to engage in a theological process that does not simply bring together after the fact what belongs together from the outset. They will not be able to hold themselves aloof from a process of "thinking God *and* world." Their whole lives will thus become invested in the process of communicative theology, their hearing and thinking, their feeling and acting, their praying and seeking, their rejoicing and lamenting—everything that defines their communication.

From the elaborations in the following chapters and the continuing extrapolating of this model it will become clear that a communicative theology as a process must constantly be broadening its perspectives. We can therefore establish a development within this process, a development that ranges from the conventional "gaze" of theological deductions and applications to church practices to efforts at reconciling traditional faith with the present-day situation, and from reconciling God and the world to the system-transforming "gaze" of a hermeneutics of difference. In order to clarify the development of the hermeneutical "gaze" we shall begin by contrasting the linear deduction-application hermeneutics (see figure 2) with our multiperspectival model. This model will be further developed and differentiated in the course of this book.

Application Hermeneutic

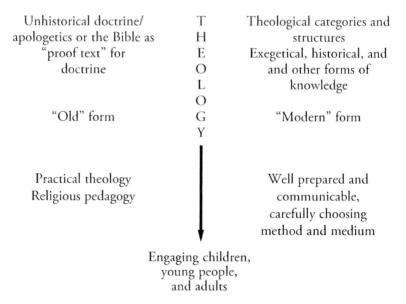

Unhistorical doctrine/ apologetics or the Bible as "proof text" for doctrine	T H E O L O G Y	Theological categories and structures Exegetical, historical, and and other forms of knowledge
"Old" form		"Modern" form
Practical theology Religious pedagogy		Well prepared and communicable, carefully choosing method and medium

Engaging children,
young people,
and adults

Figure 2

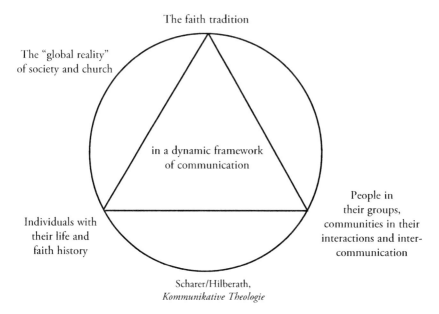

The faith tradition

The "global reality"
of society and church

in a dynamic framework
of communication

People in
their groups,
communities in their
interactions and inter-
communication

Individuals with
their life and
faith history

Scharer/Hilberath,
Kommunikative Theologie

Figure 3

This multiperspectival model makes no statement about the relationship the individual perspectives have with one another. The first thing to affirm here is that theology is generated from a communicative network of perspectives into which theologians are integrated existentially, and, thereby, intellectually as "participating theologians."

Questions for Reflection

- Which areas of theological education, research, and practice remind you of the application model above, and which of the multiperspectival model?
- Describe situations that correspond more to the first model, and to the second.
- Which questions and problems of theology fall under one or the other model, or both, or neither?
- What would you yourself choose to add to these models? And what would you alter in them?
- How would you represent your own "theology in process" in a model?

CHAPTER 2

Preliminary Observations about the Communicative Character of Human Beings

In order to better understand the significance of the academic concept of communication for theology, a further discussion of this topic is helpful.

I. What Is Communication?

The notion of communication (from Lat. *communicatio*, notification) usually refers to an interpersonal exchange of information and understanding through meaningful verbal or nonverbal symbols. As dialogical beings,[1] communication is indispensable for humans to the extent that they must rely on communication for physical survival and for psychological well-being. Communication allows humans to live in a community. Through communication in the form of daily interactions, communicating partners share a world in which they interact with one another, express norms and values, and thus develop individual identities. Therefore, communication plays an essential role in both defining and maintaining reality. "The subjective reality of something that is never talked about comes to be shaky."[2] The idea that reality can be lost reflects a constructivist position. The constructivist position suggests that reality comes into being through communication and that humans rely on communication to grasp their own and others' understanding of reality. Another possible outcome of such a constructivist view is the development of reality based on delusion. Such a false reality, when experienced collectively, is hard to escape. Totalitarian systems, seen in closed societies, are examples of the production of such destructive reality.

Doesn't a religious person construct a world that perfectly corresponds with his or her inner longing, but which does not really exist? Communication that allows thoughts of heaven (while not exclusively based on interpersonal exchanges and mutual sharing, but which also considers God's role in communication) may also be seen as a suspicious type of "reality construction."

The challenge of constructivism is this: When faced with an infinite number of potential realities, how does one come to grips with constructivism's radical relativism? Is it only by affirming with absolute certainty that one's whole being (and that of all creation) is ultimately preserved by an Other? Such a consideration is much more than a rational insight. It is a certainty that does not preclude doubt, fear, sadness, struggle, anger, desolation, and loneliness—as experienced by many biblical figures.

It is thus clear: communication, as we understand it, is by no means a mere exchange of information. It does not end with verbal expression. That which touches humans most deeply, that which absolutely concerns them is communicated in symbolic and ritual ways: through rites and gestures, with images and stories, as well as with profoundly symbolic objects. In addition, shared activities, joys, worries, losses, and responsibilities also have deeply communicative qualities.

As mentioned in chapter 1, Habermas's theory of "the communicative action" may be helpful. For our purposes, the differences between the three forms of communicative action are important:

- the instrumental, achievement-oriented, nonsocial action
- the strategic, achievement-oriented, social action
- the communicative, comprehension-oriented, social action.

The last type of action is the only form of communication that focuses on people instead of profit or outcome.

The philosophical/sociological notion of the communicative action has been theologically interpreted in several ways. One interpretation of a human person's use of dialogue stems from being a creature, who while made in the image of God was also given freedom. Therefore, the human person, who is ultimately spoken to by God, can choose to answer or to ignore God. This theological interpretation of communication seems more radical when we consider that, according to the Christian faith, the deceased remain a part of the Christian communication community. Although the living no longer do anything for the concrete needs of the deceased, they intercede on behalf of the deceased for God's saving grace.[3]

In chapter 4 we will present a thorough examination of the "communicative God" and God's communication throughout history; for now let us continue with an anthropological investigation of communication.

II. The Human Person "Cannot Not Communicate"

In this first "metacommunicative axiom," the renowned communication researcher Paul Watzlawick[4] summarizes the focus of sociology and sociolinguistics since the 1930s: Human communication is a fundamental social ability to convey meaningful messages through the exchange of culturally significant symbols. More recent sociolinguistic communication theories increasingly focus on modern communication processes made possible through technology such as the Internet and electronic mail. For our purposes, however, the theories of intrapersonal and interpersonal communication are especially important.

1. Transmitter and Receiver

One basic tenet of communication theory involves the exchange of a message between a "transmitter" who codifies the message and a "receiver" who must decode the message in order to understand it.[5] This model helps explain that messages or content can never be transmitted "neutrally." Both the transmitter and the receiver are influenced by their socialization and development, which allows for ambiguous interpretations of meaning. This can easily lead to instances where a message is understood by the recipient in a completely different way than was intended by the transmitter. Recognizing this potential problem is useful when addressing hurdles in communication in couples' therapy or in communication training. However, as we will show with regard to communication in Theme-Centered Interaction (TCI), the transmitter–receiver model does not adequately explain the dynamics of living communication. We will see how all the levels of communication—that is, the message that is communicated, the subjects who communicate, their interaction, and the actual context surrounding the communicative act—are fundamentally linked in a "dynamic balance." The transmitter–receiver model cannot handle the depth of multiple interactions of living communication.

2. The Beginning of Communication

Watzlawick's axiom that, no matter how much a human being tries, "one cannot *not* communicate"[6] is reflected in personal experiences throughout our lives. Every human being is, from the very beginning on, an entity made for, and absolutely dependent on, communication. This is also true for those living in contemplative religious orders where even verbal communication is kept at a minimum. In fact, the consideration of precisely such religious contexts allows us to expand our understanding of communication. For, both nonverbal communication among people and the communication with the mysterious, yet infinitely near, "Thou," a type of communication that we call "prayer," can help define one's personality. Communication is so essential for human beings, that early linguistic disturbances or lack of communication may lead to grave psychological or physical harm, even to the point of death.[7]

For many years developmental and social psychologists assumed that communication during the prenatal period and in early childhood was one-sided, that is, the mother and other caregivers communicated with the fetus or infant. More recent research, however, suggests that two-way communication occurs even in the earliest stages of life.[8] Not only the mother and others influence the child, but also vice versa: even in the womb, the fetus communicates with its mother and through her with the environment, thus influencing the environment. What pregnant woman does not know just how much the growing child can influence her life? Children are dependent on the loving care of their earliest caregivers. It is also true that in this "intergenerational communication," which starts during pregnancy and continues throughout their lives, children are not merely the loved, pampered, abandoned or abused objects of adults. Modern pedagogy and developmental psychology recognize the infant and often even the embryo as individual and communicative subjects. True interpersonal communication always includes interaction between people. Therefore, some type of "I-Thou" or "I-We" relationship is fundamental in a description of human communication.

3. The Human Person, a Dialogical Being

The essential relationship-based character of human communication was addressed by the Jewish philosopher Martin Buber in his description of the human person as a *dialogical being*. Buber distinguishes between the "basic words" "I–Thou" and "I–It" with regard to human encounters.

> Whoever says You does not have something for his object. For wherever there is something there is also another thing; every It borders on other Its; It is only by virtue of bordering on others. But where You is said there is no something. You has no borders. Whoever says You does not have something; he has nothing. But he stands in relation.[9]

Therefore, for an interaction to succeed, no one can become an object or a "something" in the process of communication. As Buber puts it, "It is not the pedagogical intention that is fruitful, but pedagogical interaction."[10]

This anthropology of human dialogue was successfully adapted in Ruth C. Cohn's Theme-Centered Interaction (TCI) and expanded to the levels of group, subject, and context. The "It" or subject matter, with regard to faith communication and to theology, presents a particular challenge for the TCI model. The question arises: Is this an "I–Thou" relationship or an "I–It" relationship? Most probably, it can be both: The communication of the contents of faith, that is, theological contents, would correspond to an "I–It" relationship. If, however, the human person stands before God's infinite mystery and enters a prayerful or celebrative communication, which according to the Eastern churches is the basis for any theology, this meeting is analogous to the human "I–Thou" relationship.

The well-known Hassidic anecdote of the "boy's conversion" gives an indication of such deeply meaningful or prayerful communication:

> Rabbi Aaron once came to the city where little Mordecai, who later became the rabbi of Lechovitz, was growing up. His father brought the boy to the visiting rabbi and complained that he did not persevere in his studies. "Leave the boy with me for a while," said the Rabbi Aaron. When he was alone with the little Mordecai, he lay down and took the child to his heart. Silently he held him to his heart until his father returned. "I have given him a good talking-to," he said. "From now on, he will not be lacking in perseverance." When the rabbi of Lechovitz told this incident, he added: "It was then that I learned how people are converted."[11]

4. The Importance of the "Other"

Is the communication of faith only conceivable as either the "I–Thou" or the "I–It" relationship? Is communication about faith, if we speak about interpersonal communication, to be regarded as simply an intersubjective exchange? The French Lithuanian philosopher Emmanuel Lévinas, in opposition to Buber, radicalizes the intersubjective perspective. For Lévinas, the "face" of another person is the key metaphor for the other. Radically turning toward the face of the other makes the experience of transcendence ultimately possible. Meeting the other is not confined to an "I–Thou" relationship. When the "otherness" of the other is seen, one's own freedom is questioned. Questions of compassion, justice, and mercy also arise. Lévinas sums up the central idea of his philosophy of the *Other* as follows:

> Dia-konía should precede any dia-logue. I analyze the interpersonal relationship in proximity with the *Other* as if that were his face— beyond the images I myself make of other people, the expressive in the *Other* (and in this sense the whole body can be regarded as "face") which *ordains* me to serve him.[12]

Thus, Lévinas underscores, by going beyond the mutuality and symmetry emphasized by Buber, the inequality and the asymmetry of communication. This inequality, however, does not exist as in traditional subordinate relationships (children/parents, pupils/teachers, poor/rich, and so on). Instead, the "I" is called to *serve* the "Thou."

In this sense, I am responsible for the *Other*, without expecting anything in return, even if it were to cost me my life. . . . And so, as the relationship with the *Other* is not reciprocated, I am subservient to the *Other*.[13]

In the following chapter, we will further explore the implications that Buber's "reconciliatory" approach and Lévinas's "differentiating" approach have when considering the discussion of religion and faith in society.

Questions for Reflection

- How did you previously think about communication? What is new for you now?
- Do you have a systematic or constructivist view of communication in your professional and private experiences?
- Where and how do you encounter "instrumental," "strategic," or "communicative" acts?
- What aspects of Buber's and Lévinas's approaches to communication are important for you? What are the similarities and differences between these two approaches?
- Does the story about "the conversion of the boy" help you reflect on your own communication practices?

CHAPTER 3

The "Battle of the Gods" as a Dilemma in a Communication-Conscious Society

This chapter introduces us to the theological discussion of the "Globe," that is, the overall context of communicative theology, affecting all aspects of communication in faith and theology. Ruth Cohn writes: "If you don't attend to the Globe it will eat you up." In this sense, the "working-place" of communicative theology is confined neither to the "public library" of the tradition, nor to the "private study" of individual faith experience. By the same token, however, it is also not restricted to the "closed circle" of particular group communication and its implicit theology. Within a globalized knowledge-based society, neither the tradition nor the situations of individuals and groups can be understood outside of the prevailing social understanding and practice of communication. We shall see how communicative action in the churches is closely connected to social developments that affect the very concept of how to expound the faith. As communicative communities, churches do not stand over against society. Precisely because of their communicative nature, churches are embedded in their respective societies. For this reason, we begin by inquiring how the understanding and practice of communication in the global community of knowing affects the different perspectives of faith communication and theological discourse.

I. The "Great Divide" and the Reconciling "Bridges"

The things people associate with God constitute, according to Jürgen Werbick, the decisive question regarding God-talk and thus delineate the principal task of a theology suited to the modern age.[1] As we saw in chapters 1 and 2, communicative theology thematizes the *what* (content) and the *how* (form and medium) as interwoven topics. The theological question is: *what* do people associate with God and *how* do they do it? This way of stating the question calls attention to a pivotal theological insight: There is an inextricable connection between God (or better, what we know of God on the basis of revelation and the Christian tradition) and the actual lives of people. In theological knowing it is not only the *what* of the faith that counts. The *what* is inseparably linked to the way in which knowledge coming from God is received and transmitted. In short, it is linked with the *how* of God's communication through past Christian tradition and in contemporary life histories.

Behind Werbick's formula, one senses an implicit assumption that there is an epochal separation between Christian revelation and the situation of people today. This "great divide" between revelation and situation[2] constitutes a barrier to communication that must be overcome theologically. If we correctly understand Werbick's fundamental-theological approach, we can agree with him that revelation and the believer's situation, faith and life, God and the world, fundamentally all belong together. This insight is grounded in the theology of creation and can be deepened by the theology of incarnation (the Christian belief that God became flesh in Jesus Christ).

But one may ask, is it really necessary to bridge such a "great divide" between "then" and "now," between "revelation" in the past and people's "situation" in the present? Must the two sides be reconciled dialectically? Must a synthesis be sought? Indeed, one may ask whether the postulate of the "great divide," which has long pervaded modern thought, is in fact still valid in the late-modern situation? If God and the human person are really so separated in an epochal way, there is little chance of bringing them together again simply with some "methodological-pedagogical" technique. *What* notions people have of God and *how* they are, or are not, associated first of all must be understood as a challenge for theology. This task applies to communication in every social context: in the family, in the school, in the parish. Prior to—and in many cases instead of—catechetical or pastoral endeavors, should one not ask *what* do these particular children, adolescents, or adults in fact associate with God in their respective social and ecclesial situations, that is, in their respective spheres of communication? Concretely, what kind of a "children's god," "adolescent's god," "adult's god" are they carrying "under their arm"[3] when they meet the communicative God of Christian faith?

The difficulty that traditionally educated theologians have with such a fundamental-theological approach lies primarily in the fact that *what* notions people associate with God and *how* they associate them do not manifest themselves generally in accepted theological categories. Rather, they are expressed in a "language" of profound human and religious feelings, expressed in everyday rites and gestures, in objects held "sacred," in images, metaphors, and existentially significant stories. Theologians need a new formation to enable them to "read" such expressions not only sociologically or psychologically but also theologically. Such a hermeneutical skill is no less important and no less demanding than the ability to interpret the texts of revelation and tradition.

In classical "correlation theologies" and their catechetical reception, questions were posed that aimed at overcoming the "great divide." In the logic of

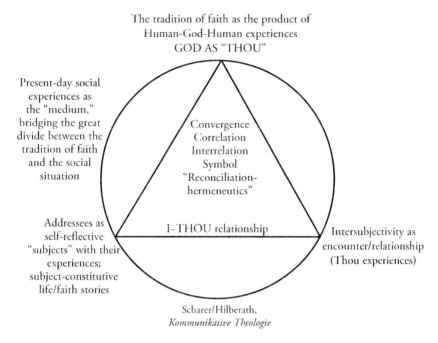

The tradition of faith as the product of
Human-God-Human experiences
GOD AS "THOU"

Present-day social
experiences as
the "medium,"
bridging the great
divide between the
tradition of faith
and the social
situation

Convergence
Correlation
Interrelation
Symbol
"Reconciliation-
hermeneutics"

I–THOU relationship

Addressees as
self-reflective
"subjects" with their
experiences;
subject-constitutive
life/faith stories

Intersubjectivity as
encounter/relationship
(Thou experiences)

Scharer/Hilberath,
Kommunikative Theologie

Figure 4

such theologies, "experience" is held to bridge the gap between tradition and situation. The tradition of faith is viewed as a collection of experiences of people with God and with one another. These experiences can be "correlated," that is, put into a reciprocal and mutually critical relationship with the experiences of people today. Obviously such "experiential bridges" do not refer to the kind of everyday experience, which has no revelatory character, such as routine actions like brushing one's teeth. What is meant here are deep, existential—even mystical—experiences that are not subject to our control but, rather, "happen" to us.[4] Thus, with Karl Rahner, one can speak of "anonymous" Christian experiences.

The critique of "correlation-theologies" and their catechetical-pastoral reception shows that both the image of the "great divide" and the notion of a "bridge" or "reconciliation" between God and the human person are problematic in several ways.[5] To examine here the "correlation" model in all of its facets would go beyond the scope of this book. At the same time, we by no means propose to go back to the pattern of theology prevailing before the advent of the "correlation" model, as, for instance, the dogmatic theologian Thomas Ruster has suggested.[6] An updated version of the "hermeneutics of deduction and application" would radically narrow our appreciation of the full richness of theology. It is only with a multiperspectival approach that the diverse angles of theology can be uncovered and viewed in their intrinsic relationships without "fusion." These angles represent the tradition of faith, the biographical aspect, the communicative aspect (group, community) in a narrow sense, and the all-encompassing "Globe." The interplay of these four perspectives shows that focusing exclusively on "reconciliation" between God and the world is too short-sighted. In order to illustrate the point of our criticism, let us attempt to fill out our familiar "triangle-within-the-circle" figure in terms of a "reconciliation-hermeneutics" (see figure 4, p. 35).

Questions for Reflection

- To what extent, where, and how, does the problem of the "gap" between God and the world, between faith and life, between church and world, play a part in your own theology and practice?
- Do you perceive a "great divide"? If yes, where? If not, why not?
- Do you construct "bridges" between God and the world through your theological thinking and practice? If so, what are these bridges made of? What makes them collapse sometimes?
- Where, when, and how do you reach the limits of bridge building and "reconciliation" between God and the world?
- How is your theology oriented? How conscious are you of the "correlation model"? Does it influence your practice?

II. The Other Pole:
Conflict-laden Confrontation "at the Border"

To begin with, we are proposing that social circumstances play a significant role in determining *what* people associate with God and revere as god-like and *how* they structure their lives around them. When communication takes center stage in a globalized knowledge-based society, theological communication is not left unaffected, however vague the concept of communication prevailing in society as a whole and in the scientific community in particular may be. "God" and "communication" are mutually related, even though many no longer explicitly avert to this connection. A theological understanding of communication is inextricably linked to the confession of faith in the One and Triune God (chapter 4). Furthermore, the nature of the human person as such and the nature of society as a globalized community of knowing cannot be understood apart from "communication." This being the case, we can ask whether it makes sense to seek new "bridges" (attempt a "reconciliation") between God's communication and human communication.

At this point, we call attention to a dangerous temptation latent in "reconciliation-hermeneutics." This approach can easily degenerate into a mere mirror imaging of the (idealized) forms of communication prevailing in a given society. When this occurs, God's communication is understood as an "image" of prevailing communicative norms, for example, the pursuit of consensus. Communicative theology, however, cannot be content to declare consensus "sacred," though in fact many theologians today do just that. It will not suffice for Christians to associate *anything whatsoever* in *any manner whatsoever* with just *any God whatsoever*, though this is precisely what many people do in their postmodern patchwork religiosity. In the case at hand, the temptation might generate the following attitude often met in the church today: wherever communication takes place in a dominance-free, consensus-oriented group, there God is present "anonymously" and "implicitly." Where, on the contrary, conflict and contradiction manifest themselves, where inequality and dominance prevail, there God has departed. No matter how attractive such an idea might seem at first sight, the "dark side" is theologically precarious: the "troublemakers" in a group or community will then be treated as outsiders and made into passive objects, and often "victims" of "successful" communication. Many church groups and communities are prone to such thinking. Naively they interpret the Gospel text "Where two or three are gathered in my name, there am I in the midst of them" along these lines. The consequences of such a theology are reflected in the inability of churches to deal with conflict and should not be overlooked.

Those who think exclusively in terms of reconciliation-hermeneutics forget that he, in whose name Christians gather, is, in fact, the crucified one. He is "the stone which the builders rejected" (Psalm 118:22, quoted in Acts 4:11 and 1 Peter 2:7). Jesus was himself a victim of the "consensus of the pious" and of the "collusion" between the representatives of "religion" and the political power represented by Pontius Pilate. No human communication saved Jesus—the one cut off from all human and religious communication, the one who cried out on the cross, "My God, my God, why have you forsaken me" (Psalm 22:1), the one who was "cursed by God" in the eyes of the pious. On the contrary, it was the wholly Other, who alone can turn death into life. It was God who made the one crucified, the one cut off from all human communication, to be the "cornerstone" and "a stone that causes people to stumble and a rock that makes them fall" (1 Peter 2:8; cf. Isaiah 8:14).

The metaphor of "bridge" and the notion of "reconciliation" that attempt to harmonize secular modernity and the biblical/ecclesial faith into an all-encompassing consensus of religions, ideologies, and religiosities (derived from Habermas's theory of communicative action) are countered in communicative theology by the metaphor of a "conflict-rich confrontation at the border." Communicative theology is guided by the assumption that the rules of communication hold equally for the ideological confrontations that take place in the theological notion of communication and the secular notion prevailing in a knowledge-based society. "Contact takes place at the borders; where there are no borders, there is no contact." The "border," however, is a place of conflict and confrontation. Between the "warm," symbiotic relationship on the one hand (a form of relating that regressively welds subjects together and makes them into "objects" of the Other) and the "cold" distance of mutual indifference on the other hand, there is an alternative; this is the confrontational, conflict-laden "meeting at the border," which is constitutive for people getting along with one another. Aggression, which arises in groups bent on harmony and which is then diverted outward in the direction of some "victim," ought not to be swept under the carpet according to a hasty logic of reconciliation but should be articulated and taken seriously. The word "aggression," from the Latin *ad gredere* ("moving toward") has a positive as well as a negative meaning. It includes not only the life-destroying forces of exclusion but also that force which can find expression in a living, loving relationship. All-encompassing peace and harmony among all creatures without doing away with their differences are ideals corresponding to the transformation of life that God promises for God's own future; they should not be hastily instrumentalized in the here-and-now.

When, therefore, we inquire about the "Globe" in which communicative theology takes place, what we have in mind is not primarily reconciliation between "God and the world," between God's communicative action and that of the world, but their confrontation and difference. A theological understanding of communication cannot be founded on a projection of human communication onto God or on a simple deduction of "divine" communication (to which we have only mediated access) to the world. The knowledge gained by combining "correlation" with a "hermeneutics of difference" sharpens our appreciation of the question: *what* and *how* do people associate things with God in a knowledge- and communication-based society?

To express this alternative view of the matter, we can revise our diagram as in figure 5 (p. 39).

In order to avoid confusion, we would like to clarify that in our schema, God's role in creation, history, and incarnation lies outside the triangle in the circle (see visual representation). This position shows how God, both as mysterious being and as human living among us, touches all dimensions of theologically significant experiences: the experiences of the individual, of the group, of the faith, and of the outside context (Globe).

We also further define communicative theology in reference to the *loci* of theology stemming from the faith tradition (as more recently interpreted by Roman Siebenrock), in terms of four intertwining locales. These dimensions form a network and influence on another:

- the locale of one's personal life and faith experiences
- the locale of church and parish experiences
- the locale of religious and biblical witnesses, living examples
- the locale of society and of world

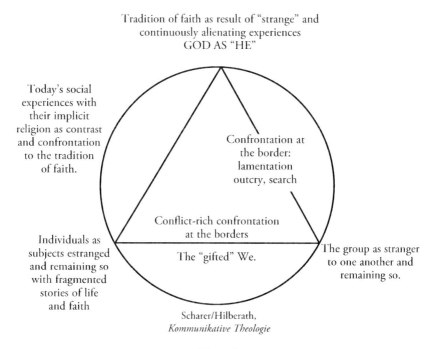

Figure 5

In situations relevant to communicative theology, this basic structure or network of dimensions can be concretely experienced and described at three different levels:

- the immediate participation level
- the experiential interpretation level
- the scholarly theological reflection level

In communicative theology, there is also always an openness for *contemplatio*, or contemplative experiences, as revealed in prayer, liturgy, and mystical experiences that serve as transforming influences on the above dimensions and levels. The central challenge of communicative theology lies in identifying, understanding, and using the theologically relevant and theologically generating dynamic that results from the interconnectedness of these dimensions and levels.[7]

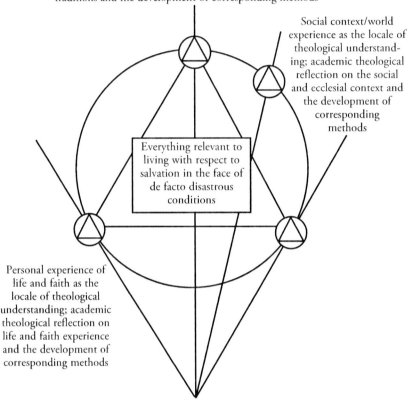

Biblical testimony in living transmission and other religious traditions as the locale of theological understanding; academic theological reflections on worldviews and religious/biblical traditions and the development of corresponding methods

Social context/world experience as the locale of theological understanding; academic theological reflection on the social and ecclesial context and the development of corresponding methods

Everything relevant to living with respect to salvation in the face of de facto disastrous conditions

Personal experience of life and faith as the locale of theological understanding; academic theological reflection on life and faith experience and the development of corresponding methods

God's self-revelation
in creation, history, and incarnation;
God as a mystery beyond human control

Figure 6

Questions for Reflection

- What sort of day-to-day situation do you think about when a "hermeneutics of reconciliation" is under discussion? What situation do you associate with a "hermeneutics of difference"?
- How and in what way does such a distinction help your theological understanding of everyday situations?
- What kind of awkwardness, what fears and other negative emotions do you experience when thinking about confrontation, difference, dispute, and so forth?

- How are such fears and negative feelings rooted in your biography? How are they connected with your personal development in faith and with your theology?
- What important insights have you gained in the course of your life by working through conflicts?

III. Ambivalent Communication in the Social and Ecclesial "Globe"

Increasingly fewer people in the Northern Hemisphere associate the Christian God with their experiences or notions of communication. The chasm between the experience of communication, its understanding, and the Christian vision of God is not merely an individual problem. It affects the whole society. Faced with this schizophrenia between normal communication and God-talk, one might well ask whether theology should not look for some other notion than "communication" in order to speak of God in today's social reality?

In a so-called knowledge-based society, communication is an unavoidable notion. Even where nothing more than raw data is exchanged, "communication" is used to describe the transaction. Especially within the context of media communication the notion of communication becomes ideologically freighted. The whole neoliberal economic system supports the modern knowledge-based society on which so many have set their hopes and is closely linked to modern means of communication and their prevailing understanding.

1. The Emotional Roller Coaster

Contradictory attitudes and feelings are linked emotionally with modern communication using the "new media." The "global village" as a metaphor for a future characterized by worldwide, boundless communication suggests the illusion that the world is in fact reduced to a village. This image fascinates many people. No wonder! It is indeed fascinating that I (Matthias Scharer) can communicate with my daughter (in India at the time this chapter was written) and can share with her the latest news via a click of the mouse. Every piece of news can reach me via the newest communication media. The very composition of this book (written by the authors—one working in Tübingen, the other in Innsbruck—almost in real time) is unthinkable without modern communication. We type our texts in the computer, exchange them by email, download relevant literature from the Internet, and so on.

Yet, however natural it is for more and more people to use modern means of communication, the notion of the global village also has a fearsome side. At the time this book was being written (2001), the European Union's economic summit meeting in Genoa was the scene of radical protest by the opponents of globalization. Protesters against globalization came together to express their fears of a "placeless society" in which all borders and barriers are eliminated. The fear that people might lose their individual and communal playground as a result of the apparently boundless freedom to communicate and might thus become victims of uncontrollable media and economic forces cannot be dismissed as being irrational and ungrounded. Shortly after the beleaguered EU summit in Italy came to an end, I, Matthias Scharer, received an email message from the same country with the following content so totally different from the reports from Genoa:

> We have been spending . . . a wonderfully, untroubled vacation in Italy. It has now dawned on me what communication for its own sake means and how important it is to cultivate it, wherever possible. It did me a world of good to discover my own needs and those of my family and to try to satisfy them without feeling the pressure of work. To live and communicate just for its own sake, without following any particular aims or intentions, that was our motto for this summer.

Feelings and attitudes toward communication have never been more contradictory than they are today. These contradictions draw attention to the ideological and religious "baggage" applied to communication. The quasi-religious hope that in the worldwide virtual world of communication humanity will be delivered from ideological and religious conflict and will enjoy worldwide, culture-bridging, dominance-free communication shows itself, in the aftermath of September 11, 2001, in its full ambivalence. On the one hand, we have the economic and cultural "real" space of the Northern Hemisphere, propagating the hope of boundless communication, but at the same time aggressively excluding the "unnetworked" from a fair share of world resources and reducing them to virtual illiterates. On the other hand, we have terrorists who take advantage of the "virtual" space in order to act on a world scale.

2. The Little Gods and the Great God

The image of the global village with its boundless communication takes on particularly religious connotations when the new media and the global market invade those areas of human life where faith and religion traditionally held sway. These are the areas of meaning and orientation, of history and the future, of right action and enduring happiness. Stopping to think about modern communication and its religious and ideological implications makes one aware of the degree to which the "little gods" of boundless knowledge, global-communicative ability, and never-ending consumption are replacing the hope for the coming of the "great God." It is a battle between "gods" who satisfy immediate needs and a God who "dries all tears" (Revelation 21:4; cf. Isaiah

65:19). It is a confrontation between the boundless freedom promised to those globally connected in the communication network and the God who communicates God's self to all people, especially to those excluded from the communication process, who calls all humankind to become one community in the freedom of the children of God. In this new world of global communication, the arguable monopoly of salvation formerly ascribed to the church appears to have been transferred to the media, so that the old adage *"extra ecclesia nulla salus"* (there is no salvation outside the church) becomes *"extra media nulla salus"*[8] (there is no salvation outside the media). Such a world obviously needs to reflect on communication from the perspective of the biblical God and God's communication with people. It is from this theological perspective that communicative theology enters critically into the (post)modern debate about communication, a debate that is growing in importance on the scientific, social, and religious levels.

3. Diversity Can Be Taken for Granted

Theology is about the relationship between God and humans and therefore about human relationships from God's "point of view." It does not treat humankind merely as the product of a media-driven market society. It follows, therefore, that the many-faceted discussion of communication in a "knowledge-based society" should begin with a critical clarification of how communication hallmarks the human person's self-understanding. In the confusing flood of information and images to which people, above all children and adolescents, are constantly exposed, the very notion of personal identity undergoes transformation. The stable ego-identity long held by developmental psychologists and religious educators to be the goal of personality development and socialization is losing ground. People are now seen to be "border crossers" balancing their way between various identities and roles, which they are offered in abundance. More and more, one uses the notion of "identity in radical plurality,"[9] a concept developed to explain the so-called patchwork or *bricollage* identities which young people increasingly manifest. Plurality, it would seem, is the hallmark of humankind's future; being embodied in the worldwide opportunities for information and communication, plurality becomes a defining factor of human self-understanding.

Such a shift in people's self-understanding and in their communication opportunities calls forth not only diversification, it also causes insecurity. In times of communicative insecurity, there is an outcry for orientation, for certitude in self-understanding, for valid roles and relationships. I want to know who I am and who the other is with whom I am supposed to communicate. I look for clarity regarding the attitudes and values that unite or separate us: what can I rely on, what can I not rely on? Many people today thus look to the church with its wealth of experience as a source of relative stability in matters of identity and roles, of norms and values. Such "stable" communication opportunities are esteemed and sought out even by people who otherwise have little to do with churches. Thus, diverse economic and management concepts instrumentalize the treasury of the church's experience for their own purposes, while ignoring important elements of the Christian message such as the call for worldwide social justice. At least in the "inner segment" of the churches, people seem, in fact, to know who they are, what they have to do, what role they have to play in different life contexts, what norms and values they stand for, and what hope directs their lives. Yet, such expectations of stability in communication may quickly tip over into a fundamentalist attitude. People then close in on themselves, seeking shelter in the convictions, systems, and conceptions they had once acquired and refuse to question them. Thus the fundamentalist refuses to go to the roots of communicative processes. Fundamentalists are "radical"—from the Latin word for "roots"—only in a super-ficial, unhistorical manner.

Over against the reactionary or fundamentalist attitude, we recognize that pluralization by the media has positive as well as negative effects. While it destroys a particular kind of self-understanding, it simultaneously opens up new possibilities in the form of "pluralism competence." This idea refers to the fact that within a person, different subjective roles and partial identities can "co-exist" in connection with one another. Thanks to the internal communication between these "foreign" elements of the personality, the ability to meet and deal with strangers outwardly, without mistrust and fear, is thus increased.

4. Identity Arising from "Gift-given" Communication

Communicative theology does not envisage destabilizing people through the dissolution of their identity and communicative ability. By the same token, it does not envisage fundamentalistic fixation of identity and communication. It does not shy away from new human developments offered by the acquisition of "pluralism competence." On the contrary, the sort of stable ego-identity that religious pedagogy postulated to be the goal of development and education has always been a fiction ignoring the fragmentary aspects that are part and parcel of human existence. This blindness for the fragmentary character of human identity gave rise to idealistic notions of communication, which were aimed at harmonious communication processes within homogenous groups.

The Jewish and Christian sources of faith and the tradition of ecclesial action open up an alternative view of human communication. In this new perspective, success is not measured by the elimination of conflict, an illusion fostered by "sweeping conflicts under the carpet." In Christian understanding, it is not communication management that generates successful communication. "Successful" communication is not something "made" but something "given"; it is a gift given by the Other, who is relationship and who spiritually indwells in each of us. God is the "wholly Other" who revealed God's self to people in diverse ways and times and ultimately in Jesus Christ (chapter 4). Thus, the faith perspective also changes the understanding of identity. An identity coming from "gifted" communication and marked by the experience of the Other as Other lives in and out of diversity in relationship. Inner and outer diversity in relationship is radically called forth by one's relationship with God. Such a "gifted identity" or "gratuitous identity" frees us from the dichotomy widely claimed to exist between "strong" autonomous subjects on the one hand and "weak," multirelational subjects on the other. The multirelational, "weak" subjects are thought to be immature, unfit for the "hard facts" of human communication; for this reason they devote themselves to the "soft facts" of cultivating relationships. Such persons are thought to be found particularly among women and religious people. In chapter 6, devoted to Theme-Centered Interaction (TCI), we will see how Ruth Cohn's axiom linking autonomy with interdependence calls attention to the problem of separating these two aspects of personality and thus opens the way for the notion of "gifted identity."

The understanding of communication suggested above is not something that falls from heaven; it is a notion that must be worked out in a dialogue between Christian faith and the (post)modern understanding of communication. For this reason, communicative theology can articulate itself only in the living interplay between communicative action and an understanding of communication. A Christian-ecclesial theology of communication thus gives particular attention in its God-talk to experiences arising from the communicative action of faith. For this reason it is articulated within the context of a communicative ecclesiology (chapter 5).

Questions for Reflection

- Where do you find the connection between the media-driven knowledge-based society and theology? How do you view this connection?
- How do you cope with the communication-oriented society? Which aspects do you find appealing? Which ones do you find threatening?
- How and where does the communication-oriented society influence your theological thinking and action? What gives you food for thought?
- How do you cope with the different understandings of identity?
- What is the basis for your own identity? What about the identity of your colleagues and other people around you?

IV. Challenges for Theology and Ecclesial Action

Ever since information has become the keyword for modern society—as its means of knowing and controlling—the communicative character of reality as interpreted by anthropology and theology finds itself faced with new challenges. The notion of society based on knowledge, information, and communication signals a transformation toward a society that generates added value less through industrial production than through virtual exchange of information. Fed by the rapid globalization processes in the economic, social, and media spheres, virtual communication is expanding explosively.

1. Extraordinary Changes in Communication

As explained above, the spoken and written word and the language of the body are no longer the sole media of communication. The panoply of communication media expands continuously. The opportunities for communication and the quantity of information exchanged are caught up in a process of rapid change. We are heading toward the "placeless society" prophesied by the British futurologist William Knoke in his book *Bold New World*.[10] Soon space and time will no longer play a significant role: the networking of information will become the new navel of the world. In the "bold new world" of the twenty-first century, nation-states, companies, trade unions in their present forms will be dissolved. The same thing will happen to schools, religions, and families. Distances will count for nothing: with a mere click of a mouse information can be sent or received, merchandise can be ordered, electronic banking transactions can be carried out. Big business conglomerates, which dominate today's economy, will break up. Small enterprises around the world will join together, amoeba-like, to offer services now performed by big business. Most work will no longer be done on company premises; instead, it will be done on private, mobile computers connected to the central office. Education too will be transformed. Instead of people having to go to school to get information, information in the future will come to people where they are. "It is indeed all too likely that in the future the figure of the teacher will take on mythical stature; the once maligned business community will become an object of longing; students will be calling in vain for the kind of personal conversation with a mentor that they know only from the stories they heard from their parents."[11]

    The big losers in all of this are those who cannot enter global communication in time, the so-called media illiterate. "Surveys show that one in two Germans is afraid of being unable to cope with the media deluge and the demands of computer proficiency."[12] If poverty has a feminine reference, the new media are deepening the gender division of society. Susanne Gaschke estimates that only 10 percent of computer users are female; women tend to see the networked computer as "an overrated men's toy."[13] But the greatest losers will be people in the so-called third and fourth worlds, the nonnetworked laborers, whose potentialities will thus lie fallow.

The development in the direction of a global, virtual communication-oriented society will necessarily lead to a transformation of people's identity. Those having access to communication media will enjoy a boundless freedom to communicate with those sharing their interests. This freedom, however, has its price: face-to-face personal encounter gives place to faceless exchange of information in an illusory community. Communication scientist Norbert Bolz, at the thirty-ninth "Salzburg Conversation," put his finger on one of the paradoxes of the new media world: because of the human desire to communicate, the new media raise the quantity of communicative activities but without necessarily "saying" anything. Thus, in the future, interpersonal, face-to-face communication will be conceivable only within the dimensions of these new communication capacities.

2. The Challenge of Effective Communication

In conjunction with the increasingly economy-driven and media-oriented "modern" world of the Northern Hemisphere, interest in effective interpersonal communication is on the rise. "How can we communicate successfully?" is the question raised by communication trainer Jerry Richardson in his introduction to the NLP (neurolinguistic programming) method.[14] Therein the author promises: if you read this book and master its techniques and strategies, you will be in a position to:

1. Take control of any situation immediately . . .
2. Establish trust and credibility . . .
3. Use the power of suggestion to get what you want . . .
4. Present your proposals in ways that are virtually irresistible . . .
5. Overcome resistance effortlessly and effectively . . .
6. Get people to agree with you . . .
7. Get other people to clearly understand you . . .
8. Avoid being manipulated.[15]

With the intention of expediting interpersonal communication, Richardson and others like him appeal to "the recent advances in the state of the communicative and the persuasive arts," which include "discoveries in such varied fields as hypnosis, cybernetics, linguistics, psychology and psychiatry, and as sales and management communication."[16] The author states his goals as follows: "In seeking solutions to communication problems, we prefer what works."[17] Talking to NLP representatives, however, we learn that such crass pragmatism has meanwhile been overcome. Nonetheless, in conjunction with the economic logic dominating our society, the trend toward quick success is apparent. Input and output must balance out. This attitude effects, as well, the whole educational sector. In our schools, technical schools, and universities, there is a tendency to measure the quality of educational aims by their empirical capacity to be operationalized and evaluated.

Against the backdrop of the developments sketched here, it is understandable that the results of information and communication theories will have a huge bearing on social development in all areas of life. But what kind of communication theories are at hand? Do the numerous anthropological and ethical problems surfacing in the knowledge-based society not reveal the shortcomings of existing communication theories? Can the social challenges of a global world really be overcome with such cybernetic/technological theories of information and communication? Cannot theology make a contribution to solving such problems by bringing to the fore the human and ethical implications in its hermeneutics? Does not the Christian God-hypothesis keep "heaven" open by postulating a communication that is "gifted" not "made"?

Aware of the unavoidable involvement of theology in modern communication, communicative theology does not approach the problems of the knowledge-based society merely from a hermeneutical/analytical perspective. By calling attention to specific communication processes and setting them in motion, it creates a theologically reflected practice with the character of a model, making transparent the interplay between social reality, ecclesial action, and theological reflection.

3. The Churches Are Involved in the Knowledge-based Society

Churches and theology cannot escape the globalization of communication nor the trend toward more effective communication. A survey of formation programs used by the churches shows clearly how complex and diverse are the attempts, which seek better to "get a grip" on the sphere of communication. The more globalized communication becomes, the more difficult are the communication problems that surface in the parish or in the school, the greater will be the desire for recipes and easy-to-learn "tips and tricks."[18]

By no means do we mean to minimize efforts to teach more effective communication techniques. Nor is it our intention to revile the enormous technological developments in the direction of digitalized communication.[19] It is precisely in view of such developments, which people will be unable to escape in the future, that church practice needs to question theological criteria for communication.

a. The "Non-profit" Option

Thinking in market terms, one might choose to apply to the churches the criteria for success designed for a "non-profit" enterprise. Obviously, the success of the church's mission cannot be measured, as in industry, by the hard facts of maximizing profit, among other factors. But the soft facts, such as effective communication, client satisfaction, high attendance rate at church events, and so on, must balance out.

In actual fact, in the contemporary church education market, one often acts in accordance with such soft-fact criteria. Such pragmatic decision making, however, shows its limitations as soon as future developments in the area of communication are taken into account:

- In the near future, it will be possible to experience immediate communication between people who meet together without pressure to achieve and work together on "their themes" without pressure of achievement.[20]
- The global communication media provide fascinating opportunities, worldwide and boundary free, to spread faith-related information and to provide access to church events. People who until now have not been reached by church education programs can be given easy access by the click of a mouse to the church's mission of spreading the faith.

It is astonishing with what naïveté otherwise conservative church personnel are jumping onto the data highway to transmit faith-related contents. Under this mantle of the modern media, however, lurks the same old instrumentalist approach to language. Such communication fails to "take hold" not merely because it blocks out the emotional aspect but also because it does not fit with the "object" of faith meant to be communicated. Numerous biblical examples show how the form of the encounter becomes itself the content: Jesus' glance alone was enough to make the denying Peter understand what was happening (Luke 22:61a); Mary needed only to greet Elizabeth and already "the baby leapt in her womb" (Luke 1:41); both women knew immediately what that meant. Unrecognized, the risen One walked at first in silence alongside the disappointed and saddened "Emmaus disciples" before entering into conversation with them and showing himself to them in a symbolic Eucharistic act (see Luke 24:13–35, esp. v. 15).

Do church leaders, we must ask, really give enough thought to the effects of media forms of communication on the relational quality of the Christian message? Do they sufficiently take into account the randomness of access to such communication? Can the fundamental Christian message effectively be transmitted in a communication system that apparently knows no borders, a system into which information can be added or modified at will, a system open to anyone and everyone, but demanding no personal commitment and allowing one to exit at will? For all the abundance of transportable information, is this not a communication that remains devoid of relationship?

b. The Meeting-and-Relationship Option

The alternative to the above option is an approach that gives priority to interpersonal encounter, which is not simply the product of communication techniques and use of media. Is this not the course for the future? Should we not direct our efforts to the I, the Thou, the tangible We (as opposed to the illusionary We of the networked world)? Should we not concentrate on transparent, directed intersubjective processes of communication involving commitment?

Not every object of faith is accessible to everyone at every given time. The transmission of faith needs the intimate space of encounter in family, group, or community. The church's awareness of these facts, however, seems now to be diminishing, though at the beginning of church history it played a leading role. One can well ask if the churches, through their use of mass communication, have not in fact fostered the typically postmodern noncommittal reception of the faith.

As we have seen, it is not merely the reflection on communication in society at large that needs theological attention, but also in the church. That is why, in an additional step, we will ask how communicative theology goes about its task of reflection, how it arrives at its insights. We will thereby assume that theology understands itself as being "God-talk" and will speak of it accordingly. The content-specific accents of communicative theology's "God-talk" will be systematically dealt with in chapter 4.

Questions for Reflection

- Which tendencies related to communication-oriented society are/were you aware of? Which were you unaware of?
- Which do you consider correct? Which do not correspond to your experience?
- Where are you personally affected by the trend toward more effective communication? Where do you fall within this trend? Where and how do you consciously set distinctive accents?

V. God in All Things: An Alternative?

In order to focus attention on contextuality, which theologians now take for granted, and to illustrate the necessary connections between contents, form, and medium, I (Matthias Scharer) will narrate an experience I once had.

Figure 7

1. God, Life, and Modern Medicine

The wife of a friend who had died of cancer was visiting me. I give her a guided tour through the premises of the old University of Innsbruck where the Theology School is located. In the course of the tour we came to the former senate meeting room, which is now used by the Department of Theology. There one finds the ceiling fresco reproduced in Figure 7. It depicts the interconnection of the sciences. In the four corners one sees symbols of the natural sciences, medicine, law, and theology. They all point to the "book with seven seals," symbolizing the mysteries of nature and the apocalypse, and to the Lamb, symbolizing the risen Christ. The intention of this arrangement is to say that creation and the history of salvation, centered in Christ's death and resurrection, are the focal point of all scientific endeavors. Science draws its knowledge from and directs it toward God's creation and revelation in Jesus Christ. Seen in this way, all of the sciences, not just theology, contribute to the search for truth about God and humans.

Silently, my friend's wife stood there contemplating the fresco. Then she said, "If science were like this today, things would have gone much better with my husband." She then told me how her husband, as a technician, had infinite trust in medical science at the beginning of his illness and how, when it became obvious that he was going to die, this trust totally disappeared. She said, "There is no longer any connection between God, human life, and medical science."

2. Can the Human Sciences Be Separated from the "Divine Sciences"?

The "old" understanding of science was, indeed, marked by the assumption that no truth about humans can exist beyond or outside of the truth about God, and God's creation and revelation in Jesus Christ. The Spirit of God ultimately made all human knowledge possible. Faith and science were inseparable.

This connection between faith and science is ideologically suspect for modern "enlightened" scientists: is faith not a private affair, which should have no effect on the work of the objective scientist? The question is, however, whether this sharp separation between faith and autonomous science does justice to the questions and quests of real human beings. (The wife of my cancer-stricken friend saw the fact that "there is no longer any connection between God, human life, and medical science" as raising a major problem.) Could it be that the theological insight expressed in the ceiling fresco of the Innsbruck Theology School is not just an obsolete paradigm after all, the insight namely that "God is in all things" and that God's revelatory communicative action becomes fully manifest only in the concerted action of all the sciences? Is the brusque rejection of any connection between faith and autonomous reason based on a certain perspective or in its articulation in scientific discourse? Is it not rather a reflection of the past history of injuries suffered by the "new" sciences at the hands of theological hubris which treated them as mere handmaids of theology instead of as disciplines in their own right? The fact is that in every scientific discipline one finds even today scientists who, motivated by their own faith, are open to the possibility that, in their scientific work, be it in the natural or cultural sciences, they can sense the "ineffable" though they make no attempt to articulate it directly within their scientific endeavors; for them, the knowledge of faith has its primary place in the personal sphere of their lives.

3. Life Sciences without God?

The questions raised here touch on a recent development at universities. Under the label "life sciences," the attempt is made to counter the trend toward further fragmentation of scientific research by bringing together under a single roof all the diverse sciences dealing with the phenomenon "life" in all its aspects. Such experiments, however, generally leave out theology. On the one hand, theology itself is reluctant to adopt the label "life science." On the other hand, prejudice against a "science of God and faith" is so great that theology's indispensable relevance for the life sciences is hardly appreciated.

4. Communicative Theology and Human Sciences

If theology understands itself as a reflection on communicative events, it cannot refuse cooperation with other sciences, especially with those that, explicitly or implicitly, deal with human communication. Theology can well assume that scientists, even when they do not explicitly acknowledge this to be the case, are in fact led by the Spirit of God in the quest for truth and for genuine knowledge of the world and the human person. When properly used, the rational procedures of the sciences do not contradict the truth of the Triune God. To acknowledge God in all things and thereby to understand both the world and humans in their genuine meaning is the aim of all scientific endeavor.

VI. The "Private" God and the "God-less" Science

The plausibility of the image of "God in all things" has long been shattered. Indeed, it would appear to have been turned into its opposite. The sciences obtained their freedom of research and thought by cutting themselves loose from the churches and "their" theologies and by banishing religion from the public sphere of society and science.

1. Autonomous Science

Following a dramatic history of condemnations and defensive isolation, the churches and theology have found their way to a new understanding of the relationship between science and faith. A classic text dealing with the relationship between the autonomous study of "earthly things" and the faith in God treated by theology is article 36 of the Second Vatican Council's pastoral constitution *Gaudium et spes*:

> If by the autonomy of earthly affairs is meant the gradual discovery, utilization and ordering of the laws and values of matter and society, then the demand for autonomy is perfectly in order: it is at once the claim of humankind today and the desire of the creator. By the very nature of creation, material being is endowed with its own stability, truth and excellence, its own order and laws. These, as the methods proper to every science and technique must be respected. Consequently, methodological research in all branches of knowledge, provided it is carried out in a truly scientific manner and does not override moral laws, can never conflict with the faith, because the things of the world and the things of faith derive from the same God. The humble and persevering investigators of the secrets of nature are being led, as it were, by the hand of God, even unawares, for it is God, the conserver of all things, who made them what they are. We cannot but deplore certain attitudes, not unknown among Christians, deriving from a short-sighted view of the rightful autonomy of science; they have occasioned conflict and controversy and have misled many into opposing faith and science.[21]

The drive toward research autonomy, the concentration on the scientific and technological paradigm of taking things apart to explain them, the privatization of religion, and the substitution of new dependency on markets and media for the former dependency on religion have all contributed to the marginalization of theology in the information society.

2. "Court Jesters" of Science

In an "educational society," where utilitarian pragmatism reigns, theologians are increasingly reduced to the role of "useless servants" or even "court jesters" of science. Yet, possibly, the conscious acceptance of this fact can make a "redeeming" contribution to the explanation of communicative reality and to the better appreciation of meaningful connections, without which no science worthy of the name "human" is possible. For such a role can only be played in the form of a selfless, critical service in the concert of the sciences, uncorrupted by the scientific power structure and its sponsoring mechanisms. Communicative theology is predestined for this role by its biblical foundations and its future-oriented capabilities.[22]

3. The "God-hypothesis," a "Private" Articulation of the All-determining Reality?

The modern context into which scientific theology is inserted has a large bearing on the question of how theologians come to their knowledge and what theology can mean as a reflection of a communicative event. Given the Council's demand for a "methodical investigation within every branch of learning . . . carried out in a genuinely scientific manner and in accord with moral norms," it follows that theologians share in the prevailing scientific standards of the scientific community. According to Wolfhart Pannenberg's interpretation of science, theologians, together with the representatives of other cultural sciences, make an important contribution to overcoming the traditional separation between the law-like explanations of the natural sciences and the hermeneutical interpretations of the humanities. This contribution takes the form of a "system-theory rather than merely a nomo-logical notion of explanation."[23] With such an expanded notion of under-standing, it becomes possible to locate the individual within the whole and so to integrate the disparate units of meaning within increasingly larger con-texts, reaching out for an "ultimate sum total of meaning":[24] "Because every individual meaning depends on this whole (*Sinntotalität*), the latter is implic-itly invoked in every experience of particular meaning."[25] Thus, the question of truth coincides "with the internal coherence of the semantic totality (*Sinn-totalität*) which embraces all experience."[26]

But even if each meaningful experience refers to this sum total of mean-ing,[27] it does not necessarily follow that reality contains within itself an all-encompassing, unbroken meaningful whole. After all, there are the experiences of "meaninglessness" and "senselessness" to account for. The quest for an all-encompassing meaning of reality as "truth" points beyond this world. It is, according to Pannenberg, identical with the quest for God. The "God-hypothesis," that is, the postulate of an all-determining reality, must be measured by its own implications and must be confirmed in people's experi-ence. Such a reality is something that "happens" to people. It can be recog-nized indirectly, never directly in the accounts of human witnesses to such "happenings" within time and history. The clear and direct manifestation of God is possible only from the perspective of the end of history, as Jesus, for instance, anticipated in his hope-evoking announcement of the coming of the reign of God. The confirmation of such hope by God, as manifested in Jesus' resurrection, must be maintained throughout history by integrating ever-new experiences into the central Christian perspective. For this reason it must be treated scientifically only as a hypothesis.

4. Traces of the "Communicative" God

Communicative theology looks for parameters with which we can identify those meaningful experiences, impossible to produce, that befall us. Such experiences help us to escape meaninglessness because they contain within themselves the seeds of an all-encompassing, meaningful whole. Reflection on communicative events makes possible some important distinctions based on the specifically Christian "God-hypothesis" and the communicative structure of the church, whose mission it is to keep alive the hope in the coming of God's reign. The Christian "God-hypothesis" is not an abstract philosophical theory. It is instead a "communicative reality," in which the truth of God is perceived as a being-in-relationship. God is a God of life and freedom; God *is* relationship, and God has communicated God's self to humankind. The church is thus a "sanctified fragment," despite all its fractures and sinfulness; it represents that form of communication in which the hope for the coming reign of God shines forth as the all-encompassing communicative reality of God.

When, therefore, it is a matter of communicative experiences, which continue to generate meaning and hold open the future for God, then it is appropriate to "reflect" on communicative events in the church and society in the light of such experiences. Such reflection does not take place in a void or in a laboratory. It cannot take place in isolation from the concrete societal and ecclesial forms of communicative activity. Communicative theology must be grounded in model events of communication of the sort that we practice in our training courses in communicative theology. All this underscores the indissoluble connection between theory and practice and the ecclesiological anchoring of such a theology.

5. Possibilities and Limitations of Communication Sciences

Such processes show that theologians cannot rely solely on scientifically qualified, primarily hermeneutical procedures as a scientific methodology for analyzing details and interpreting isolated facts. In its dependence on religion and belief in God, theology must always look to the all-encompassing horizon of meaning. This means that in concrete communication processes theology has to pose the decisive questions regarding meaning, orientation, and future survival of the world and of humankind. Such questions tend to be overlooked due to the increasing specialization and fragmentation of detailed research. Potentially, therefore, theologians can counter with their questions the growing mistrust of modern science generated by its failure to provide orientation. The "God-hypothesis" is like a thorn in the side of modern science's specialization. It is a call not to limit science's truth claim to the closed horizon of the "next to the last," but rather to open up scientific thinking to the "open horizon" that encompasses the whole reality of human experience, including religion. Furthermore, it is an invitation to go beyond this horizon to anticipate the possible future of the human person and the world and thus contribute to a rationally founded hope.

Questions for Reflection

- How do you see and experience the differentiation and interconnection of the sciences?
- Where and how do you encounter the sciences or their results as isolated elements in your life context? What effects of this encounter do you perceive?
- What role can theology play in the future development of the sciences? What do you expect from theology here? What do you not expect?

VII. Revisiting the Question: How Is Theology Done Communicatively?

Against the background of these reflections we repeat the question already raised in chapter 1: How is theology done communicatively?

As an undivided and indivisible, transcendent and communicative reality, God is not immediately accessible empirically or phenomenologically. Using only the explanatory methods of natural science and technology or the hermeneutical paradigm of the cultural sciences, theologians can learn nothing more than linguists studying texts or anthropologists and historians of religion studying the rites and usages of different cultures. On the other hand, historical-critical, comparative, interpretative approaches, among others, to the study of the religious expressions of humankind, including the Jewish-Christian expressions of faith, are indispensable for theology. Equally indispensable is the scientific understanding of contemporary religious phenomena, inside or outside Christian denominations, insofar as they are studied by religious phenomenology and religious sociology.[28]

1. Knowledge Coming from Identification and Communication

Is the linguistic, cultural, and social scientific preparation of theologians sufficient to enable them to grasp what is essential in "God's communication with humankind," which culminates in the incarnation of God in Jesus Christ as the central act of liberation/redemption valid for all persons and cultures? How can the "central core" of the Christian "God hypothesis" in its narrative and symbolic expression be accessed scientifically? The answer is: only from within! The texts of life and faith divulge their meaning only in the process of reflection on human speech-acts. This presupposes an identification that is open to the meaningful connections inherent in the communication between God and human beings. The form of this disclosure, however, depends on the object of the knowledge gained. The notion of communication is thus not arbitrary; it is analogous to the Christian understanding of the One and Triune God, who in God's self represents the "form of communication"[29] par excellence and who, by God's very essence, is directed toward communication with the world and with people in such a way that this communication finds its binding human expression in creation, in the covenant, and ultimately in Jesus Christ.

Theological knowledge may never be isolated from the others, be they acquaintances or strangers, who are also involved in the communication process, but it is always encompassed in the actual communicative community of the churches, where the "grace" of communio "happens" within the context of permanent otherness. Theologians do not attain their knowledge by working solely in the ecclesial and social isolation of their study, on their computer or in the library; of vital importance is their participation in the joys, sorrows, and conflicts of real men and women whom they encounter in Christian communities critically confronted with the Gospel. The communio of seeking/believing Christians united in their living witness of faith, in their service to one another and to society, and centrally in their liturgical celebration is an indispensable source of theological knowledge.

The truth of God-talk, which theologians are always trying to approach, does not, therefore, lie in an ideological insistence on this or that position to the exclusion of some other position. Neither is it to be found solely through critical interpretation of some canonized text. Theology as all-encompassing understanding of communication is itself based on communication. This theological communication does not—not even in the face of the fiction of apparently boundless communication inside a global village—refrain from bringing into scientific discourse the event of grace, which befalls a person open to the gift of transformation. From a hermeneutical point of view, we see that the quest for the truth of what it means to be human from the perspective of the Jewish-Christian God goes forward in a tension between an understanding based on a common horizon, on the one hand, and, on the other hand, the challenge to be open toward a communication process in which speaker and listener appear not to share a common horizon. This is an experience that people can have not only with a "God as stranger" but also, intersubjectively, with other people perceived as strangers.[30] The Other, as the stranger, indeed the wholly Other, is conceivable as a "communication partner" in an encounter in which the human person and world are open toward a horizon that makes empirical limitations obsolete. This experience of horizon expansion can befall one explicitly in the ritual "game" of liturgy, in which past, present, and future come together, making the "real presence" of God's history of dealing with humankind become tangible as a salvation history.[31] But the expansion of the horizon also becomes visible in other "communicative actions" in which the working of God's Spirit shines forth, for instance, in the witness of one's life or in service of one another

2. Who Is Welcome at the Table?

An example helps illustrate how traces, however fragmentary, of such comprehensive events of communication manifest themselves in concrete situations and lead to an immediate, theologically relevant insight.[32]

> *Near the Innsbruck railway station, some Catholics were celebrating Mass. The Mass was well under way, when a woman, easily recognizable as a prostitute, entered the chapel. She was evidently rather tipsy. Loudly she shouted, "Do I get something here, too?" She obviously meant the Eucharistic bread. The priest presiding over the Eucharist was speechless at first, then hesitantly he said, "Yes, certainly," in the secret hope that the woman might eventually leave the chapel before Communion would be distributed. She stayed, however, and at communion took the Eucharistic bread in her hands, broke the host in two, consumed one half and put the other in her pocket. Then she left the church. It turned out that she went straight to the mission station at the railway depot, where a sister who had often helped her in the past was on duty. The woman gave the sister the other piece of the host, saying, "Look what I've brought you! I know how you love to eat it."*

Sociologically, this incident is about a group of people gathered together for a ritual action expressing their group identity who are suddenly confronted with a dilemma when their interaction is unexpectedly disturbed by an "uninitiated" person. To understand the group's reaction, one can appeal initially to theories of group sociology. Humanly speaking, the more a ritual action is ideologically freighted, and the more it expresses the group's identity existentially, the greater is the likelihood that the "stranger" will be excluded as a disturber of the ritual action. The plausibility of such exclusion can be verified by a study of the manifold exclusion mechanisms practiced by traditional religions. Jesus himself was a victim of a process of exclusion. The "new" religions are no less exclusive when it comes to identifying who is "in" and who is "out." The global selection processes of the market and the media, processes that are unconsciously mirrored in the way science is done in the Northern Hemisphere, do not merely exclude individuals, but produce instead hosts of marginalized victims.

What made it possible for the liturgical community near the Innsbruck railway station to overcome its initial hesitation and refrain from excluding the stranger? And what made it possible for the woman to act spontaneously in a theologically relevant manner? This incident bears a significant resemblance to the stories of Jesus' eating and drinking narrated in the New Testament. That all human beings were welcomed by Jesus and that he did not hesitate to eat and drink with "tax collectors and sinners," that is, with people in moral disrepute, left such a strong impression on his early followers that it found unmistakable expression in the portrait of Jesus painted by the New Testament witnesses. Therefore, it belongs to the prophetic heritage of Christianity that, in the social and ecclesial response to others and to strangers, any exclusion of people runs contrary to the "Word of God" incarnated in Jesus Christ. Such a theological insight, more implicit than explicit in our example, acquired within and by means of the church's central celebration, suggests further steps to be taken theologically.

3. Theology Born of Contextual Attention and Authentic Vulnerability

In the congregation's sensitivity to this woman's situation and her question, as well as in the woman's sensitivity to the deep meaning of the Eucharist, we find an example of the practical significance of "contextualizing theology" in scientific "God-talk." As we see in this case, taking the theological context into account is not a matter of subjective or intersubjective aloof analysis of the life world (*Lebenswelt*). It demands authentic involvement in the joys and hopes, the grief and anguish of the people of our time as a source of theological insight.[33] The sympathy (literally, "suffering with") of the biblical God with the hardships and opportunities of both the human person and society may well stimulate the use of intersubjectively oriented human and social-scientific methods of "analysis of the life world" in order to "see" better what is happening. Yet, theological "seeing" confronts the problem of truth at a level on which it is no longer simply a matter of verifiable or falsifiable partial elements of human reality but rather of human reality as a whole, in view of the sustainability of humankind and society in the one world for all. If the church, according to Vatican II, understands itself as a "sacrament," that is, as "a sign and instrument, of communion with God and of the unity of the entire human race,"[34] then Christian theology, contextually attentive and authentically involved, is able to gain the knowledge that is given to it by the Spirit of God's presence in the world, outside as well as inside the church's proclamation (see chapter 1).

4. Theology Born out of a Capacity for Guilt and Acknowledged Powerlessness

In such a learning process, theology in a living relationship to church history, is not allowed to shrug off the burdens of the past, for example, unresolved confessional divisions, remainders of anti-Judaism, culturally ignorant mission campaigns (in Latin America, for instance), discrimination against women. No theology stands out as a "pure" representative of a truth claim. To make such claims means to ignore its involvement in the historic guilt of humankind. Precisely as a critical science, theology examines its conscience and acknowledges its guilt. Theology is impelled to deal critically with its historical failures and faults by its abiding trust that, in the eyes of our loving God, no guilt is so great, no fault so disastrous that it should be hidden from enlightened reason.

Theological group processes can bring to the fore the global entanglement of the churches and of theology in guilt and can give expression to the individual and communicative powerlessness of those touched by individual and collective suffering. Such emotionally moving moments and scenarios have their place in existentially significant theological processes. One must learn not to fall into individual or collective depression, but also not to repress feelings of vulnerability either. Our example puts us on the right path.

5. Theology Born of the Gift of Transformation

Contrary to all canonical and sacramental-theological standards of worthiness of those receiving Communion, the priest in our example agreed to the woman's request, evidently not without a bad conscience: "You too will get something to eat here!" For both the priest and the community, the Eucharist is far more than just "something to eat." Under the form of the holy bread that the celebrating community eats together and the cup from which they drink, the whole history of God's dealings with human beings is made really present, most notably God's presence to Jesus in his death on the cross. That God should be present on the cross is no more obvious for people today than it was for the early church. The Hebrew Bible says: "Anyone hung on a tree is under God's curse" (Deuteronomy 21:22; cf. Galatians 3:13). For this reason, the fate of Jesus, signified in the Eucharistic celebration of the Christian community, is "foolishness" from a human point of view (1 Corinthians 1:18), but for Christians, it is an expression of "God's power" (1 Corinthians 1:18): "For as often as you eat this bread and drink the cup, you proclaim the Lord's death until he comes" (1 Corinthians 11:26). The fact that the priest, notwithstanding his hesitations, gave the Eucharist to the woman and the fact that the community, contrary to all logic of social conventions, accepted this social and theological provocation without indignant protest, reveal a theological insight of central importance to the communication between God and human beings. Even a ritualized communicative action can be broken open for the sake of an individual, when both priest and community let themselves be transformed toward new insight by the inner mystery of the celebration.

6. Theology as Distinction

At present, Christian theology can only be done in a context of plural religious experiences. From the point of view of a functional understanding of religion it is clear that the religious field is becoming increasingly blurred. New social institutions are forming which, like a kind of "super-religion," determine the lives of more and more people. They take on functions that traditionally belonged to the domain of religion. The market and the media, as pseudo-religious phenomena, dominate ethical and ideological orientation and the quest for meaning, even to the point of becoming the life-and-death horizon for more and more people. For the sake of their own freedom, there is need for a debate between these new "gods" and the One and Triune God of the Bible and Christian tradition. The information- and communication-based society, in particular, calls for such a debate.

Whenever worldviews are set against one another, the temptation to engage in an ideological battle is particularly strong. Each side accuses the other of being ideologically closed to impartial rational argument. The biblical story of the prophet Elijah (see 1 Kings 18) illustrates the effects of such ideological conflict. Elijah engaged in a bitter ideological battle with the priests of the false gods and called down on them divine punishment. Though he carried the day, his subsequent fate leads us to think of the theological depression that can befall even the victor of such ideological battles. Fleeing from the queen who persecutes him, he wished himself dead (see 1 Kings 19:4). It took God's angel to encourage him to get up and go on, in order to be transformed by the new, unfathomable intuition of God expressed in the gentle breeze, which breaks through the old theophanies of storm, fire, and other violent natural forces.

How can one distinguish between God and idols? In the first chapter of his letter to the Romans, Paul expresses his theological conviction that the knowledge of God is revealed and accessible to human reason. The quest for truth is thereby inextricably linked to the quest for justice. Injustice suppresses the truth. God's glory cannot break through; people will exchange it for temporal images:

> For the wrath of God is revealed from heaven against all ungodliness
> and wickedness of those who by their wickedness suppress the truth.

For what can be known about God is plain to them, because God has shown it to them. Ever since the creation of the world his eternal power and divine nature, invisible though they are, have been understood and seen through the things he has made. So they are without excuse; for though they knew God, they did not honor him as God or give thanks to him, but they became futile in their thinking, and their senseless minds were darkened. Claiming to be wise, they became fools; and they exchanged the glory of the immortal God for images resembling a mortal human being or birds or four-footed animals or reptiles. (Romans 1:18–23)

Theologians are confronted ever anew with the truth of God and thereby with the truth of humankind and the world. That is to say, they come to their knowledge by identifying what people set their hearts on and what they make into their gods. The scientific debate about the true God in the form of argumentation makes sense only if we place our trust in the ability of all men and women—not least in the intersubjectively intelligible insights of science—to gain access to the intuition of the One who, as St. Paul puts it, "can be recognized in creation" but who remains at the same time the transcendent Other. If we were to look for a formula to sum up the way in which theologians gain their insights, we could speak of "intersubjectively comprehensible interpretation in anticipatory communicative actions." Such an understanding keeps heaven open for human reality and does not mistake mere images of passing realities for the "glory of the eternal God."

Questions for Reflection

- What image of theology do you bring from your theological formation?
- Is your image of theology and of theological insight confirmed, irritated, or changed by what you have just read? If so, how?
- What existential consequences do a participatory theology capable of accepting responsibility and transformation make possible?

CHAPTER 4

The Communicative God of Christian Revelation and God's Communication in History

In this chapter, we will deal explicitly with the content or the "It" aspect of theology—the faith tradition in its theological meaning and its relationship to other perspectives of the communication of faith. In this way the question of God will explicitly come into view.

I. God—a Communicative Being

The previous considerations compelled us to reflect on God as the subject, that is, the starting point, the permanent reference, and the final goal of every theological effort. It has already become clear that the decisive (constitutive) and communicative actions of the community have God as a subject, albeit in a primary and basic sense. It has also become clear that even a fully theocentric theology, such as Karl Barth's dialectical theology, cannot avoid speaking of people, even as it speaks of God. This means, in reverse, that to speak of God is to speak of God as relating to humankind.

It may seem a bit strange and questionable that, in this place, we should speak here about God as a communicative being. One might suspect that—yet again—God is being identified with some theological concept, that we and our "communicative theology" are imposing on God the kind of "mirroring" of human experiences of communication and longings that we criticized in chapter 2. This danger is real, and it can be withstood only by a rigorous negation of the concept itself. We could exclude misunderstandings resulting from a narrow conception of communication, but that would be irritating within this context and give the impression that we are sanctioning mere talking about God. Silence before God, meditation, liturgy of various kinds, spiritual conversations, sharing of biblical faith were and are constant ingredients in our courses in communicative theology. That is to say, we are dedicated to a holistic understanding of communication, combining talking about God with listening to God's Word and with talking to God in response.

Another serious objection to the concept of communicative theology might be raised here. Is God's otherness being underestimated? A first partial answer is: indeed, God is also someone who is silent, someone who talks in such a way that people do not understand God, someone who escapes even those who turn to God with trust. God is not someone who can be reached on a hotline at any time! A theology that does not take into account that God is also the wholly other, the silent one, the concealed one, the absent one falls short of its task. A second partial answer is: this does not mean that theology also has to be totally strange, totally concealed, or totally wrapped in silence. Theology's task is to speak even when drawing attention to the fact that, on this or that point, every speech must become silent. To do otherwise would be to risk cutting off speech and thought prematurely. It is certainly right that concerning some decisive theological questions (e.g., how can God allow suffering) there is no answer that can satisfy our human reason. Theology's task is not to keep silent on such questions; rather, it is to look for reasons for the lack of an answer. One should, therefore, make a distinction between God and theology. The situation we have just sketched puts theology—insofar it as remains within its actual scope—in a posture of humility.

If we look once again toward the God of whom theology speaks, we can further clarify the definition of God as a "communicative being." For the believer, God is a relational being. This is no human invention; rather, it is something made possible by God's own revelation of God's self. That is to say, God enters into a relationship with the world as creation and with people as created beings, as sinners and redeemed, and as beings on the way to perfection. Only in this way can we speak about God as relational. Even in Christian theology, we can make no statements about God *in and for God's self.* This God *in and for God's self* we can meet only as God *for us.* But we cannot draw the conclusion that God *in and for God's self* does not exist. It is really a question of drawing a line to mark the limits of theological reflection and expression. With regard to the concept of communicative theology we can say: it is only because God enters into a relationship with us, because he wishes to be in communion with us and makes contact with us, that we can speak about and with God. We can also add further precision to our description by saying that God is *the* communicative being par excellence. It is first and foremost God who makes possible communication and community, which keeps us alive. This is our faith in God the creator of heaven and earth, of all things visible and invisible. It is not, in the first place, God's self-revelation in history that shows God to be *the* communicative being; this is already manifested by God's self-revelation as creator.

What this means for God's revelation in history will be examined in detail in section IV of this chapter. It has been necessary here to consider briefly the revealing action of God both in creation and in history in order to emphasize what we are saying about God as *the* communicative being par excellence. We cannot make any reliable statement about God independently of God's self-revelation. In this way we are trying to avoid the misunderstanding that theology can be developed "from above," that is, by first developing an abstract concept of God in and for God's self and then bringing this concept into contact with history. Thus, if we here speak of God as *the* communicative being, before considering revelation and history, then we will never lose sight of the starting point of our discourse, which makes this discourse possible.

Under the assumption that we can speak about and to God only because God has spoken to us and continues to do so, we can take a further step that for Christian theology is as crucial as it is controversial. It is clear that God may be understood as a communicative being with regard to creation as a whole and to humanity in particular. Christian proclamation of God, however, goes on to speak of God as a thoroughly, intrinsically relational being. This is the core of the Christian faith in the Triune God. But it poses a serious challenge to theological explanation. In our communicative theology courses we have tried to highlight this core truth by presenting the topic of the communication of the Triune God as "In the Beginning Is Relationship." Such a motto is true with regard to creation and humanity, as stated above. Is it also true about God? Must we, can we, may we say that God, the origin of everything, is in God's self originally a relational and communicative being? Abstract speculation on the concept of God does not bring us any further. In dialogue with strictly monotheistic religions, such as Judaism or Islam, we can say that God, with regard to creation and humanity, is a relational and communicative being even if one thinks of God in a strictly monotheistic fashion without speaking about relationships *within God*. But how does Christian theology come to speak about relationships within God as well?

Questions for Reflection

- Is it easy for you to speak about God or does it make you stammer?
- If you think about God, do personal images come to mind, or rather symbols of transcendence?
- What does "relationship" mean for you? Do you also link relationship to God?
- Where do you experience God as near and familiar and where as "other" and unapproachable?

II. How Did the Christian Community Come to Profess the Trinitarian God?

The Christian image of God has developed by means of a process of experiences and communication. Its final formulation defined by the Councils of

Nicaea (325) and Constantinople (381) represents what we described as a constitutive communicative action. This action is renewed not in new synodal or conciliar gatherings but in each celebration of baptism and often in the Eucharistic celebration.

How did Christians come to their profession of trinitarian faith? How did they come to say "God" and understand the Father of Jesus Christ, Jesus the Christ, and the Holy Spirit, the Lord and the Giver of Life?

The starting point, the *locus theologicus* from which the Christian experience of God gains its communicative explanation is decisive. In the traditional doctrine about God, a fatal medieval partition of this doctrine is reflected. Before speaking about the Trinity (*De Deo Trino*), one dealt with "the One God" (*De Deo Uno*). This gives the impression that a philosophical, metaphysical doctrine of God could be developed without regard to the experience of the Triune God. Christian theologians started their reflection with the Creed. The intention behind this approach was to be able to debate this Creed also with monotheistic Jews or Muslims and to find common ground for the discussion about God. In these debates the question arose whether traces of the Triune God or only of the One God could be found in creation. However well intentioned this approach might have been, it fostered a division that, as we have said, is fatal. By the fact that in the treatise on the One God decisive things were already said about God's essence, the impression was given that in dealing with the Trinity, nothing essential would be added. Indeed, some treatises dealt with the Trinity as if it were some higher mathematics or weak and naïve symbolism.

Even today we tend to start our discussion about God by developing a sort of general feeling for transcendence. Still, it is crucial that the respective communicative processes manifest the roots of the Christian experience of God. For the formation of the Christian profession of faith in God, the experience of God which Jesus of Nazareth himself had and then shared with his disciples is decisive. It was Israel's experience of God that Jesus of Nazareth shared and articulated—albeit in a provocative way—within the mainstream of the Old Testament tradition. We have to state this with the greatest precision: the starting point and permanent reference point of the Christian faith is Israel's experience of God as taught and lived by Jesus of Nazareth until his death. In the resurrection God the creator was made known by witnessing to Jesus as God's own son and ultimate messenger. From that moment on, the followers of Jesus could no longer speak of God without speaking of this Jesus of Nazareth. In the confrontation with strict monotheists, they had to strive to give a twofold answer to the crucial question of whether Jesus is on the side of God or of humankind. First, Jesus of Nazareth was like us in everything but sin, that is, he always remained in communion with God; and, second, at the same time, God communicated God's self as our salvation through this very man Jesus.

Another fundamental experience for the Christian profession of faith was added to the insight into Jesus' relationship with the Father. Jesus, who understood himself as fully dependent on God, his Abba Father, acted in the holy/healing Spirit of God. Jesus revealed to his disciples what kind of child of the Spirit he was and is. This revelation took place through faith communication, by means of prayer, meditation, reading of the scriptures, in theological discussions "on everything that happened in Jerusalem," in constitutive communicative actions such as the table fellowship and service with his disciples (see the Emmaus-account in Luke 24). In this way the disciples found out that it was the Spirit of God who proclaimed Jesus as savior of Israel at his baptism. It was the same Spirit who took him to the desert and helped him withstand the temptation to exchange his mission for earthly power. Through the same Spirit he expelled evil spirits and freed people from their oppression. The same Spirit united him with God who is Father, Creator, and Savior. This same Spirit helped him in Gethsemane to remain faithful to his mission and to the love he had for his friends. In the same Spirit, he entrusted his life into the Father's hands, despite all human despair. What the disciples experienced living with Jesus during his time on earth, they understood fully only after having experienced him risen and living in their midst. Then it became clear to them that it was God's Spirit who raised Jesus from the dead and placed him at the right hand of the Father as judge of the living and the dead. They realized that it was in the Spirit that God descended so deeply into creation that God became incarnate in the actual person of Jesus.

Thus, the disciples were compelled, when speaking about God, to refer also to Jesus and to the holy/healing Spirit of God. Just as at the Council of Nicaea it was said that in Jesus Christ the Word of God had become flesh, so in the Council of Constantinople in 381 it was decided that the Holy Spirit is the Spirit who comes from the Father, who is Lord and Giver of Life and, as such, a divine Spirit, who is worshipped and glorified with the Father and the Son. It was not philosophical theories or metaphysical speculation that moved the people of God, with their bishops and theologians, to explain this triune, communicative notion of God. It was an experience based on the conviction that only God could save us, restore our broken communication, and sustain our coexistence. To this first conviction, that only God could save us, a second conviction emerged: only if God came among us and dwelt within us would we be saved. An axiom of patristic theology said: "What is not assumed is not redeemed; but whatever is united to God is also saved."[1]

Questions for Reflection

- Where do you find yourself in the Emmaus episode?
- Can you experience the fact that God is close to you in body and spirit?
- Do you yourself speak about Jesus and the Spirit when you speak about God?

III. Features of the Communicative Understanding of God

Is the essence of God a communicative one? When we say that Jesus is consubstantial with the Father, does that mean that he has a share in this communicative essence? Is that also true of the Spirit who is not explicitly called consubstantial in the Creed but is implicitly affirmed to be co-essential ("together worshipped and glorified")? The fact that God communicates God's self in Jesus of Nazareth and in the Holy Spirit reveals God to be a communicative being, a relational God. This was not easily understandable for Judaism and even less so for Hellenistic culture. A strict version of monotheism maintained the transcendent, unchanging, and unmoved character of the divinity. A descent from the divine sphere into the worldly sphere meant nothing short of a degeneration of the divine condition.

Greek philosophers also conceived unity as very strict, without diversity and without differentiation. Christians, however, wanted to hold fast to the fact that God communicated God's self in Jesus of Nazareth through the Holy Spirit, without thereby ceasing to be God. In the confrontation with the Greeks, it was not a matter of replacing One with Three or finding symbols that would explain tri-unity in order to replace the symbol of unity in the rigorous sense. Rather, it was a matter of convincing them that God can enter this world without ceasing to be God. God can really come into and be present in our midst without diminution of God's divinity. Admittedly, the Christian ideal is the homecoming to the heavenly house of the Father. The motive for this return, however, is not the rejection of matter as somehow evil but instead the perfection of creation.

For Jews, then as now, the idea of a living diversity in God posed no problem as long as the concretization of this relational diversity does not become independent "persons." The Old Testament speaks about God's Word, God's Wisdom, in the sense of messengers going about the exercise of some divine mission or of an entity like God's Wisdom, which accompanied God before the world was created. In this sense, pastor and poet Kurt Marti could speak poetically of a "social divinity."[2] We should bear in mind, however, the limits of such a characterization. What the God of Israel and the God of Christians is cannot be thought of by means of a general concept of divinity. The richness of relationships in God cannot be conceived by means of weak analogies of social life.

But, with regard to any dialogue with Jews or Muslims, we should bear in mind that it is not just when we speak about the Son of God or the Holy Spirit coming from the Father (and the Son) that we start to speak of God as a communicative being. In our dialogue with Jews or Muslims we can maintain that *in and for God's self* God is *for us* and that God is always such a God who expresses God's self through communication and communion, that is, through shared life and relationship. For our part, we Christians will say that God's self-revelation, as the divine communication through the Son and the Holy Spirit, is essentially an expression of what we have experienced about God. Speaking of God and calling God Father, Son, and Holy Spirit are therefore by no means the abolition or the dissolution of monotheism into polytheism (tritheism) but is rather the symbolic presentation of what we know about the communicative essence of God.

At this point all the concepts and images we apply to God—even the best ones—reveal their limits. Indeed, the very notion of person and the notion of communion are limited and can lead to misunderstanding and error. This is why in interreligious dialogue it makes little sense and it is not usually productive to operate with one-, two-, or three-God conceptions. It is far more productive to ask ourselves: which intention provides the background for each image of God, for each theo-logy? In our courses, we have learned to distinguish between the theme and the intention behind it. We are constantly reminded that such a distinction can also be helpful in ecumenical dialogue, as well as for faith and for theological communication in general.

Which intention, then, provides the background for a Christian's faith in the Trinity? It is the profession of God as a communicative being. God is a God who, by God's own volition, expresses God's self through relationship, communication, and the expansion of this communion into the sphere of the nondivine. This is not something inferred or invented. It is neither wishful thinking nor a mere projection of an idea onto the divinity. We Christians—just as Jews or Muslims in their own specific ways—are convinced that God communicated God's self. For us, Jesus of Nazareth is the climax of this communication, which, through the Holy Spirit, is shared with us permanently and which continues to live in us. Instead of speaking about "three persons," Father, Son and Spirit, we can try to articulate the basic intention underlying our creed by speaking of the source of divinity, its eccentricity (*Exzentrizität*), and its concentration, its centrifugal and its centripetal force. In this sense, Jesus Christ stands for the concentrating and centripetal movement (tending towards the center) and the Holy Spirit for the eccentric and centrifugal movement (tending outward from the center) within the dynamic of the One God.[3] In other words, God is a communicative being inasmuch as God is oriented per se toward the communication of divine self to that which is not divine and, in this communication, God always comes back to God's self. God exteriorizes and interiorizes God's self at the same time. Therefore, the fact that God is not dependent on the communication of someone else in order to come back to God's self accounts for the divinity of the communicative God. This idea that the existing one returns to itself through the other is fundamental to Hegel's three steps: thesis, antithesis, synthesis. In Christian trinitarian theology, this basic idea is deepened insofar as God fulfills God's self in the three steps of self-communication, self-finding, and self-being. This is a limit notion, which should remind us that God does not depend on us to be

God. All the greater then is God's gratuitous gift of depending on us to perfect creation and to live in communion with God.

In our Christian perspective the Holy Spirit stands for this eccentricity of God, for God's going out of God's self toward creation and the world, toward the nondivine. Therefore, God is to be found in God's Spirit in all creation. Jesus Christ is the concentration point of this eccentric movement, the point in which the eccentricity is condensed and concentrated, made concrete. God's going out of God's self is always, at the same time, a bringing home, a concentration, a meditation, a movement toward the center. In dialogue with other religions, we can seek similar experiences of God's going out of God's self, of God's coming toward the center. Particularly interesting is the question whether or not in other religions there are such experiences of God's becoming human, becoming flesh, of an incarnation, of a manifestation of God as a centripetal force, that is, the force that is oriented back toward the center.

We have explained the Christian understanding of God, which resulted from experience, meditation, and reflection. It is not something inferred from something else but a development of self-communication. It is assumed that both revelation and faith, as well as transmitting and living the faith, can be understood today only as communicative processes. If the communicative God reveals the divine self, this revelation can only be a communicative event. The transmission of this communicative event can take place only in the form of communicative processes. We will elaborate on this theme in the next section.

Questions for Reflection

- Do you have any experiences of talking about the things of God with people of other religions?
- Can you verify in your own experience a centripetal and a centrifugal force, a drive toward ecstasy and a drive toward concentration?
- Do you find it easy to give up the word "person" when you speak about God?

IV. Revelation and Faith as a Communicative Event

Earlier, in section II, we stated for a fact that we can only speak about God because God revealed God's self to us. To speak about the communicative God assumes God's communication with people. The two sides of this communication are theologically termed "revelation" and "faith." They are like the two sides of a coin: God reveals the divine self in order for people to believe; people come to believe because God has revealed God's self. These two notions are relational concepts. They depend on each other. Still, they do not constitute a symmetrical relationship. Faith does not constitute revelation but vice versa. Revelation would miss its goal if no one were to believe. Faith is revelation's raison d'être. Since they are relational events, revelation and faith are events of freedom. That is to say, even God cannot force anybody to come to faith. God invites a free response. Still less can the faithful compel God's revelation. What holds for interhuman relationships holds all the more when we consider God's relationship with the human person. The dialectical theology of the younger Karl Barth, which we previously have mentioned, so radically contrasted revelation and faith that the Triune God in God's very self became the recipient of revelation, because, on the human side, there could be no point of contact with revelation. Such a concept is invalid, because in this case revelation would not be revelation at all if there were no one to whom it could be revealed or who would be invited as a free being to believe in the One who reveals the divine self.

In the following, we are going to consider revelation and faith as the two sides of the same communicative event.

1. Revelation as God's Self-Communication to the Creature

For our conception of communicative theology, an interesting parallel presents itself. With regard to what the church sees as revelation, we notice an important shift of accents between the statements of the First Vatican Council (1869–1870) and the Second Vatican Council (1962–1965). Roughly speaking, the accent shifted from a strictly unilateral communicative action on God's part toward differentiated and mutual action involving also the human respondent, thus making the communicative event more clearly recognizable as the defining feature. The striking parallel is in the development of the concept of theological teaching and learning, which has thus been released from a one-sided, mainly cognitive and authoritative, approach to discursive actions, and moves along the lines of what we could term a communicative theology, involving the interaction of various subjects.

In the Dogmatic Constitution on the Catholic Faith, Vatican I spoke about the revelation of God to the creature, which, as a matter of principle, makes it possible for people to recognize God as the origin and the goal of all things "by the natural light of human reason."[4] The Council text goes on to say, "It was, however, pleasing to his wisdom and goodness to reveal himself and the eternal laws of his will to the human race by another, and that a supernatural, way."[5] The role of this so-called supernatural revelation is therefore to make the acknowledgment of God in creation easier; it is not, however, absolutely necessary to that end: "the reason is that God directed human beings to a supernatural end, that is a sharing in the good things of God that utterly surpasses the understanding of the human mind."[6]

Etymologically, as well as literally, to reveal means to uncover something that was concealed. This can happen in various ways: above all, by pointing to what was previously hidden or by speaking about things hitherto unknown. In this context, Vatican I chose to quote the Epistle to the Hebrews: "In the past God spoke to our forefathers through the prophets at many times and in various ways, but in these last days he has spoken to us by his Son" (Hebrews 1:1).[7] Thus Vatican I interpreted revelation as a form of God's speaking to people. This revelatory speech took place, for our ancestors in faith, through the prophets; in the Christian understanding, it occurred in an eminent and final way through the last prophet, Jesus Christ, the Son of God. Admittedly, it belongs to the tradition of scholastic theology to speak of revelation in word and deed, but deeds were seen only in their function of confirming the words. Such "deeds" were above all, the miracles of Jesus. Therefore, both the accomplishments of the Old Testament prophecies and the miracles of Jesus are viewed primarily as a confirmation of the divinity of his mission. To sum up, it can be said that, at the time of Vatican I, "revelation" was taken to mean the authoritative address of God to people.

But what was the content of this address? In the wording of Vatican I's Constitution on Revelation, God wished "to reveal Himself, as well as the eternal decisions of his will."[8] Vatican I, therefore, was acquainted with the notion that was to become the keynote of Vatican II, "God's self-revelation." But Vatican I withdraws behind the concept of revealing hidden things and decrees hitherto unknown. This interpretation is confirmed by the continuation of the above-quoted text, where it speaks about the absolute necessity of supernatural revelation, insofar as the human person is designed for a supernatural purpose. This supernatural purpose is explained as the share in "the good things of God," "that utterly surpass the understanding (!) of the human mind."[9] Certainly, "the good things of God" can be taken to mean a share in divine life, insofar as this obviously surpasses human understanding, but, with regard to the general context, it is significant to note that one looks first of all to the cognitive aspect of revelation. This is further confirmed by the assertion, in this connection, that this supernatural revelation is contained "in written books and unwritten traditions."[10] The cognitive moment is thus predominant; revelation is seen as a communication of truths, of dogmatic propositions.

Vatican II in its Constitution on Revelation starts from the same motif of God's revelatory action, which it sees in God's goodness and wisdom. Also, when it comes to the content of revelation, the text speaks of God's self-communication and about God's will. This is the exact wording:

> It pleased God, in his goodness and wisdom, to reveal himself and to make known the mystery of his will (see Ephesians 1:9), which was that people can draw near to the Father, through Christ, the Word made flesh, in the Holy Spirit, and thus become sharers in the divine

nature (see Ephesians 2:18; 2 Peter 1:4). By this revelation, then, the invisible God (see Colossians 1:15; 1 Timothy 1:17), from the fullness of his love, addresses men and women as his friends (see Exodus 33:11; John 15:14–15), and lives among them (see Baruch 3:38), in order to invite and receive them into his own company. The pattern of this revelation unfolds through deeds and words which are intrinsically connected: the works performed by God in the history of salvation show forth and confirm the doctrine and realities signified by the words; the words, for their part, proclaim the works, and bring to light the mystery they contain. The most intimate truth thus revealed about God and human salvation shines forth for us in Christ, who is himself both the mediator and the sum total of revelation.[11]

God reveals God's self and communicates to people the mystery of God's will. But Vatican II no longer speaks about the eternal decrees of God's will; it does not stress that God communicates these decrees to people. Rather, the Council speaks of mystery (Latin *sacramentum*). Here biblical and patristic terminology is used again. As in other Vatican II texts, one speaks of *mysterion/mysterium/sacramentum*. Revelation is a communicative reaching out by God, who has decided in favor of the redemption of humankind and of all creation. This saving plan, this *mysterion* of God's will, has been revealed by God and enacted throughout the history of salvation. The mystery of God's will is understood by Vatican II not as a communication of decrees and statements of truth but rather as a revelation of the share humans have in the life of the Triune God, through Christ, in the Spirit, with the Father.

In a second stage, Vatican II likewise speaks about God's speaking. This is understood, however, not as a communication of statements; rather, it is an address to the people. The accent placed on God's communicative revelatory action lies, therefore, not in the fact that God communicates some thing. The primary relationship is not of the "I-It"-type; rather, it is an "I-Thou" relationship. Stated even better, it is the relationship of the Triune divine "We" to the human "We." It is not a mere association in a community of knowledge but rather a union in the community of life, peace, and love. The motif of freedom is comprised in this, inasmuch as the text speaks in terms of an invitation and inasmuch as God is said to be the one who makes acceptance in this community possible, that is, by the acceptance of the invitation.

The text of Vatican II does indeed speak about the act of revelation taking place in words and deeds.[12] But, what appeared one-sided in the vision of scholastic theology and of Vatican I is raised to another level here: that of a mutual relationship of deeds and words. We should note that deeds are mentioned first and words last. Revelation is, therefore, God's self-communication above all in deeds, that is, in God's action for people. Revelation is thus a communicative event. More accurately than as mere speech, revelation can thus be described as God's "communicative action." We concur with Max Seckler that "the Council's notion of revelation is a communicative-participatory one." The Tübingen fundamental theologian explains this notion as follows: "While the 'communio' aspect is aimed at personal relationships made possible by God's self-revelation, the idea of participation expresses the granting of a share in the 'divine good,' that is, truth, justice, love, peace, and so on, that is to say, it expresses a social and objective component."[13]

One can demonstrate that communication, communio, and participation have, in a theological context, the same basic structure. There are three relational aspects, which make for a clear succession. First of all, there is God's self-communication, God's initiative in opening the communication, inviting into community, and offering a share in God's love. Second, there is the human person's trust in God's call. The human person allows him- or herself to be spoken to, grasps the hand that reaches out for communion, and accepts the offer of participation. Third, there is the life that corresponds to this basic structure of the mutual relationship between God and the human person. The human person becomes fulfilled as a communicative being. He or she lives in the communio of human community and participates in carrying out the communicative practice of the trinitarian community of life (reign of God).[14]

2. Faith: From "Assent to Truth" to Entrusting Oneself to God's "Communicatio" and "Communio"

Faith, as we said, is the other side of the coin, where God's self-revelation reaches its goal and people come to faith. As a result, it is obvious that a particular concept of revelation involves a corresponding concept of faith. We will now consider the notion of faith with a closer look at what the two Vatican Councils had to say on the matter.

The relevant passage in Vatican I's decree *Dei Filius* reads:

> Since human beings are totally dependent on God as their creator and lord, and created reason is completely subject to uncreated truth, we are obliged to yield to God the revealer full submission of intellect and will by faith.
>
> This faith, which is the beginning of human salvation, the Catholic Church professes to be a supernatural virtue, by means of which, with the grace of God inspiring and assisting us, we believe to be true what He has revealed, not because we perceive its intrinsic truth by the natural light of reason, but because of the authority of God himself, who makes the revelation and can neither deceive nor be deceived.[15]

As we can see, the supernatural revelation of faith corresponds to a supernatural virtue. In accordance with the asymmetrical relationship between creator and creature, there is also an asymmetrical relationship between God's revelation and the human person's faith. This asymmetry was particularly underscored by Vatican I. The text speaks about total surrender and submission. The reason for faith lies in the authority of God who reveals. Given that God cannot deceive God's self and—as the God of truth—does not wish to deceive anyone else, the revealed truth must be accepted solely on the basis of God's authority.

This definition of faith is expanded in the formula that post–Vatican I theologians saw as a quasi definition of dogma in a solemn and formal sense. The relevant paragraph reads as follows:

> By divine and Catholic faith all those things are to be believed which are contained in the word of God as found in Scripture and tradition, and which are proposed by the Church as matters to be believed as divinely revealed, whether by her solemn judgment or in her ordinary and universal magisterium.[16]

What is to be believed by divine and Catholic faith is a truth revealed by God ("divine faith") or put forward by the church as a truth of faith ("Catholic faith"). A dogma in the strict, solemn sense is, therefore, a statement by the church, wherein the church declares that the stated truth is part of God's revelation and is proposed for belief. From this definition, it follows—surprisingly for many—that the resurrection of Jesus is not a solemn dogma of the Catholic Church. Of course, no one in the church disputes the fact that the resurrection is an element of God's revelation. But in its 2,000 years of history, the church has never had the occasion solemnly to define it as such. By implication, to ask, therefore, what dogmas must be believed unconditionally is to reduce the content of faith only to those few truths, which, for historical reasons, happen to have been the object of solemn definition. Moreover, since Vatican I's quasi definition of what constitutes a "dogma" comes from 1869–70, it is not immediately clear what constituted "solemn proclamation" in the 1,800 years prior to this proclamation. Likewise, the provision that defined truth must be contained in revelation is not unproblematic. De facto, what is a solemnly defined truth of dogma has been a point of contention in diverse disputes between academic theology and the magisterium, particularly in an ecumenical context. What is important for us here is that Vatican I solemnly defined "revelation" and "faith," as did scholastic theologians well up to the mid-twentieth century, as the communication of truths of faith that people have to hold as true by reason of authority. One should note, moreover, that this one-way communication of revealed truths is continued by ecclesiastical mediations. The authority of the self-revealing God is made present by authorities in the church (Scripture, tradition, magisterium). The extent to which Vatican I envisages an asymmetrical, hierarchical gradient within a hierarchical society, instead of a communio made up of baptized persons sharing, as a matter of principle, the same dignity, is made clear by the following Vatican I text.

> So that we could fulfill our duty of embracing the true faith and of persevering unwaveringly in it, God, through his only begotten Son, founded the Church, and he endowed his institution with clear notes to the end that she might be recognized by all as the guardian and teacher of the revealed word. To the Catholic Church alone belong all those things, so many and so marvelous, which have been divinely ordained to make for the manifest credibility of the Christian faith. What is more, the Church herself . . . is a kind of great and perpetual motive of credibility and an incontrovertible evidence of her own divine mission.[17]

We do not by any means wish to question the fact that the church can in itself bear a credible witness to God's self-revelation. But we have to give careful consideration to what we understand by church, especially how we define the life of the church and how we respond to Jesus' invitation, "Come and see!" Even in our present time, in the aftermath of Vatican II, it is difficult to experience a church structured after the pattern of hierarchical communication as being a credible witness to the participatory self-revelation of God. Vatican II repeats the words of its predecessor and also states that submission of intellect and will must be given to the God of revelation. With this statement, the Council holds true to its intention expressed in the introduction to *Dei Verbum:* "following . . . in the steps of the councils of Trent and Vatican I, this synod wishes to set forth the authentic teaching on divine revelation and its transmission."[18] The general impression is that when describing the reverse side of the revelation/faith coin, Vatican II is more in line with Vatican I than it is when speaking about the obverse side, namely, the side of revelation. *Dei Verbum,* however, starts with a quote from the beginning of the First Epistle of John, which makes clear that in the twofold communicative event of revelation and faith the Council has in mind a communicative and participatory community of life. In this community, assent to the truth of statements based on authority is acknowledged but is not the primary model for understanding the event of faith and revelation. *Dei Verbum* begins thus:

> Hearing the word of God reverently and proclaiming it confidently, this holy synod makes its own the words of St. John: "We proclaim to you the eternal life which was with the Father and was made manifest to us—that which we have seen and heard we proclaim to you, so that you may have fellowship with us; and our fellowship is with the Father and with his Son Jesus Christ" (1 John 1:2-3).[19]

This is what the communicative-participatory understanding of revelation and faith events is all about. God invites people into a communion with God. God takes the initiative. God moves toward people and gives them the Spirit, who enables them to live in and from this communion. The church comes as the vanguard of God's reign, a sign and an instrument for this communion. This is what is meant by *mysterion/mysterium* and by *sacramentum*. Through the communion of people with one another, communion with God comes into existence. We proclaim to our fellow humans, through word and deed, this divine invitation to communion. When people have communion with us, they have communion with God, because the holy/healing Spirit of this communion lives in our midst and moves us to follow in Jesus Christ's footsteps until we reach God the Creator.

V. Living Tradition as a Communication Process

When we considered Vatican I's understanding of revelation, we noted that if revelation is taken to mean the mere transmission of statements to be believed, then it is to be found chiefly in the written and orally transmitted revelation. Of course, Scripture is *the* source and norm of faith and is not normed by any other source. This is still valid in the new perspective of revelation and faith presented by Vatican II. Admittedly, Scripture is not to be understood as a collection of statements of faith from which one picks and chooses this or that proposition to prove a doctrine of the church. The tradition of the church is not understood to be a second material source of authoritative proofs of doctrinal correctness. The authority of Scripture and tradition is still valid, but the Council relativized it by putting it in the larger context of communicative-participatory revelation. At the time of Vatican I, the crucial question was who, as the ultimate instance, represents the decisive ("infallible") authority in the church. In connection with the communicative-participatory understanding of revelation developed by Vatican II, theology has rediscovered the multiplicity of subjects involved in the church's teaching authority. In technical terms, one speaks again about various *loci theologici*, recalling the work of the early modern theologian Melchior Cano, who, in the context of Reformation controversies, called attention to the diverse witnesses to revelation and faith. Along with the oral tradition of Christ and the apostles, there is, for example, the universal church (*ecclesia catholica*), the ecumenical councils, the Roman Church, the fathers of the church, the theologians as such, and the magisterium. Along with the *loci theologici* in the strict sense, there are other sources that are not genuinely theological but have a legitimate place in theology: these are natural reason, philosophers, and human history.[20] In the next chapter, devoted to the gift of the "We" in the church, we shall speak more about the distinction and the abiding interrelationship among the various subjects of faith communication.

It is important to bear in mind in our context that, according to Vatican II, tradition is taken to be a living process. We no longer speak about two material sources of revelation (Scripture and tradition) but about tradition as the transmission of the apostolic faith as witnessed to by Scripture as an answer to God's self-communication in Jesus Christ through his Spirit. The scriptural Word does not explain itself but must be proclaimed and become alive in hearing, reading, and action. This is the tradition process of the faith community called church. Because tradition is all about the transmission of the Word of life (see the beginning of 1 John), the tradition process must also be a communicative-participatory one. In this new perspective, Vatican II took important first steps, but these steps represented only a first stage in the development—also from an ecumenical perspective—of a truly communicative-participatory understanding of tradition. The Council opened the door; now is the time for resolute steps forward.

Questions for Reflection

- How do you use the words "I believe" in everyday life?
- Are you still influenced by an understanding of faith reduced to merely holding statements to be true? Were you educated that way or is such a remnant from the past from which you hold yourself aloof?
- Do you recognize yourself in the biblical episodes about persons of faith (Abraham, Sarah, Zechariah, Mary, Peter and Paul, John the Evangelist)?
- What do you value about the tradition of the church? Do you consider it a resource without which we could not survive?
- To what extent do biblical accounts of revelation (Abraham's visitation [Genesis 18], Moses' experience of the burning bush, the baptism of Jesus, the wedding feast at Cana, the conversion of Paul, the visions of John) correspond to your own experience of God?

CHAPTER 5

The Church as a Community of Communication: The "We" as Gift

When God reveals God's self, God calls a human person to faith. This person has the freedom to answer. Whenever human persons let themselves be led by God, the way of faith begins, a way of faith that also may include doubt and even lack of faith. The way of faith is the way to Emmaus. While a decision is demanded of each individual, one can only follow in the footsteps of Jesus as a community. God self-revelation takes place again and again in every moment anew, and people must give their answer of faith in every moment anew. Thus the "We" of the community of the faithful is constantly being reconstituted. This does not mean, however, that the *communio fidelium* must be reinvented each time. The connection in the here-and-now is given by the tradition. The church is always synchronic and diachronic at the same time, contemporary yet fully conscious of its tradition. The church does not re-invent itself and does not let go of the riches of tradition. However, just as faith does not simply happen, so too, the living tradition does not "automatically" happen. Whether or not the transmission of the communio is success-ful, both synchronically (with contemporary people) and diachronically (with one's mothers and fathers in faith), depends ultimately on the church's culture of communication.

The church becomes real, wherever the communicative God transmits God's self and wherever God's revelation is met with faith. This history of communication is transmitted in a living tradition and is continuously being structured anew by God. Therefore, the church is either a community of com-munication or it is no church at all. The church does not live out of itself, but out of God's events of communication. The church does not live for itself, but shares *communio* and *communicatio* with others. For this reason, the essential and decisive elements of the church are not what it has made of itself, but what it has received as a gift—not a self-arranged communication but the surpris-ing and freely given communion of people who of themselves would probably never have come together.

In the course of this chapter, two aspects must be kept in mind: on the one hand, our efforts to develop a structure of communication and a culture of communication appropriate to communion, and, on the other hand, the experience of the gifted We.

I. Developing a Model of Communication for the Church as Communio

Vilém Flusser (1920–1991) taught philosophy of communication at the University of São Paulo in Brazil. In his book *Kommunikologie*,[1] he distinguishes six types of communication, that is, four types of discourse and two so-called dialogue models. To the four types of discourse he gave the names: theater discourse, pyramidal discourse, tree-like discourse, and amphitheater discourse. We will take up the dialogue forms later.

1. *Theater discourse* is Flusser's name for a communication situation in which a sender transmits a message to one or more receivers facing them. As in a theater, the sender stands on a stage alone in front of a projecting wall. There is no sender behind them; the person alone functions as the sender. The backdrop shields from outside noise and projects the message toward the receivers. The recipients of the message are themselves pure receivers; they do not become transmitters in turn.

This form of communication we find in the church *de facto* and, in some cases, *de jure*. Whenever authoritatively (in the person of Christ or the power of the Spirit) God's gift of salvation is promised to men and women, the speaker, by the authority of office or of prophetic charisma, functions as a sender addressing receivers. Behind the speaker is not another sender but rather the protecting and projecting wall of the theater of God's drama of salvation. The speaker, as sender, has a mission to fulfill. In virtue of this mission one speaks with authority. This is the characteristic form of discourse in the liturgy and in sacramental celebrations. In the sacrament of reconciliation, for instance, the central message consists of three speech-acts: (1) a faith-inspired statement, (2) a corresponding request, and (3) a consequent official performative declaration. The faith-inspired statement is: "God, the Father of mercies, through the death and resurrection of his Son, has reconciled the world to himself and sent the Holy Spirit among us for the forgiveness of sin." The prayerful request is expressed in the sentence: "Through the ministry of the church may God grant you pardon and peace." Thereupon follows the performative declaration: "I absolve you from your sins in the name (!) of the Father, and of the Son, and of the Holy Spirit."

It is important to note, however, that for the integral celebration of the sacraments, other forms of communication may be involved as well. Thus, the central act of absolution described above is preceded by a dialogue between penitent and confessor, the "confession conversation." On the basis of this first example we see that communication in the communio of the faithful can take many forms. They are legitimate when they correspond to what is being communicated; they are illegitimate when they do not correspond to what is being shared. Thus, I cannot absolve myself of sin; I need the authoritative declaration of the confessor. There are times, however, when this authoritative form of communication is not appropriate. This is the case when it comes to ascertaining the *consensus fidelium*, the agreement of believers in matters of faith. In this case, every believer is an authoritative witness to the faith. Real consensus requires that every believer be allowed to give his or her testimony. Consensus cannot be verified by one-sided communication.

2. *Pyramidal discourse* is characteristic of a hierarchical structure of communication. The original sender passes on a message to receivers who function as relay stations to transmit the message unchanged to additional receivers, who may in turn relay it further. Typical for such pyramidal discourse is the concern for the integrity of the message. The relay stations are not creative subjects in the process of communication but mere repeaters. Feedback serves only to control the purity and integrity of the message transmitted. It allows no room for innovation and modification. Flusser identifies examples of such communication in all hierarchically structured organizations, which see control as the central factor in the communication process.

In the communication processes of the communio of the faithful, fidelity to the original message, to the gospel message of salvation, plays a central role. This marks a liberation from enclosed forms of communication that excludes others. It envisages an open, inviting form of communication that does not harmonize all differences but instead stakes out borders, which it respects. The original sender in this case is the Triune God, the author of our salvation. Everyone who in faith trustingly commends him- or herself to God and God's salvific communicative action becomes a "relay station," a messenger of the gospel. Only on the basis of this fundamental equality, then, is it possible to recognize differences that give rise to diverse forms of communication based on charisma and official responsibility. In this context, the concern for the faithful transmission of the original message has its place, but the original message can be transmitted faithfully only when it is translated into the respective present situation. This requires sensibility and innovation. Thus the Second Vatican Council rightly remarks that the people of God has received a gift of discernment in matters of faith (*sensus fidei*). "By this sense of the faith . . . the people of God unfailingly adheres to this faith, penetrates it more deeply through right judgment, and applies it more fully in daily life."[2] It would be false, however, to attend only to the note of "progress" expressed in this statement, at least if by "progress" one understands only a positive process in the history of the church. There is also "progress" in a negative sense, a going astray, a movement down false paths. Such errors are corrected not only by the relay stations represented by the papal/episcopal magisterium. Church history contains examples where ordinary women and men among the people of God were closer to the original gospel than many ecclesiastical hierarchs. For this reason, the model of pyramidal communication is of limited use in describing the form of communication typical of the church.

3. In *tree-like discourse*, the original sender no longer plays any significant role. In reality there are no longer any communicators at all in the strict sense, only a progressive spreading out of information, branching out impersonally in ever-new directions. It is difficult to see how Flusser can still speak of "dialogue" to describe the role of intermediaries in spreading information according to this model. In any case, there is no face-to-face communication here. Flusser himself describes this form of communication as unimportant and inhuman. His description of it reminds one of impersonal forms of communication in the Internet, where information is transmitted without reference to the personalities of the sender or the receiver. Such transmission of pure information deserves neither the name "communication" nor "networking." For the communion of the faithful, this type of "discourse" can be seen only as a warning against what should not constitute communication in the church.

4. Flusser's next model, *amphitheater discourse*, is inspired by the architectural structures patterned after the Roman coliseum. The audience here consists of an inarticulate mass of passive recipients exposed to an ongoing stream of messageless sound, like the mix of music and advertising broadcasted impersonally in all directions in a supermarket. In this form of discourse, the persons of the sender and the receiver play no role at all. There is neither an "I" nor a "We," indeed, there is not even a clear message, no "It," and the "Globe," or environment, is such that the audience remains at best a loose collection of passive individuals paying little or no attention to what is being broadcasted. Thus, there does not take place the interchange between the receiver and the sender that is characteristic of true communication. Indeed, what takes place hardly deserves the name communication at all. Obviously, this form of discourse is not appropriate for the communio of the faithful. On the contrary, it is a warning example of what should not take place in the church, and it should make us careful in our use of modern communication techniques.

5. More appropriate than these four models of discourse for describing communication in the church are Flusser's two models of *dialogue*. Characteristic of the dialogue forms is that, in dialogue, pieces of information are synthesized into something truly new.[3]

The first model is the so-called *circle dialogue*. The circle dialogue has the structure of a round table and is the communication setting found in committees and laboratories. Flusser describes this type of dialogue in the following terms:

> The memories of the participants in dialogue differ from each other, not only in terms of the information which is to be discussed (or the problem to be decided upon), but also in terms of their respective competencies (the quantity of information each has available), the codes in which information is stored, and the individual levels of awareness. The "common denominator" which is sought is not, therefore, a piece of information already shared by all participants prior to the dialogue, but is rather a synthesis which only emerges in the course of the dialogue; it is thus something truly new. This should explain why dialogues are such difficult forms of communication and why "liberal democracies" function so badly. They are based on conflict, rather than agreement. But it is this very disadvantage that provides the legitimization for this form of communication.[4]

One problem with the circle dialogue is the limited number of participants. This is why Flusser calls it an elite form of communication:

> According to all appearances the lowest number of participants is two, and many regard this situation as the basic dialogue form (e.g. between lovers, between mother and child, between master and disciple, or even between the human person and God). Plato went so far as to think that the real creation of information took place in an "inner dialogue," that is, in the restriction of the participants' number to just one. However, such a schizophrenic state is more of a division of memory, a dialogue between two parts of the same subject. By reason of its speculative character, "reflection" as a form of dialogue puts the synthesis of information into question and thus breaks out of the consideration here under discussion.[5]

Flusser thinks it is possible to determine the optimal number of participants on the basis of the constitutive goal of the dialogue: "In any case, those wishing to 'participate' should be able to state the type of circle dialogue they wish to take part in and the competence they have for the processing of new information."[6] Of course, this assumes in the case of the church that the participants really have a voice in order to be able to express themselves in this way. Flusser thinks that circle dialogues are seldom a success. However, when they are, "they represent the loftiest communication form which people are capable of."[7]

6. To assure that this most human form of communication not be lost when the circle of participants is extended beyond the round-table setting, Flusser introduces a second dialogue model, the *network dialogue*.

In recent decades, it has become fashionable in various areas of sociology to speak of "network structures." This term and the social pattern it designates have likewise entered theology in connection with strategic pastoral reflections. Attempts have been made to link communio theology and network theory. Flusser understands network dialogue as collective memory, "the reservoir into which all information ultimately flows, albeit sometimes making complex detours."[8] Unlike circle dialogues, network dialogues are open and "in this sense genuinely democratic."[9] Also unlike circle dialogues, they are always successful. This looks particularly interesting to us with respect to communication within the church. However, Flusser goes on to qualify his statement:

> Our elitist tendency to despise "common sense" compared to "generally valid human reason" and to join Trotsky in his assumption that "the majority is always wrong" is not the right way to investigate network dialogue. But the reverse, still equally elitist tendency to adopt the *vox populi, vox dei* thesis, that is, the voice of the people is the voice of God, or to consider the "silent majority" as the decisive authority is just as inappropriate to describe the function of network dialogues.[10]

Starting from a basic anthropological assumption, Flusser comes to the following political conclusion: engagement.

> It goes without saying that people were always aware of the fact that network dialogues were the basis for communication and hence of human resistance in the face of death. In this sense, political commitment, which is also a commitment to communication, can be seen as a commitment to network dialogues. The aim of politics must basically be that of "informing" and "forming" the network dialogue and so contribute to "new information" (the "new human person"). Seen in this way, demagogy is exactly the opposite of politics, since it relies on repeating existing information. Through redundancy it works against the penetration of new information in the network dialogue and thus prohibits a change of the human person.[11]

7. A structure of communication for communio. In God's salvation-historical dialogue with the human person, which is continued by the church as the vanguard of communication for God's reign, what is at stake is precisely the process of people being informed and as a result formed. It could well be that from this notion of communication, talk about infused grace, infused virtues, and formation through grace can take on new meaning. In any case, however, the goal of the reign of God is concretely conceived. It is clear that the structure of communication, information, and decision making in the

church is not arbitrary. Although no specific system can be deduced from revelation, it is possible by way of a negative theory of communication to exclude certain forms that are clearly contrary to the goals of the system of communication which is the church. This is not the place to elaborate a complete doctrine of communication in the church. It is clear, however, that the direction must be that of a network dialogue. Thus, it is important to attend to the significance of the diverse intersections involved in the church's system of communication. Moreover, one needs to inquire when and how other forms of discourse find a place in particular sectors of the church's system of communication.

Nonetheless, what is common to many modes of discourse in the church is a situation of inequality because of an asymmetrical relationship between the subjects involved in the communication process. This can be seen in the church's hierarchical structures and in the differences between clergy and laity. Although we readily acknowledge the legitimacy of such forms of communication within given limits, we cannot accept any of these models of discourse as constituting the principal form of communication for the church as a communio. At first, in fact, we tried to use the model of a pyramid positively to explain the church's system of communication. This pyramid was built up "from below." Each higher level was based on the lower level as its minister and as its representative. But on further reflection, we have come to see that this conception raised many problems and unanswered questions and gave rise to misunderstanding. Can a pyramid really be built up "from below"? If we are to avoid the impression that the subjects on higher levels are only official speakers for the lower-level communities, it is necessary to clarify the responsibilities of those on the "higher" levels. These remain unclear in this model.

So we were forced to develop a model that more accurately illustrated the responsibility of the "higher" levels in order to support communication and communio. Some of the main tasks would be to give dignity and support to each one of the faithful, to appreciate each one of them as an authentic subject and to give guidance as well as to allow them to participate in the process of community building. Such a ministry can be characterized as one of communication. Thus, we would now situate the different subjects and their communities on the same plane, instead of locating them (as a pyramid would) vertically above one another in a hierarchical fashion. This leads to differentiation within one and the same plane. The former "higher levels" have to be understood in their responsibility for the connection of the former "lower levels." They have to oversee the whole community network and to link the different participants. The local community is indeed church, but only in community with the other churches. Thus, mutual recognition and ongoing communio are essential for an ecclesial community. Church exists in the basic communities, in parishes, which are linked to dioceses. The bishops, as the witnesses and the teachers of their own local churches' faith, meet collegially in synods or conferences and, in exceptional cases, in councils.

Then they are in communion with the pope as the first minister of communication.

So in the following figure we try to illustrate what the Second Vatican Council means when it says that the church exists in and is based on the local churches. We deny neither the bishops' responsibility nor the special ministry of the pope. But these must be conceived as ministries of service within the whole community of the church. The church cannot be characterized as a pyramid from top down nor from bottom up. It finds its identity in a structure of networking, which rests on different committed participants taking up various responsibilities and functions. Karl Rahner has trenchantly commented on the relevant statements of the Constitution on the Church *Lumen gentium*, where the hierarchical and the communitarian perspectives are juxtaposed:

> One must soberly admit that for the Council a different perspective was inherited from traditional theology and that this perspective necessarily had its effect on the decree. It was virtually impossible for the decree to use both aspects as its structural principle. In any case, the *Constitution* does not exclude the other perspective. One *may* start from the concrete community in which God's Word is preached, in which His saving death is proclaimed in the Eucharist and in which He is made present in mutual service and brotherhood. In this way, eschatological salvation is made present and the church becomes church in the true sense of the term. From this perspective, it is thus possible to gain an understanding of the church as a whole, because the church is *truly* present (*vere adest*) in the local community. Thus the possibility of developing an (ecumenically highly significant) ecclesiology starting from the community of Word and Altar is opened up by this paragraph and acknowledged to be legitimate.[12]

At the moment, therefore, the following figure (p. 88) appears to us the best expression of the structure of communication in the church as communio.

This figure reflects, of course, only the principal forms of communication in the church. Other forms, as described by Flusser's theory of communication, are not thereby excluded. They must be integrated, however, into this principal model. In this figure we no longer have a three-dimensional structure like a pyramid, but rather a two-dimensional structure in which all active and passive subjects (the I and the We) are arranged on the same level. The task of networking is not something on a higher level, but belongs to one and the same level on which all the participating subjects are situated. Those responsible for maintaining the network are themselves located within a network.

Concretely, this means the following: the Christian community (the territorial parish, a "floating" parish, a hospital or campus ministry, and so

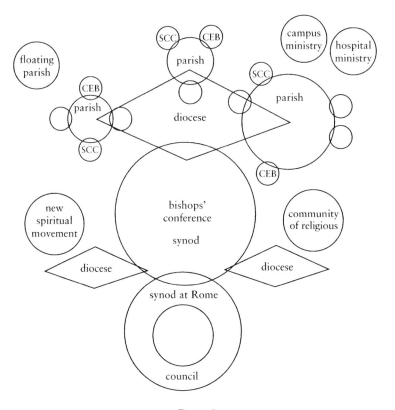

Figure 8

forth) exists in a collection of basic communities (clubs, organizations, neigh-
borhoods, youth groups, family circles, local religious communities, and so
on). Since Vatican II, a special type of ecclesial base community has come
into prominence, the CEB (*comunidades eclesiales de base*), which originated
in Latin America, and the SCC (small Christian communities), which originated in southern Africa and spread widely, particularly in Asia.[13] The leadership of the Christian community exercised by an individual or a team has
the task of linking these groups in a network. It is not the point in these
groups that everyone get along well with everyone else, but that no one
should be excluded ("excommunicated"). Leadership is especially called for
when communication fails or schism threatens. "Floating" parishes, campus
and hospital ministries, communities of religious with pastoral outreach,
groups associated with the so-called new ecclesial movements, and so on are
diversely related to the networks represented by territorial parishes, dioceses,
and the church as a worldwide organization.

Together, the parishes within a city or territory are linked to form a diocese, which constitutes a "local church" under the leadership of a bishop.[14] Several dioceses can be linked to form a "particular church" of a region, a nation, or a continent, whose leadership is then represented by a bishops' conference or by a synod. Such particular churches are further linked among themselves on different levels. The traditional expression of such linkage is likewise the synod, which, when it represents the whole of Christianity, is called an "ecumenical council." In the strict sense, only a synod representing the whole of Christianity merits the name "ecumenical council." Thus, a meeting like the Second Vatican Council is not "ecumenical" in the full sense of the term—a point most important to the Orthodox churches—but is more properly termed a "general synod" of the Roman Catholic Church. Vatican II, the most recent such "general synod," whose proceedings and results are published in the *Acta synodalia*, called for the revival of some old and the development of new forms of network in the Roman Catholic Church. Particularly notable among these new forms is the so-called Roman Episcopal Synod, an ad hoc assembly of bishops elected by regional episcopal conferences or nominated by the pope. From the point of view of communio ecclesiology, the relationship of the personal subjects of church leadership (in particular the bishops, acting individually or in synodical assemblies) to the Roman church's administrative offices and tribunals (in particular the Vatican congregations and *nuncios*) has not yet been satisfactorily resolved. The whole problem of relating ecclesial ministry and service in terms of exercise of ecclesiastical power remains to be resolved. It is to be hoped that further development of communio ecclesiology will help to diagnose the problem more clearly and contribute to its resolution.

II. Communion and Communication

In this section we will try to expand our inquiry into the relationship between communion and communication. We begin by asking about the theological importance of communio ecclesiology and then consider the relevance of Theme-Centered Interaction (TCI) for understanding this relationship.

Communio ecclesiology understands the local community as the *communio fidelium,* that is, the community of the believers, and it treats the "higher" levels of the church as networked communions (*communiones*). Thus, the communication principles of communio theology apply also to the relationship of local churches (represented by bishops) to one another and to the central church leadership represented by the organs of the Petrine ministry. It is precisely here that international public opinion cannot fail to notice that the communication structures of the Roman Catholic Church fall short of the ideals proclaimed by the Second Vatican Council's people-of-God theology/communio theology. The question has thus been raised: is the very concept of communio to blame for this discrepancy?

1. Communion—Ideal or Caricature of Communication?[15]

It would indeed be a fatal development if the notion of communio, which was singled out by the 1985 Extraordinary Synod of Bishops as *the* main idea of Vatican II twenty years after the Council, was in fact turned into its opposite. To be sure, this key concept of communio is all about the communicative-participatory realization of the revelation structure in the church. The notion of communio has the advantage of providing a theological basis for this structure of communication. Our concern here is not to assimilate the church into a modern democratic structure and its corresponding theories of communication. Our appeal to the structure of communication of the *communio* church is theologically based. We start our reflection with the vocation and mission of all who share in the task of building the reign of God. As we noted in the section on revelation, the notion of communio has a threefold structure. First, it indicates what is the basis of communion. The basis is the salvific action of the Triune God, God's self-communication in history, which takes concrete shape in the mission of people to give individual and collective witness to the Good News. The second dimension is the acceptance of revelation by men and women who put themselves at God's disposal. Ecclesiologically, one can speak here of the church as the fruit of God's salvific action. On the third level we would place what we consider to be the mission of the church, that is, the church as an instrument of salvation. On this third level it is appropriate that we speak about our sharing in the responsibility for the reign of God.

Seen in this way, it becomes clear that the concept of communion and its corresponding structures of communication do not refer only to the third level, the instrumental level. Our task is rather to extend what we have said above about revelation into the concept of church. By God's invitation the church becomes a community of people called to witness to the whole world about God's salvific action. This communion is a gift, the gift of *koinōnia*. By sharing in this gift, symbolically effected in the Eucharistic celebration, we build together a body, a community of persons.

If this is so and if it can be biblically warranted, we can ask, where the resistance to the concept of communio ecclesiology comes from. Resistance to this notion is based on the fact that "communio" is often used like a magic formula without defining clearly what is meant thereby. Not infrequently, the notion of communio is used to clothe an understanding of the church according to the pattern of pyramidal or theater discourse. Every one of us is acquainted with the phrase "we are all brothers and sisters," which is often used to cut off unpleasant debates about church structures. The fact that the 1985 Extraordinary Synod of Bishops selected "communio" rather than "people of God" as *the* main idea of Vatican II fits well with this argument. A large number of bishops attending the synod suspected that the notion of "people of God" implied an inadmissible democratization of the church. They preferred the notion of "communion" in order to emphasize the church's sacramental character, its essence as *mysterium*. Others saw in this position an immunization strategy to block necessary reforms of the church's communication and decision-making structures. Unfortunately, this controversy has led partisans of communio ecclesiology, on the one hand, and of people-of-God ecclesiology, on the other, to mutually "excommunicate" each other. In reality, they are not that far apart. They share a common concern. The interpretation of the Council's intent is not arbitrary. It should take its orientation from the intentions of the overwhelming majority of the conciliar fathers and should follow definite rules. On this basis, one can say with certitude that the concept of communio ecclesiology must correspond to a communicative-participatory structure of communication in the church. It may be for the moment that this aim can be better expressed under the heading of "people of God." One should bear in mind, however, that it is not self-evident that the structure of communication implied in the notion "people of God" is communicative-participatory. This too needs to be worked out in further detail.

The call for communio and for a more adequate structure of communication in the church moves in the tension between an ideal to be striven after and a feared distortion. For this reason it is necessary to beware that whatever ecclesiology is under discussion, be it communio, people of God, or Mystical Body, the concrete concept invoked must reflect the communicative-participatory structure of God's revelation.

As indicated in the introduction, it is our belief that the attitudes and patterns of Theme-Centered Interaction (TCI) developed by Ruth C. Cohn can provide a useful framework for the working of a theologically adequate structure of communion and communication in the church. Some of these impulses will be noted in the next section of this chapter. Chapter 6 will then take up TCI in more detail.

2. The Attitude and Communication Pattern of TCI as a Means of Focusing Attention

TCI thrives on the ideal of integrating self-awareness, group dynamics, and working together on a common topic. For a communio ecclesiology and a corresponding structure of communication the following three moments are important:

1. the acknowledgement that individuals are independent subjects whose decision making and responsibility in matters of faith cannot be substituted for by others;
2. the recognition that the group is more than a mere sum of individual "redeemed" subjects; that it is in the group that individuals are given or denied the opportunity for making decisions of faith; that commu-

nity with one another is not a secondary consequence of faith, but rather the real symbolic form of faith itself; and that the generation of real faith is necessarily constitutive of community;

3. the awareness that concentration on a "theme" is understood as a faith-response to the self-communication of God.

In the terminology of TCI, these three factors, the "I," the "We" and the "It" form a triangle encompassed in a "Globe."[16] It is admittedly a limitation of the communio notion that it is so inwardly focused. In the future, communio theology and its corresponding structures of communication must be expanded to take into account the Globe, which defines the borderland wherein Christian men and women live their faith. The world is not "outside" the church; lack of faith is not "outside" faith. On the contrary, the individual subjects—the "I"-factor—participate in the We and are oriented toward faith (It) as their response to the communication of God in the ambivalent situation marked by the Globe. The protective wall of theater discourse in the church should not be thought of as a "gated community," which isolates and cuts off all interaction with the world outside![17]

Other postulates and rules of TCI will be treated in chapters 6 and 7, where the relevance of TCI for communion and communication in the church will be considered in more detail. For now, we call attention to the following four rules:

1. One must attend to everything that is vital for developing a sensitivity for each individual's life of faith and for each individual's corresponding competence in matters of faith. In our courses we have been enriched when people have spoken of their faith in their own terms as independent subjects. And this happens on a much larger scale than the one-way communication of theater discourse or pyramidal discourse associated with the traditional forms of teaching and learning.

2. Paying attention to the balance between tradition and progress is, in our opinion, an important rule of communication in a communio church. It means, among other things, that participants in an authentic communicative process be encouraged to be selective in what they contribute. They should contribute to the interaction only to the extent that each individual is prepared to take personal responsibility for what they say at any given moment and with respect to the others in the group.

3. That each participant should be his or her own "chairperson" is a maxim that sums up everything that has to do with the participation of all believers in the church's life of faith.

4. Finally, the rule that disturbances should take precedence is particularly relevant for communication in the church. Clearly, this does not mean that "troublemakers" are allowed to torpedo communion at will,

but it does mean that the gospel cannot take root and become incul-
turated unless obstacles along the way—the thorns, thistles, and
stones—are taken into account and removed as far as possible. A rough
guideline might be so formulated: it is not important to say all that
could be said, but it is important to say what is decisive in a way that
strikes home. This corresponds to the significance of the revelation of
God's self-communication to human beings for their salvation as an
invitation into the community of the Triune God.

III. What It Is All About: The Gifted We

When we spoke above about the necessary balance between the individual
subjects of faith and the group/community within the ecclesial-social Globe,
we already called attention to the gift character of the group/community's We.
In this chapter we have been discussing the communication structures of communion of the faithful in the light of Flusser's philosophy of communication.
At the end of this discussion, the gift character of the We should again be
underscored. This is not just some pious conclusion. Speaking about the We
as a gift is not intended to blot out the diversity of subjects within the group
or to minimize the individuality and personal responsibility of those individual subjects. We dealt with this in detail in the previous chapters. The social
and ecclesial experience of the last decades has shown that there are indeed situations in which one can speak about a We without distinctions since it is precisely the collective identity that is meant to be accentuated. Thus, we are
reminded of the slogan "We are the people," which was the motto of the East
German "revolution" of 1989 or the "We are church" movement within
German-speaking Catholicism that began in the mid-1990s. True, many individuals show a certain uneasiness about being "absorbed" into a collective We.
This has often been our experience in working with groups. We take this sensitivity seriously and do our best to create conditions in which aggressive
potential within a group can be vented. This caution is especially necessary in
church groups, because conflict and dissent are often branded as things that
have no place in the church. However, our experience shows us over and over
again that only by venting such conflicts and dealing with them openly do we
really serve the group. Thus, as we have continually emphasized in our reflections on the notion of communion, we are not interested in any sort of
homogenized We.

What we are interested in is what has been validated in our experience
working with groups and which we rate as fundamental for the church's system of communication: the gift character of the We! The emergence of a We
in a group is not something that happens accidentally; it is not a surprise package given to any one individual. When people come together for a one-week
theological communication course something occurs in the group process that

they can neither foresee nor plan nor produce themselves. The fact that in the group another person is able to open him- or herself up to me, that we are able to open up to one another, that we are able to suffer and rejoice together and enrich one another, all of this we experience time and again as a gift. The liturgical celebration at the end of such a week is not just an obligatory thanksgiving ritual, but it occurs exactly at the right time. And the hugs (and sometime tears) that take place during the departure the next morning are never something planned. That such groups generally do not come together again, despite their best intentions to go on seeing one another, is a healthy thing. This fact demonstrates the autonomy of the individual subjects and does not put into question the We that was experienced together in the group.

With regard to the church as a whole, we cannot help but conclude that those who are frustrated, disappointed, and without hope would benefit from these group processes. Were some of our bishops, priests, lay pastoral ministers and theologians to have this opportunity, then they would be in a better position to know what could really carry us forward. Of course, not all that shines at the grassroots is gold! But there is so much readiness to believe, so much joy, courage, and commitment in faith, so much genuine living of the faith, all of this can only be experienced as enriching and upbuilding. In this sense, a communio church lives indeed from the bottom up. The church lives foremost at the grassroots and is not constituted only by information and commands that come down from above and call for hearing and obedience. In the We of the church there is much less mistrust and opposition than many are inclined to believe. Quite the contrary, church authorities who are genuine, that is, those who are truly devoted to promoting truth and life in faith, will find enthusiastic reception when they allow themselves to enter into such group processes.

It goes without saying that what we have experienced in our study groups and what we here recommend to ecclesiastical authorities is of fundamental importance for ecclesiology. As already stated, the church is not simply the sum of redeemed subjects. The church is not the kind of We that people by themselves can produce. To be sure, we can "do" a lot, and it is necessary that we do our part! But group experience is something that belongs to the core of our faith, the experience of God's gift calling so many different people to the discipleship of Jesus Christ and giving them life in his Spirit. Precisely because this gift is not of our making, because we can't control it, it liberates and enriches us. We are a gift for one another; therein is rooted the free character of the We that constitutes church.

With regard to the ecumenical movement, one often hears the warning that we ourselves cannot bring about unity. Church unity is something given to us as a gift. Admittedly, this proposition is true, but it is also true that overstressing it can make it false. Such a statement is false when it tends to reconcile us with the status quo or console us in our inactivity. Certainly, church unity is a gift. Certainly the We of the church is a gift for us. But this has nothing to do with the kind of pious appeals to brotherhood and sisterhood so often voiced in the Catholic Church to avoid facing up to latent differences of opinion. No indeed! Such a gift requires openness, attention, sensitivity, interest in the other as other. It calls for what TCI terms "selective authenticity," "the chairperson principle," and "the targeting of group conflict." Paradoxical as it may sound, only those who trustingly let themselves become involved in the group's interaction are able to experience the group as a gift-given We. The paradoxical wording is by no means opposed to the gift character of the We. It is only when we really become involved that we discover what we cannot achieve by ourselves.

Recalling the story of the two disciples on the road to Emmaus can help clarify what is meant here. Obviously they know each other, and they are journeying together. On the way they discuss what has happened; they read the Scriptures and meditate on them. Into their group they invite a stranger. The entry of the stranger, however, is something that disrupts their twosomeness. The stranger opens up for them all that had hitherto been closed off in their relationship. When he breaks bread for them and their hearts are enflamed, can we not say that they suddenly experience We as a gift? Furthermore, the Emmaus account teaches us that we cannot "stay put" when we receive this gift. The We requires reaching out to others, to the You, inviting them to share in the communion. This is what the Emmaus disciples did! This passage from We to You is found as well in the prologue to the First Epistle of John, where the author exhorts the "You" to have communion with the "We" so as to have communion with the Triune God. Likewise, the hymn in Ephesians 1:3–14 shows the same structure: the leading subject is God, who acts in Jesus Christ and in the Holy Spirit. The active subject throughout is God, the Father of our Lord Jesus Christ. Wherever the "We" of the community of believers serves as the grammatical subject, it is always in a passive sense; "We" are the recipients of God's action, the receiving ones. And at the end of the hymn, a third subject is introduced, a "You" standing for those to whom the epistle is addressed. Ephesians 1:13–14 puts it thus:

> In him you also, who have heard the word of truth, the gospel of your salvation, and have believed in him, were sealed with the promised Holy Spirit, which is the guarantee of our inheritance until we acquire possession of it, to the praise of his glory.

Thus the church is a gifted We, the *communio fidelium*, that which Vatican II stated at the beginning of *Lumen gentium* names a sacrament, that is, a sign and instrument for the innermost union with God as well as for the unity of humankind.

CHAPTER 6

Communication as a Practice of Theological Awareness: The Perspective of TCI

In this chapter we consider the same issues we addressed in the previous chapter from a systematic theological point of view from the perspective of TCI. Just as the TCI perspective was latent in the preceding chapter, so in this chapter the theological perspective will not be absent. Our intention is to foster a practice of theological awareness and participation inspired by TCI.

One of the outstanding features of communicative theology is that it does not take place solely at the desk or in the library. As a "theology in process," communicative theology comes to its knowledge through reflection based on participation in processes of communication. In particular, we regard those processes that we called "faith communication" as being important not only pedagogically but also theologically. In communication between human beings, an awareness of meaning and orientation proper to the Christian message becomes manifest. When "communicating" becomes an object of theological attention and participation, theological knowledge broadens in a twofold sense:

- The content and the "form" of communication belong together inseparably as the object of theological knowledge. Neither the one nor the other can be thought of except in relation to the other. This means that participation in the communication event and the (interpretive) attention given to the event together make theological understanding possible.
- The theologically significant field of "faith communication" is not restricted to communication processes within the Christian churches/communities: "the Spirit blows where it wills," and the hope for the coming of the reign of God extends beyond the boundaries of the churches. Thus, communication processes taking place outside the churches should also be thought of in terms of their implicit potential for Christian hope and so be evaluated in terms of their theological

significance. In this specific perspective, communicative theology connects with general communication research, which is constituted by a network of diverse scientific fields.

How then is it possible to attend to and participate in processes of communication that take on theological significance? Is there a "method" that corresponds to the theological understanding of communication presented in this book?

The specific "method" of communicative theology in the sense of the (scientific) attention to and personal involvement in communicative processes is founded, on the one hand, on the Christian understanding of God and the church (developed in chapters 4 and 5) and is related, on the other hand, to Ruth C. Cohn's Theme-Centered Interaction approach (already in focus from chapter 1 onward).

The specific perspective of the theological hermeneutics of communication is determined by the fact that the communication of the "communicative God" with people through history becomes the norm. The understanding of communication gained from the tradition of faith changes the "angle" from which present-day communication experiences and processes are viewed. Admittedly, contemporary experiences of communication are not identical with the experiences of communication in the faith tradition, but these two experiences are also not so radically different as to have nothing in common. In order to look theologically at human communication one needs a range of hermeneutical instruments that make transparent, on the one hand, the incarnational "reconciliation" between God and the world and, on the other hand, the enduring difference between them. Such instruments cannot be developed as a purely speculative hermeneutic cut off from actual processes of communication. In the awareness that there is an unmixed and inseparable relationship between divine and human communication (see chapter 7), we present here an approach based on the model of communication from Cohn's Theme-Centered Interaction. This approach is designed to relate the relevant theological and communication levels to each other.

The communication processes that we employ in the "Course in Communicative Theology" offered by the Theology Department of the University of Innsbruck utilize the approach and method of TCI and serve as our experiential research field. In these processes central anthropological and theological concerns and themes come to the fore. We do not claim that Cohn's Theme-Centered Interaction is a panacea for successful communication. It does not magically create a "communicative" heaven on earth. It is merely a particular value-oriented attitude and a methodological tool that focuses attention on context and gives a genuine and personally relevant form to processes of communication. Although one must clearly distinguish between processes of biblical/church communication and processes of TCI, on closer examination an astonishing congruence between the two types of processs

becomes evident. This congruence may well have been intuitively appre-
hended by the early European followers of Ruth Cohn, among whom there
were some priests and theologians. Since these beginnings the work with and
the scientific reflection on TCI have expanded widely and now extend into the
following fields:

- psychotherapy and supervision[1]
- schools[2]
- group dynamics[3] and educational activities
- economics[4]
- pastoral care[5]
- theology[6]

Out of desire and intuition, we as second-generation TCI mentors and
practitioners are faced with a difficult task. Many have already published
reports on what was or was not accomplished in various groups, schools, universities, companies, associations, and so forth when they endeavored to communicate according to the attitude and method of TCI and to structure work
and learning processes accordingly.[7]

Moreover, Ruth Cohn, the founder of TCI, has described this approach
in diverse publications. Her immediate followers and students have developed
it further, applied it and reflected on it academically in various fields. We are
confronted, therefore, with abundant primary sources and with a rich history
of reception that we must take into account.

Are we satisfied with this history of reception? Communicative theology,
which applies TCI as a model of communication suited to communio ecclesiology, understands itself as a "living theology" in the sense that "thinking
about God" is closely linked to group processes in which communication is
structured according to the manner and method of TCI. We have in mind
concrete men and women, above all those who are theologically educated,
with whom we have been working in TCI seminars for more than ten years
and whose existential engagement with central theological themes we have
been privileged to witness. When they first come to our courses and encounter
a more genuine and existentially oriented form of serious theological reflection
than they have previously been used to, the question naturally arises explicitly
and implicitly: what role does TCI play in this theological process? This question has at least two perspectives:

- The clarification of what TCI is or can be: what special attention
  should be given to the "communicative world" in theological processes
  by virtue of TCI's image of the human person, its manner, and its practice?
- What opportunities and limitations does the TCI "technique" offer for
  theological processes relevant for church and society?

The first perspective will be the object of this present chapter. The second will be dealt with in chapter 7.

I. Questions Which Those Trained in Theology Taking Part in TCI Courses Raise That Might Guide the Reader

As a rule we avoid saying very much about the methodology of TCI when introducing communicative theology. The reason is not to withhold information. Nor do we intend to leave them in the dark until the "big surprise" occurs and they positively experience what happens in the group process. Quite the contrary! TCI relies on a high degree of transparency in all of the planning and group processes for the participants. We have learned, however, that the experience of a group process structured according to the attitude and method of TCI after several days raises more concrete questions and produces better results than an abstract discussion beforehand. Such concrete questions are:

- How seriously am I taken as a participant with my experience, conflicts, denials, and my demands on the group?
- How much do I reveal of myself, how much do I hold back? How does the group influence the positions I take?
- What is the value of the group? Is it an instrument for more effective work? Is TCI possible outside the group?
- When will we get "to the core of the matter"? Does "theology" come up short in comparison to the experience of the individuals and the group process?
- What is the role of "the theme" in the group process?
- How much was planned in advance by the leadership and how much is being developed in the course of the process?
- What is the role of the leaders? Why does the leadership consist of two or three people? How does this team cooperate?
- Why is the group process structured in this way and not otherwise?
- Who is this Ruth Cohn who is so often quoted?

These are but a few of the more important questions that emerge when groups begin working with communicative theology. The reader of this chapter, however, may have other concerns.

- Perhaps you are looking for an introduction to TCI or to communicative theology.
- Or perhaps you have some previous experience with TCI groups and processes and you wish to read something more about them.
- You may be fundamentally interested in theology employing group processes and you want to know what kind of role TCI can play in it.

- Or perhaps you have had bad experiences with theology using group process and you want to understand why.
- Maybe you are looking for practical instruction about how you can make use of the attitude and method of TCI.

The following introduction to TCI aims to offer the reader enough information about what is important in Cohn's approach in order to appreciate its relevance for theology as a whole and communicative theology in particular. The TCI theory is not an abstract construction, however, but rather derives from the historical form of reflected experiences that actual people have had in interactive processes centered on major topics of human interest. At the same time, it evokes particularly for those who have studied theology an engagement with certain questions that are basic to its approach. This chapter will take both aspects into account.

In order to have access to TCI, let us first look at how it arose and its central conceptuality.

II. Tracing Everything Carefully from the Beginning

When we discuss TCI we need to turn our gaze to the woman who initiated this approach. Ruth Charlotte Cohn was born in August 1912 as the second child of a well-to-do German-Jewish family in Berlin. Her father, Arthur Hirschfeld, was a bank officer. Ruth Cohn remembers him as a serious, loving person, but also a man with a superior attitude who was definitely the head of the house. Her mother, Elisabeth Hirschfeld, formerly Heiden-Heimer, was a pianist. Ruth remembered her, by contrast, as a person with a sunny temperament who was a bit of a dreamer. To upset her was a "sin" for Ruth.[8]

In her sympathetic description of Ruth Cohn, Silvia Hagleitner cites one of Ruth Cohn's later poems as a key to understanding her life:[9]

> *Star-coin child*
> *Star-coin child stood still.*[10]
> *She ran her fingers through her hair*
> *And over her own body, no longer covered with a shirt.*
> *She ran no longer. Now she had time.*
> *She looked up towards heaven to see: a sparkling gown*
> *Descending carefully around her shoulder and gaze—*
> *A dress of draped cloth with golden stitching.*[11]

Ruth Cohn received an honorary doctorate from the University of Hamburg in 1979 and was honored in 1992 by President Richard von Weizsäcker with Germany's Grand Cross of Merit for her work in the fields of psychology and pedagogy. Even in old age, she has remained true to her childhood dream of writing poetry, poetry reminiscent of her own biography:

- Reminiscent of the homeless star-coin child: *"If this woman had not suffered so much through emigration, poverty, problems with her children, injustice, etc., she —and we—would never have come to her simple, yet consistent insights."*[12]
- Reminiscent of the child who standing still, accepts gifts, understands reality, and transmits this inner attention to other people: *"I can only be fully myself when it becomes clear to me in each moment what is happening to me, what is stirring in me, what is distracting me, what is crippling or blocking me, what is lifting me up and giving me courage. In her appeal: 'Come to yourself, discover what you really want, stand up for yourself!' Ruth Cohn is unrelenting."*
- Reminiscent of the sparkling gown, which clothes the person and changes her own gaze and that of others: *"I could express the results of my meeting Ruth Cohn in one brief sentence: I became more alive. I now force myself to think more clearly and to feel more deeply. I have become both younger and older: younger, because I no longer hide behind the bulwarks of my former stance; older, because it is now clear to me which values I will and must stand up for."*

1. How Does One Fit the Market?

The personal relevance of the learning processes described here can be confirmed by many people who have worked together with Cohn or have gotten to know TCI through courses or training programs. Yet TCI is not limited like other similar group processes only to the personal and communicative level; it has a social political agenda as well, which is a heritage rooted in the biography of Ruth Cohn.

My own (Matthias Scharer) last encounter with Cohn took place during one of the yearly meetings in which TCI course participants regularly come together. We were talking about the "marketability" of TCI in the booming market for psychological, organizational, and educational techniques. In a heated debate, some colleagues suggested that TCI could be better "marketed," and they made appropriate suggestions how this might be done. At first Ruth only listened to this debate and kept silent, but she obviously became increasingly nervous. Then she said: "I have never considered the question of how TCI should be fit to the market. My question has always been, how can the market be fit to people?" This intuitive shift of the theme toward what is essential shows a typical ability of Ruth to get to the point and reveals a focal point for understanding her approach. Ruth Cohn was never interested in setting up a system of rules and methods for group leadership. Neither did she intend to develop a pedagogical technique to communicate painlessly dry and difficult information to students. Admittedly, TCI has often been misused in this way or so misrepresented in the literature. Her intuitive transformation of the question, "how can we make TCI fit the market?" into the question "how do we fit the market to people?" explodes the prevailing logic of success and gives an example of how focusing the theme, one's personal commitment, and methodological-communicative ability are bound together in her approach. We shall see more of this in chapter 7. This transformation of the theme reflects the way in which Cohn has shifted the therapeutic point of view away from individual repression mechanisms to focus on social repression mechanisms, in particular the repression of human exploitation and ecological destruction.[13] As Cohn grows older, her warnings have become ever more insistent, and she has become ever more vocal in protesting against the exploitation of humanity and nature. Against the background of her experience as an immigrant, she said in an interview:

> Today I feel just like I did in Germany back in 1932. I am absolutely convinced that anyone who is not blind can see what awaits us, and if we do nothing to oppose it, it will soon be too late. . . . Not long ago I was in the USA, where I met—more strongly than in Europe—the attitude that it is not all that bad, or that some miracle will deliver us, or that there is nothing we can do anyway; that those in charge are too powerful. And I can only repeat: if something decisive does not happen now, it will soon be too late.[14]

How does this woman see the battle against the exploitation of humanity and living things? She often gives the answer based on the ancient Greek fable about the two frogs fallen into the milk jug: one of them cries out in despair, stretches out its legs, and drowns. The other frog stomps with his legs until the milk turns to butter. Totally exhausted but alive, it then climbs onto the clod of butter and frees itself:

> I am the stomping frog. The rest is not my business; nor is it yours; it is beyond our power. Naturally a mass movement is needed; but I cannot create this by myself. I can promote it by doing everything within my possibilities. I am neither omnipotent, nor powerless; but I am indeed powerful in part.[15]

The fact that in TCI groups everything can become a theme does not mean that it doesn't matter which topic comes into play. Theme-centered communication is founded on an image of the human person and on an ethos that is very near to the Judeo-Christian concept of humanity. Asked about her most important legacy to the world, Ruth Cohn answered:

I have tried to express the Judeo-Christian message of reconciliation and love as a humanistic value for our age and I wish that both TCI and everything else that can lead us ahead will be carried over into the twenty-first century.[16]

Apart from the actual life experience of the founder, the connection between attitude and method in TCI cannot be understood. Ruth Cohn herself thinks that her intention was there "from the very beginning":

I think I have grown into that which I now represent because it has been my intention from the very beginning to advance my own self-improvement and to improve the exercise of my profession (in relation to my patients and students), so that there will be less cruelty and better relations with one another, that what today we call self-realization will be promoted, that is, the creative note which is the specific character of humanity.[17]

2. The Early Experiences

How did Ruth Cohn's life go on before she discovered TCI? Let us listen to her own words:

I was born in Berlin in 1912. It was a time in which everything looked pretty peaceful. I came from a bourgeois Jewish family. My childhood was like that of other children from such families. My parents were nice and good people. We began in moderate circumstances, later we became better off. I went through school and earned the diploma that qualified me for university studies. My personal wish, and also my firm conviction, was that I was a born poet. I had written poetry from the age of seven and I wanted to make a career of it. But I was told that one couldn't make a living as a poet. My father believed that even if a girl married she should have a profession by which she could make a living should it become necessary. This had to do with the fact that he was forced to care for his two sisters after his father died. That a woman should have a profession presented me with no difficulties, but to have a profession that would be lucrative was more difficult to accept because what I really wanted was to be a poet. When I was nearly grown up, adults suggested that becoming a journalist might be an acceptable compromise to my question of what I should become if I still wanted to be a poet. But what should one study to become a journalist? Economics was the answer. Economics was to be sought after; it was what was expected of a journalist. So I started studying economics in Heidelberg.

Already in the first semester I knew that this was not my subject. But it was at Heidelberg that I met Gundolf, the great author who had written about Goethe, who was my idol. Gundolf died, however, in the course of that semester during which I attended his lectures. Then I went back to Berlin for the second semester and there I met my first boyfriend. His mother was a psychoanalyst, and this was the first time that I heard the word. Nowadays we can't imagine that, but at that time psychoanalysis was not a dictionary word. I liked very much what she told me, and so I came home one day and told my mother: "I don't know if I'm going to marry Fred, but I am going to become a psychoanalyst." I was nineteen at the time, and I stood by my decision. But at the same time a lot of other important things were going on. It was 1932—my friend was politically active and was also Jewish. I wasn't into politics myself, but I was Jewish, and what the Nazis were doing was very hard to take. I wasn't attacked personally, but around me I saw how houses were being searched and how Jewish students at the university were being attacked by the Nazis. For the time being they left us girls alone. Nevertheless, it became clear to me that I couldn't study in Berlin anymore, so I went to Zurich to continue my studies. I went there as a student, which meant that I didn't have refugee status in Switzerland. Thus, I couldn't stop studying because they would then have expelled me—and where would I go? So I continued to study for many years in order to avoid being expelled.

3. From (Therapeutical) Distance to Encounter

The decisive experience in Zurich was Ruth Cohn's training in psychoanalysis:

> Between 1933 and 1939 I spent six times a week for fifty minutes on the couch. My analyst listened to me patiently. He was young and attractive. I knew that, however, only because I saw him when I entered or left the room, when we shook hands.[18]

The irony of the last sentence of this quotation reveals a point of criticism that Cohn subsequently came to direct against classical psychoanalysis. It was this criticism that opened up her lifelong quest for alternative therapeutic opportunities and procedures. She was horrified to realize that during the analysis, her psychoanalyst had become the center of her life:

> My thoughts and my feelings revolved around his person, his questions, his statements, his attitudes. I believed that he had some spe-

cial knowledge and that he was leading me infallibly, so that, if the analysis did not go well, it would be all my fault.[19]

The "positive" therapeutic transfer neurosis, which Cohn suffered from during her years of psychoanalysis, was fostered by the dogmatically maintained psychoanalytical setting. It reminds one of the phenomenon of ethical-religious regression even though it is precisely this sort of phenomenon that psychoanalysis is directed against: "Essentially I had been a submissive child and now I had become an equally submissive patient."[20]

The resolution of this therapeutic transfer dependency took place because of events from outside the psychoanalytic setting. Her analyst had advised her not to make any existentially important decisions during the analysis. She had to marry her boyfriend, however, because it was the only way to save his parents from the gas chambers. After this, Ruth's analyst was called up for military service as a doctor. When her analysis was thus ended by the political situation, "an analytical miracle took place":[21]

> Personal letters began arriving from my analyst who had formerly been so very orthodox and abstemious. He had never spoken about himself and almost never expressed any of his own feelings. Now he wrote about his experiences as a doctor and as a border guard, about his feelings about this activity, and about the problems of the time.
>
> A second miracle happened when my first child was born. My former analyst happened to be on leave just then and he brought me a huge bouquet of flowers. He was very touched and told me why the birth of a child was so very important to him—now, at this time, and in this situation.[22]

This overcoming of therapeutic distance through "normal" communication proved to be a foundational experience that would never leave Cohn. For the development of her own approach this experience was crucial. At the same time her long confrontation with classical psychoanalysis led to important learning experiences:

- Apart from poetic intuition, philosophy, and religious faith, scientific methods exist to investigate inner reality. Such procedures are no less valid than the methods of the so-called empirical sciences. Indeed they are the only way of accessing scientifically the reality of inner phenomena: "Freud's combination of the theory of the unconscious with its dynamic connections to the subconscious and the technique of free association has turned inner experience into an object of science. . . . The fact that inner processes may be researched only from within increases the subjective responsibility for their contents and does not diminish their character as reality."[23]

- The specific procedure of psychoanalysis is the analysis of transference. As such, the transference of earlier onto later experience is a vital function that "shortcuts" our ways of knowing and intuition. In psychoanalysis, transference is applied to unrealistic "illusionary" childhood experiences that had led to pathological attitudes. Transference analysis teaches how to "deal with universal transference phenomena in the fields of human relationships."[24] At the same time Cohn learned "to question the notion of transfer neurosis as a tool."[25]
- The analytical principle that resistance should be tackled before dealing with contents led Ruth Cohn to develop a specific notion of how to deal with disturbances in TCI groups. We will come back to this point later.

4. "To Give Too Little Is Theft; To Give Too Much Is Murder"

One cannot understand Ruth Cohn's approach apart from her close relationship to children and education. This relationship was conditioned by having to raise her two children alone after she separated from her first husband.

> Nobody taught me more about human relationships or pedagogy than my own children. From the time they were born (in Heidi's case until she got married; in Peter's case until he went to college) they were at one and the same time the object of a loving relationship and my most important task in life.[26]

Despite this closeness Cohn does not become nostalgic about her children and their education. Quite the opposite, she writes openly about the doubts that she had in her everyday decisions regarding their education. For years the idea that she had to be a perfect mother who could make no mistakes stood in the way. For a long time her pedagogical approach was directed to the future of her children rather than to their present.

> Only slowly did I come to learn from and with my children to treasure the present moment, to trust that the guidelines of my action would always be revealed in becoming, that is, in the process of living. . . . Parents and children are both teachers and learners. If solutions for conflicts are sought in openness, humility, and love, errors on both sides will not be disastrous. The tools for the dialogue are not violence but rather the inner and outer vision of reality.[27]

Also the political and social conditions with which Cohn was confronted earlier in her life brought children into the spotlight of her interest. During her analysis in Zurich she worked in a kindergarten in order to complete her analytical practicum with the direct observation of children. Her most intensive time with children was after her departure for America. Let us listen to her own account.

> My mother migrated to America in 1938, and so we—I had meanwhile married another German Jewish refugee in Switzerland—could also migrate to America as part of a German contingent. So I came to America as a psychoanalyst but without knowledge of the language or of any of the other things that one needs to know about people when one wishes to work with them in a strange country. I also discovered that without belonging to the medical profession I could not become a professional psychoanalyst. I could, however, work as an educator. And because I had always been interested in children and schools this is what I did, without entertaining any ambitions to become a child therapist. I went to a progressive teacher training school—"progressive education" is what they called it—and there more than in any other place was where I learned about people, about children, about America. . . .

The Bank Street School was a teacher training facility that had its own preschools, kindergartens, and elementary schools, patterned on the program of "progressive education." With hindsight, Bank Street was for Cohn "*the source of living learning*."[28] With utmost attention and engagement she took part in the learning processes and immediate experiences of the children:

> . . . to track the steps of a child's interest from the crib down to the floor, from the floor over to the doorway, from the doorway on into the next room, to mother's feet and then up to her knees above them, then up to the table and over to the dangerous stove, from the kitchen over to the doorway opening onto the street—with all its noisy cars, buses, building sites—out to the playground, to the trains, the subways, to the airport. All these stations along the road lead from *one* here-and-now to the next, to another. . . . For it is in the here-and-now of experience that lies the starting point of all learning. Learning is not something imposed from above, but rather it is something to be grasped in a living way with body, soul, intellect, and spirit.[29]

Nevertheless, Cohn judged certain aspects in the Bank Street School's educational system as problematic, for example, the exclusively technical orientation of the school, the repression of personal feelings on the part of the teachers, the children's power over teaching staff. She calls for a balance between "giving too much" and "giving too little": "To give too little is theft; to give too much is murder."[30]

5. "The Couch Is Too Small": Therapy and Pedagogy for Society

For Ruth Cohn it was a long road as she switched from doing therapy with individuals to working in and with groups. In the process she came to develop a "broad" as opposed to a "depth" therapy, an approach that not only served to heal certain personality and group disturbances but above all worked preventively to help people help themselves. Increasingly Cohn foresaw the application of her method "to large sections of the population"[31] or even "to society" as a whole. Having lived as a refugee, this middle-class woman had experienced social needs first hand: "This is how I moved from individuals to society; the circumstances forced me to do so."[32] Already in her pioneering work *Von der Psychoanalyse zu Themenzentrierten Interaktion* she wrote:

> The couch was too small. The new world of the discovery of the psychodynamic laws could as a matter of principle lead to a conscience-expanding, humanizing pedagogy, but how? For over thirty years I have worked in the historical process of personal and mental interaction on a systematic attempt to integrate pedagogical-therapeutic elements in teaching as well as other groups of communication.[33]

Her immigration to America in 1941 gave Cohn the possibility to get to know newly emerging forms of therapy. As a member of the American Academy for Psychotherapy (AAP) she became acquainted with both the most important therapists and with the new psychotherapeutic methods. Her work was first influenced by the method of conscious body experience devised by Elsa Gindler's school of bodily reeducation.[34] She used this method of body sensitivity initially as a complement to her own method. She then applied it as a "psychosomatic analytic technique."[35] For the TCI group work it is not, however, the therapeutic application of conscious body experience that takes center stage.[36] Characteristic for TCI is the involvement of the body's reality in the perspective of the fact "that the sensitization of a person for the reality of him- or herself will bring one to a deeper understanding of one's life and of the mutual dependence that connects one to other persons."[37]

For the integration of analytic and body-therapeutic procedures, it was the holistic vision of the human person as a unity of body and soul that was of paramount importance. For Cohn this is linked to the interdependence inherent in humanity and the anchoring of the human person in a universal whole (see the TCI axioms below, III.2).

Apart from psychoanalysis and body-oriented therapy and the holistic principle, several forms of group therapy had a significant influence on Ruth Cohn's concept. In the United States there were primarily four directions that were widely applied:

- psychoanalytic group therapy
- experience therapy in groups
- Gestalt therapy in groups
- encounter groups.[38]

In 1965–1966 Cohn completed a supplementary course in Gestalt therapy with Fritz Perls. Just how much she appropriated for her method in a critical confrontation with that therapeutic direction and its dogma of autonomy, and where she differed from it in balancing autonomy with the human person's interdependence and social responsibility, is shown by her alternative formula, which she developed into her "Gestalt Prayer." Like many other supporters of the third way in psychotherapy to which they gave the name humanistic psychology, Perls had said:

> I do what I do and you do what you do.
> I am not in this world in order to live up to your expectations.
> You are not in this world in order to live up to mine.
> You are you and I am I.
> If we find each other by chance—wonderful!
> If not, there's nothing one can do about it.[39]

Perls's way of thinking in terms of "I am I and you are you" and his notion of "self-support"[40] were taken by Cohn in another direction:

> I want to do what I'm doing. I am I.
> You want to do what you're doing. You are you.
> The world is our task. It does not meet our expectations.
> However, if we commit ourselves to it, it will become beautiful.
> If we don't, it won't.[41]

In the so-called first axiom[42] of TCI, Cohn's differential conception of autonomy comes to expression; it is unthinkable without a comprehensive involvement of the person.

6. TCI "Is Born"

Again let us listen to Ruth Cohn:

> With the children I just stumbled into what I call "living learning" without really thinking about it at that moment. I taught in psychotherapy institutes, and my teaching was obviously influenced by the group therapy that I was participating in. Soon enough students

would approach me and tell me time and again that my work had given them their best learning experiences, and at first I didn't quite know why. Then I started studying closely what it was that I actually had been doing. And I realized: What I was doing was: first, listening carefully instead of lengthy lecturing. Second, I observed the individuals . . . how they embarked on a theme, how they learned, and how they learned from one another, so that there was a kind of interaction taking place between them that could not generally be found in schools and universities. That is to say, the cooperation principle, that is, that people learn together and from one another, now came clearly into focus. Then, I tried to see how I managed it, that both myself and my students were so lively in these courses and seminars that we didn't "hold lectures" but just talked to one another. And I reflected a lot. Yes, it is difficult to invent such a thing: What are the criteria? What are the procedures? Why is it so lively? I reflected for a long time about that.

The moment TCI was born was actually in a workshop on transference led by Cohn in 1955. Her aim was to expand psychoanalysts' capacity to recognize and resolve group transference. In the lengthy clarifying process on how to teach this approach, a dream played a major role. In this dream Cohn saw a four-cornered pyramid, which she interpreted as the pattern of each group process:

> Now it looks awfully simple, so simple that I can say it in two or three sentences: I insist that each person, the teacher and the students, is equally important, that they see themselves as important, that they see their entrance into the subject matter as important and that they see that what they tell one another is important. I see to it that the theme does not get stifled by the importance of the individual persons and their relationships. All this can be summarized in a formula: I (= the individual person), WE (= the group), IT (= the matter at hand, the task or the theme) are all equally important. That sounds extremely simple, yet it is difficult to put into practice. But this is exactly what makes a group to be a living one. Moreover, one should add, there is no such thing as a group in a void. Groups are always imbedded in a certain environment. Now, this environment can be viewed either as this particular space and moment, or it can be thought of as being as big as the universe. In any case, we always find ourselves caught up in an environment. Symbolically, we can imagine this idea as a triangle, with all angles and sides equal, and enclosed in a sphere representing the infinity around us. . . . And this is the idea: any group is basically a triangle, consisting of I, YOU, and IT. But the specific method that we call Theme-Centered Interaction, is

an interaction, an interplay between people around the topic. This method has the characteristic that these three points are seen as being equally important. You see, if you have a lecture, only two elements are important: the lecturer and the subject matter. And the listeners sit in a row, and they don't see each other; they're not supposed to; it is the same case in a classroom. Perhaps in a classroom the students know one another; however, the system forces them not to work together, but against one another, to see who are the best among them, for only the best, second best, third best, and so on, has a chance in life. In order to counter that tendency—now I come back to therapy—let me say, we should nowadays do population therapy, saying, we are all equally important; we are all human beings. And wherever we find ourselves in groups, in families, in villages, in communities, in schools, in parishes, everywhere we are all important human beings with different functions and different tasks.

How did one come from individual and group therapy to develop the method called by Norman Libermann, an early colleague of Cohn, "living learning"? Supported by Libermann, Frances Buchanan, and others, Cohn founded in 1966 the Workshop Institute for Living Learning (WILL) in New York City. WILL is to this day the international association that promotes and guarantees authentic TCI training and application.

In 1968 Cohn attended the International Congress for Group Psychotherapy in Vienna, Austria, and presented this new therapy form developed in America. It was only after this initial phase that she began to propagate TCI among therapists, teachers, social workers, and pastoral theologians. In 1972, some German and Swiss colleagues founded WILL-Europe. At the same time, the first formation curriculum was devised for TCI group leaders. In 1973, Cohn closed down her American practice and moved to Switzerland, where she settled in the vicinity of the Ecole d'Humanité, an alternative school in Hasliberg, in the Bern Highlands, where she still lives part of the time. In what she calls the "big view with a small apartment"— her description of her tiny forty-square-meter apartment in a farmhouse— many a disciple, friend, and acquaintance has gone in and out. Her hospitality, her mastery of dialogue, her attractive openness, but also her capacity for political commitment, were something that I (Matthias Scharer) myself experienced some time ago while on a visit with a couple of theology students from Linz. In a matter of minutes, she involved the students in an intensive discourse on their relationship to church and society. With her long flowing hair, the then-almost-eighty-year-old Ruth, sitting on her "bouncing ball" cushion, looked like the youngest member of our group, but also like the most mature member of the group. Nowadays, she lives most of the time with Helga Hermann in Germany.

In order to get a deeper appreciation of what communication is according to the manner and method of Theme-Centered Interaction one needs this biographical information. It shows clearly the inextricable link of this method to the founder's life as well as to social developments and to the history of psychotherapy.

Questions for Reflection

- What did you already know about Ruth C. Cohn's biography, and what was new for you?
- What fascinates you about this woman? What amazes you about her life? What does not particularly impress you?
- What connections do you see between her life and Theme-Centered Interaction?

III. Communicating with Attention to Theme-Centered Interaction

After having thus situated TCI in the biography of Ruth Cohn, we now go on to reflect systematically on this communicative approach and to confront it with concrete challenges arising within the process-oriented, theological approach that constitutes communicative theology. The TCI method can serve thereby as a heuristic and hermeneutical framework for themes that must not be ignored in an anthropologically oriented theology because Christian God-talk is always a discourse about people in relationship. The leading questions of this section are, therefore, the following:

- What are the main theoretical assumptions and methodological considerations for communicating according to the manner and method of TCI?
- What marks the value-oriented attitude of TCI without which, according to Cohn, TCI is "as dangerous as a lighted match in a haystack"?[43]
- Which concerns or themes are highlighted when the anthropological-ethical assumptions of TCI become effective in theological reflection groups?

1. "Slowing Down" in TCI, the Anthropological-Ethical TCI Assumption

Ruth Cohn's approach does not contain a systematically developed anthropology. Helmut Quitmann, however, has shown that underlying Cohn's anthropology is the Heideggerian understanding of *Dasein* in the sense that "I am, because I exist, because I live and die."[44] In a critical confrontation with psychoanalysis's disregard for the body—a general feature of Western culture—and with the pressure of achievement, Cohn's concept of the human person in this respect becomes recognizable:

> An attitude that stresses existence rather than achievement is unknown to those poor souls who have been trained to achieve, to perform, and to compete.[45]

Cohn never tires of maintaining the inseparable "interdependence between human and spiritual values and her specific methodological approach." Thus, she has always resisted attempts to reduce TCI to a mere technique for directing group processes.[46] This value reference is most clearly expressed in the "axioms" of TCI, which formulate the "irreducible presuppositions" of the TCI approach and contain "elements of faith."[47]

- As existential, value-dependent statements, they provide a basic orientation for human action; the intention being to alter inner and outer reality constructively in terms of this value orientation.
- As a starting point for the reflection of the human person on his or her experiences and on his or her environment, they make people aware of their expanded possibilities.
- The vision of the human person and his or her possibilities becomes clear only in their connection with each other. The axioms are not to be thought of separately; they are linked in an interdependent relationship.

Ruth Cohn has continued to develop these so-called axioms of TCI. The most elaborate presentation is contained in a work she published with Paul Matzdorf.[48]

What effect do the axioms have on actual group processes? To answer this question we report on our own experience with such groups. As a TCI week draws to its close, we sometimes lay out on the floor a big chart of the "TCI system" with its axioms, postulates, and with the figure of the triangle within the sphere. Then we read slowly the week's theme and ask the participants to position themselves near the element that for them was most important as they worked on a given theme. Initially, "I"-centering predominates. The individual participants put their own concerns in the center and expect the interaction process to yield tangible results as soon as possible. With time, however, other elements of the TCI attitude take on greater importance.

The anthropological-ethical basis of communication processes through the TCI attitude "slows down" group processes. What counts is not the speed with which a result is achieved or the absence of conflict and disturbance. What marks the communication processes according to TCI is respect and attention toward those values that are important for each individual, for the group, as well as for humanizing the prevailing ecclesial and social contexts. Detours and even erroneous paths that individuals or the group as a whole might take are not viewed as tragedies or as a waste of time and energy. Rather, they are accepted and taken seriously as learning opportunities that should be thematized as such. Such an approach to communication, which involves "slowing-down" and attending to values, heightens the confrontation with the prevailing social, ecclesial, and scientific performance paradigm. The expectation of quickly acquiring information and mastering a method of effective communication dominates initial expectations even with groups of people trained in theology. The empirical performance paradigm, according to which only that which is "produced" is measurable, is deeply rooted in the minds of academics and church people alike. This effectiveness expectation—sometimes traumatically marking the beginnings of a group—manifests itself in theologically oriented TCI groups in at least two ways:

- One must quickly "get down to business."
- The "TCI method" must be learned effectively in the shortest possible time.

Taking each individual seriously in his/her biographical development and future possibilities and taking group processes seriously, including their blockages and disturbances, are hardly factors that can be captured with techniques of quantitative measurement. However, this attitude opens up a new horizon of attention to what theological themes are all about, that is, not knowledge as something that remains exterior to the human persons in their relationships and that can be acquired theoretically, but rather an assurance encompassing the whole person that marks human existence. This assurance can be gained by the individual as well as by the group only gradually in a step-by-step process. Analogous to a theme in Erich Fromm, one could say that theological knowledge is not a knowledge "to-have" but a knowledge "to be." Theology takes the form of a life-long process of seeking the "truth that gives assurance to life."[49] This process can take place only in a communicative way with leaders and participants alike.

For those accustomed to efficiency-oriented communication approaches that are exploited "in terms of whatever works," and are more or less cut off from their anthropological-ethical background (chapter 2), it is clear that the TCI approach will be experienced as a detour or as an impediment in the communication process. But as Cohn used to say, "the more you have to do, the slower you need to go." And this piece of advice should encourage TCI group leaders not to separate the TCI attitude from its methodical consequences but rather to use the TCI attitude as the actual method.

We can see that such attitude-oriented, "decelerating" group work has a significant bearing on the whole life of those trained in theology by reading the following excerpts from interviews conducted by an Innsbruck student as part of a thesis. Those interviewed were participants in a course on communicative theology held in the Theology Department of the University of Innsbruck.[50]

> *K:* Well the first thing that strikes me is that things were different than I expected. We had no lectures at all. There was a brief "input," which is what an unnamed individual called it about the method of TCI in combination with theology and what that would look like. It was exciting and interesting, but the real communicative theology, which is what this is all about, I would say, that's us, you know, ourselves. . . . That is to say. . . . well, we are here to develop the themes in a process-oriented way, to attain knowledge about them. And this is really very exciting, and during this week I thought a couple of times about our conversation at the beginning of the course. And I realized I had said that I wanted to experience something exciting and to learn something and so on. And this is just what is happening. I am very happy to be here. It is also very meditative and what happens here is extremely moving.
>
> Without exaggeration, it's a life-changing experience. I felt really challenged personally concerning problems in my faith, my life, my theological constructs that I carry around with me. And this went on day after day! And that goes for things very deep inside of me. And this is . . . this is not easy to do. It's all very exciting.

> *Interviewer:* You have just said everything went differently than you expected: there were no lectures and it was moving. How would you describe the first part of the course?

> *K:* Yes, well, if you think about a normal large university lecture: one hundred and fifty people in an auditorium, the professor comes in, paces to and fro, as many do, or sits at his desk, as others do; people write things down and go home with more or less newly acquired information.
>
> Here, it's exactly the opposite.
>
> Here we sit with our chairs in a circle. We only leave our chairs for group work, but there too we also sit in a circle. Naturally, there were also some individual activities. We had some tasks, to reflect on some questions on our own, which we then brought back to the group. But, I should underscore it yet again: we never really left the circle of chairs. There was no change in seating order! Oh yes, there was one exception. Yesterday afternoon we had a presentation on computer history, in which we saw the university's homepage, where we can also learn some things virtually. Then we sat in rows, because the image was projected on the wall, that is to say, for purely techni-

cal reasons. Otherwise, it was all so communicative and everything was done together and everything was marked by this being done together.

Oh yes, in fact, with hindsight I would say that this was almost necessary.

If it's a matter of connecting biography and theology, then there's no one who can make this connection for me. The only person in the whole world who can connect theology with my biography is myself. But of course, guided, in a group, led, yes, a little—directed is too strong a way of putting it—motivated, accompanied by other people, who are on the same path as I am.

What's really cool is . . . or better, another strong point of this way of learning is that the man and woman leading the course—later on other members of the group will assume this role—are always doing everything together with us. There is not a single process that they weren't a part of. When there are small groups, you can be assured that they'll be there taking part also. . . .

And they are there with heart and soul, with their questions and problems just like all of us.

I: So, there's no trace of the classical teacher/student distinction?

K: Absolutely not! It is a completely new way of learning and teaching. The team reflected on this once again with us yesterday. Also with regard to exams, how they should take place, as well as the master's thesis and the other things that will be necessary. Also about the overseas project that is going to take place. So, it's a very well-thought-out concept.

It's something more than what we have . . . I mean there are, of course, very good lecturers. I am one of those who would travel far and wide to hear a good lecture. . . . I mean, here it's more than a principle of educational psychology; if, actually, one gets the chance to live it. And here we've got such a chance, . . . to experience it ourselves.

Of course I have to think it through more. . . . I mean, there are a lot of people here who have a lot of education and professional experience. But, I mean, it is now clear that I would like to make some changes in the direction in which I go about my professional activities.

I: So you received some impetus here in order to do just that?

K: Yes, I did.

I: I'd be interested to know whether the topic for this week, "Theology and Biography," interested you? Did anything change for you along these lines?

K: Well, to get to the point, it was about breakdowns and break-throughs in life. We first had to reflect on our biography and tell some stories from it. That really makes your life seem vibrant, if I may say so. It happened to me. And then it just . . . ah . . . deep-ened—"increased" would not be the right word—yes, it deep-ened. . . . And we poured out our minds and hearts . . . or rather stretched our minds and poured out our hearts.

We pondered how our theology corresponds to our biography, in what relationship do they find themselves? So we looked at our biog-raphy, our theology, and vice versa. And what was really interesting is how many similarities there were between the dark moments of life and the bright ones. . . .

Although we were always in these groups. . . . I mean we were a good mix, and, with one exception, when we happened to be the same four people, we were always with new people, which, if I may say so, was very challenging. Sometimes you feel a need to stay together: oh, I worked so well with those guys, it would be nice if we could go on together. But they planned it differently here and that can have its good side, I think. And one gets to hear new stories each time, from other people, and one learns things differently each time, from another perspective.

I: So you constantly switched groups. Always new faces, new stories. . . .

K: Yes, I can hardly think of anyone from the big group with whom I had not at some time interacted in a small group. And this makes the whole thing very challenging, even tiring. In the evenings, I felt very tired. It's certainly more fatiguing than just sitting there listen-ing to lectures.

B: I hadn't really thought about "communicative theology" before, but I did sense something, and perhaps that's the way I am. In the first conversation round I told how I had experienced theology in the monastery and then in the university. And, to my mind, commu-nicative theology goes on in the monastery—where we got into one another's hair, where we prayed together, where we celebrated Mass together. Somehow all this accompanied me throughout my whole life. Simply the experience of it back then, the way we related to one another, but also the way we discussed things like religious issues. Even putting into words our deepest religious convictions. Yes, expressing convictions, that is what I experienced so strongly back then. And this experience has stayed with me. I learned the name communicative theology only much later, but I think it is what hap-pened to us back then, at least at times. I think, a lot has happened here. I think I sense what communicative theology is. But I cannot put my finger on the specifics or on the individual stages according to which it develops.[51]

Questions for Reflection

- How do you experience the relationship between efficiency and "a depth dimension" in your work, your studies, your groups?
- What expectations and experiences expressed in the interviews of participants in the communicative theology course are comprehensible for you, which ones are not?
- To what extent would a "decelerating" concept of group interaction help you or not?

2. The TCI Axioms

After these introductory remarks about TCI, we will now consider the individual axioms and their significance for theological group work.

(a) The human person's autonomy and relational character are dialectically connected.

The first axiom, the so-called existential-anthropological one, contains explicit statements about the nature of being human. How autonomous are human beings and what does their autonomy mean? How much does the human person relate to other persons and to other things, and what do these relationships mean? In the existential-anthropological axiom, a holistic vision of the human person is clarified in a twofold way: "the individual per se and the individual as part of the environment together make up a single whole."[52] Human persons cannot ask about themselves, therefore, in a way that makes sense without involving all other persons and all other things. This holistic autonomy refers to thoughts, feelings, and actions.

Cohn cautions against a false understanding of autonomy, which focuses solely on the human person's independence. This distinguishes her approach from those methods which, like TCI, belong to humanistic psychology but which overemphasize autonomy. Biologically and intellectually, the human person is indeed autonomous: the person is a living unity. But she or he participates in a mutual interdependence with other people and the circumstances that comprise "the world." Autonomy and participation are dialectically linked: "The more I consciously allow the world to enter into me, the more autonomous I am."[53] An increasing self-awareness leads to an increasing awareness of the world and vice versa.

In terms of the dialectical linkage of autonomy and interdependence, the first axiom, in its original form, touches the question of the relationship between past, present, and future. In humanistic-psychology approaches such as Gestalt therapy, attention was directed almost exclusively to the here-and-now: the only thing that counts is what I experience "totally" in this very moment with "hand, heart and brain"; everything else is irrelevant. Contrary to this attitude, for Cohn, events in the past, present, and future belong together:

> My here-and-now is merely one of my human dimensions. The here-and-now world without the awareness of the future lying within it is shallow.[54]

It is against this background that Cohn articulates her existential-anthropological axiom:

> The human person is both a psycho-biological unity and a part of the universe. Therefore the person is autonomous and interdependent to the same extent. The individual's autonomy will be all the greater the more he or she is aware of his or her interdependence with all other persons and things.[55]

To complete the first axiom: Human experiences, attitudes, and communication are subject to universal laws of interaction. Events are not isolated happenings, but they condition one another in the past, present, and future.

For the theologically educated the tension between a human person's autonomy and interdependence would seem to be resolved. The free human being exercises one's freedom in a loving relationship. The person's conditioned freedom offers no ground for the assertion of autonomist dreams of power, nor is one's interdependence a prison cell in which one must sacrifice one's life's blood for others. Clear as this theory about the human person might be in a Christian anthropology it is very difficult to live concretely the dialectics of autonomy and participation in theological or ecclesial practice. The challenge posed by this dialectic takes various forms which recurrently surface in TCI groups with those trained in theology:

- as a confrontation between human-centered "liberation" theologies and God-centered "pious" theologies;
- as a battle between autonomy-minded, emancipated theologians and pastors, on the one hand, and "self-sacrificing" church workers, on the other;
- as an emphasis on love of self as opposed to love for one's neighbor and love of God;
- as a proclamation of a gospel that liberates from established roles and

promotes independence, rather than a gospel that imposes acceptance of an ecclesial system of norms and values.

If those trained in theology come into TCI groups, they get entangled in existential confrontations with their image of themselves and of their roles, which are often based on an image of the human person that tries to set limits on the dialectic of autonomy and interdependence. A "fatal" alternative comes into play between "divinely willed" self-sacrifice, on the one hand, and "autonomy infatuated" self-protectiveness that refuses to open up to others, on the other hand. We shall come back to this point in section 5.

(b) Option for life

In the second, so-called ethical axiom, Cohn formulates an evaluative judgment about the meaning and value of human life and action. She writes:

> Respect is due to all living things and their growth. Respect for growth determines value judgments. What is human is valuable; what is inhuman is value threatening.[56]

This unequivocal option for the value of life includes respect for nature. What is human may be recognized in terms of a loving, respectful, interactive attitude; what is inhuman shows itself in a marginalizing, "sinful" and disrespectful attitude.[57] The question arises of how Cohn distinguishes between "good and evil" with respect to the ethical axiom related to life and to being human.

> I don't believe that an *absolute* good or evil is revealed to any chosen people. But I do believe that an "indispensable" good and evil leads us, whose direction is not static and inflexibly mandatory, but is rather ordered to inner and outer circumstances. From an ethical point of view, we can understand an act and its actors only within their overall context. Ethical values are unalterable *and* yet they are dependent on the process. Whoever understands oneself as a perspective-bound person, that is, as a person with a limited capacity of perception, knows that good and evil look differently from different perspectives. I can only describe *my* truth, never *yours*. Yet I believe that there would be no differing aspects of the ethos if they were not related to the reality of an unalterable center; even though the interpretations thereof can be misleading.[58]

Ruth Cohn supports the hypothesis of an "innate," "organic" sense of values, whose development is a question of survival for humanity and which corresponds to the autonomous and yet interdependent character of the human being. Only when this innate sense of values is preserved, elaborated, and developed can the increasing rationalization and fragmentation of the world be halted and atomic destruction avoided.

> I believe it possible that the development of values and meaning takes place not only at the slow pace proper to evolution but also in transformational quantum leaps. Both Judeo-Christian and humanistic ethics teach values of goodness and humanity. When smirking pessimists of every age express their regret that human nature has always been inclined toward the survival of the fittest and that nothing will change this, then I protest by saying: the fact that something has been like this in past history does not mean that it must always remain like that. . . . Animals may well be ancestors of our ethical capacity; they may have a "sense" of ethics. . . . Yet between them and us there is a qualitative difference that offers us freedom and responsibility, music and ethos, leaving us with the task either to build community or to destroy ourselves.[59]

Theologically the second axiom raises the problem of human conscience. In the Second Vatican Council's fundamental statement on conscience we read:

> Deep within their consciences men and women discover a law which they have not laid upon themselves and which they must obey. Its voice, ever calling them to love and to do what is good and to avoid evil, tells them inwardly at the right moment: do this, shun that. For they have in their hearts a law inscribed by God. Their dignity rests in observing this law, and by it they will be judged. Their conscience is people's most secret core, and their sanctuary. There they are alone with God whose voice echoes in their depths. By conscience, in a wonderful way, that law is made known which is fulfilled in the love of God and of one's neighbor. Through loyalty to conscience, Christians are joined to others in the search for truth and for the right solution to so many moral problems which arise both in the life of individuals and from social relationships. Hence, the more a correct conscience prevails, the more do persons and groups turn aside from blind choice and endeavor to conform to the objective standards of moral conduct. Yet it often happens that conscience goes astray through ignorance which it is unable to avoid, without thereby losing its dignity. This cannot be said of the person who takes little trouble to find out what is true and good, or when conscience is gradually almost blind through the habit of committing sin.[60]

Between the Christian notion of conscience and Cohn's option for life and humanity, her position on the distinction of good and evil, and her "organic"

conception of the sense of values, there are points of agreement as well as differences. The most crucial difference is the Christian's dependence on God.
This is the point where the concept of communication based on exclusively
human interdependence is radically transformed. It is in conscience understood as a human person's hidden center and sanctuary that God speaks to
every person whether or not they are subjectively aware of this fact. Neither
consensus in a domination-free discourse on values nor the natural tendency
of each person to do good are comparable to the communicative "quality" of
the human person's confrontation with "one's" God. From the biblical
accounts of people being called, through the stories about people struggling to
do good, up to Jesus' call to conversion in view of the coming reign of God
(see Mark 1:15), there is an impressive tradition of communication that
expresses the conflicting position in which human beings find themselves
when confronted with God's speaking to them.

As the Council notes, fidelity to conscience links Christians with other
human beings "in the search for truth and for the right solution to so many
moral problems that arise both in the life of individuals and from social relationships."[61] This connection between all human beings through the authority of conscience shows congruity with TCI's awareness of values. In
religiously and ideologically "mixed" groups, themes that have to do with
value awareness, with the basis for values, and with conscience become particularly acute. For people who base their judgments of conscience on the communication between God and human beings, the honesty with which some
so-called humanists motivate their ethical choices can be most challenging.
Ruth Cohn herself can adequately serve as an example of a lifelong authentic
search for the values of humanity and for the deep commitment to people and
to the world, that goes with this search.

(c) To act responsibly within a conditional freedom

The third (pragmatic-political) axiom calls for a certain pragmatism, that is,
for a realistic approach, as opposed to the dream of unconditional freedom. It
connects the inner and outer aspects to each other and connects the three
axioms together:

> Free decisions take place within conditioning inner and outer bound-
> aries. Expanding these boundaries is possible. The measure of our
> freedom is greater when we are intelligent, healthy, materially secure,
> and psychologically mature as opposed to sick, limited, poor, and
> subject to violence and insufficient maturity. The awareness of our
> universal interdependence provides the basis for our human respon-
> sibility.[62]

The paradox of conditional freedom marks the reality of human existence. In all situations, inner and outer boundaries are involved. But it is crucial to know that boundaries can be expanded. Once again, the historicity of human existence comes to expression here. One acts in a humanly responsible fashion precisely when one is fully aware of the universal conditioning of freedom, but at the same time one makes good use of the "free space" available within the conditioning globe.

Questions for Reflection

- With which TCI axioms can you identify? Which ones would you rather modify or give only qualified assent to? Which would you reject altogether?
- Where do you see correlations between TCI axioms and Christian conceptions? What coincides in the two sets of values? Where do they differ?
- What significance do you attribute to a communicative attitude taking account of values? Where do you experience the opposite attitude, either within or outside of the Christian churches?

3. Indispensable "Playing Rules" for the TCI Attitude: The Postulates

The anthropological-ethical implications of the TCI axioms give rise to two indispensable rules known as the "existential postulates"[63] of TCI. They mark the point of intersection between the axioms, that is, the existential-anthropological, the ethical-social, the pragmatic-political basis and the "TCI methodology," aimed at a living, holistic learning process. These postulates should not be misunderstood, however, as though they were recommendations of "those in the know" to "those still ignorant."[64] They are meant as "recommendations of equals addressed to equals."[65]

(a) "Be your own chairperson"

How does one live out the outer and inner attention promoted by the TCI attitude? How is it put into practice in group communication and group leadership?

- An attentiveness to bodily sensations, changing feelings, basic dispositions, intuitions, fantasies, evaluations, and so forth, as well as
- An attentiveness given to other individuals, to the group process, and to everything happening in the world at the moment.

How can one remain capable of action and not be torn apart in the flood of different perceptions, feelings, and ideas? First of all, one need not "do" anything at all outwardly, One begins simply by perceiving and accepting oneself as one is. At the same time, the chairperson postulate calls one "to make decisions and take responsibilities in the awareness of oneself and of the situation."[66] This is how Ruth Cohn phrased it:

> Be your own chairman/chairwoman, be a chairperson for yourself.

This means:

- Be aware of your inner circumstances and your environment.
- Take every situation as an opportunity for your own decision. Give and take as you wish with responsibility for both yourself and others.[67]

Cohn remarks that some time ago in American linguistic usage the word "chairman" was unambiguous and designated a group leader who was not a neutral person outside the group. It was replaced by "chairperson," which does not have quite the same connotation. Perhaps we could rephrase the chairperson postulate as: "Be your own leader," or "Decide for yourself."[68]

Analogous to the old notion of chairman, a "chairperson" is the one in charge of his/her "inner group" making realistic and conscious decisions. Faced with the (post)modern challenge of the most diverse life possibilities, which are communicated through the media, the chairperson postulate is a suitable opportunity to live "identity-in-plurality" (chapter 1). The diversity and contradiction between various life projects are not blocked or denied in any way. They are taken seriously and permitted. But one does not thereby become the ping-pong ball of plurality. He/she is challenged to make a concrete decision each time. How the balance between diversity and nonambiguity can be found is made clear by another older formulation of the postulate:

> *You are your own chairperson, your own leader.* Listen to your inner voices, to your various needs, wishes, motivations, ideas; use all your senses, listen, see, smell, observe. Use your spirit, your knowledge, your power of judgment, your responsibility, your capacity to think. Weigh your decisions carefully. No one can take your decisions away from you. *You are the most important person in your world, just as I am in mine.* We must be able to express ourselves clearly when we talk to each other and listen to each other carefully as this is the only bridge between one island and another.[69]

Because the chairperson postulate includes not only the I but also the We and the You, Annedore Schultze, an early collaborator of Cohn, expands the chairperson postulate with the sentence: "I lead myself and I allow/create a possibility for others to lead themselves."[70]

According to Matzdorf and Cohn, the central therapeutic and political intervention of TCI is expressed in the chairperson postulate. It makes possible human individuality and solidarity.[71] Even as it recognizes human diversity, it makes it possible to have community on the grounds of a genuine dialogue. Thus, the TCI concept excludes both individualism and collectivism.

The chairperson postulate also "regulates" the human tendency to swing between arrogance and resignation. It encourages one not to give into the temptation to be narcissistic and become one's own god and thus to fall into the modern god-complex. At the same time it protects one from the crippling despair that can befall people faced with inscrutable economic forces and media influences. In a realistic fashion, it makes a person aware of the room for action available in any concrete situation. In Cohn's words: "I am neither omnipotent nor powerless; I am partially powerful."[72]

Our room for action is by no means static; it changes according to age and situation. Despite the fact that one is responsible for oneself and is one's own chairperson, there are situations when one has to exercise responsibility for others, especially when others lose their consciousness or have not fully attained it:

> If I should tell a five-month-old baby: "Be your own chairperson: go, if you will, or remain in bed if you will," that is obviously absurd. The baby can neither understand the words nor can it decide to go. I must therefore take up and carry the baby or the disabled person to wherever they should go when this is necessary or desirable for the person's existence. In a similar way I must take responsibility for others even in less radical circumstances when I think—and have responsibly checked my belief—that the child's maturity or the disabled person's disability and my own responsibility for them call for me to make decisions for them.[73]

(b) Disturbance and passionate involvements take precedence.

It is proper to human communication and growth that they do not take place without disturbances, that is, without inner and outer resistance and without varying degrees of involvement. As an academic psychoanalyst, Cohn well recognizes the learning opportunities that people have in the face of resistance and the overcoming of resistance. Therefore, the original wording of the so-called disturbance postulate does not have the negative character suggested by everyday usage. By "disturbance" we generally understand events or ways of behaving that block us, that are inappropriate and irritating. The formula "Disturbances and passionate involvements take precedence" or, in other words, "Disturbances and passionate involvements claim their precedence," recalls the counter-transference workshops in which TCI was born. This postulate refers to an observation about the reality of human interaction: disturbances do not "ask for permission"; they are simply there as "pain, joy, fear, distraction,"[74] and so on. If they remain unexpressed or are suppressed, they give rise to "the kind of impersonal, 'disturbance-free' classrooms, factory halls, auditoriums, conference rooms" that are "filled with apathetic and submissive or desperate and rebellious people, whose frustration ultimately leads to their own destruction and that of their institution. The postulate that disturbances and passionate involvements take precedence means that we acknowledge people's full reality."[75] It is precisely this acknowledgment of the reality of disturbances that makes it possible to change them.

Although the notion of disturbance priority takes its origin in the fundamental psychoanalytic principle that resistance should be dealt with before the contents, the TCI context develops a broader notion of disturbance. "In a TCI sense, disturbance sources are not only those arising from unresolved intrapsychic anxiety. Disturbance sources can be all inner emotional processes and outer circumstances that stand in the way of addressing the theme."[76] Early on, a notion of disturbance with sociopolitical significance made its appearance in TCI:

> *We believe that many of us fall victim to a disturbance in which we forget about the humanly possible because we let ourselves be crippled by the humanly impossible.* Maybe this is our most important generative theme: "What do I do as individual or as small group when confronted with the inscrutable factors that seem necessary for solving sociopolitical problems?" The disturbance says, "It is impossible, it is too much. We cannot find a solution for all the destructive, senseless, unjust things that are happening."
>
> *Is it possible that this very way of phrasing the question causes such disturbances? . . .* We believe that the disturbance ("it is too much, too complicated, too depressing to do something political") may be countered with a policy of small steps and with the belief in humane values.[77]

According to Anita Ockel and Cohn, the first steps toward overcoming the disturbance of political incapacity consist in becoming aware of one's possibilities and powers and in thinking about the possibilities for joining together with others to attack the problem.

> When do I need peace and quiet in order to think or meditate and *when do I seek peace and quiet as an escape* from something that is in actual fact more important for me? When do I need action and solidarity in view of a constructive attitude and when is *action only an escape from the awareness of other conflicts* and priorities for me? *Which*

*priorities do I set for myself as a private "I" and which priorities corre-
spond to my political participation in the "We"? How can I realistically
engage my possibilities, my knowledge, and my current psychosomatic,
spiritual, and familial situation?* [78]

The following figure summarizes the axioms and postulates and connects
them with the TCI working principle.

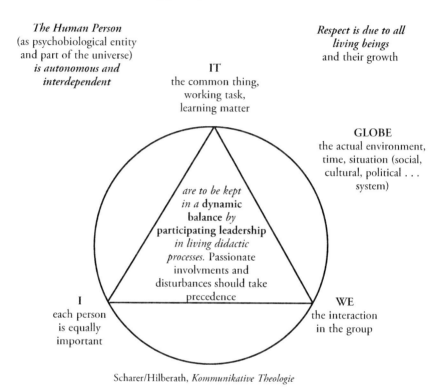

Scharer/Hilberath, *Kommunikative Theologie*

Figure 9. Free decision takes place within certain
inner and outer borders. Expansion of borders is possible.

Questions for Reflection

- What does the chairperson postulate tell you about your everyday
  communication practice? When are you aware of your chairperson
  and exercise it and when do you not do so?
- In which situations do you experience "the group" of the different
  "inner voices"? How do you reach authentic decisions?

- What "disturbances" are normal for you?
- What are "disturbances," according to the TCI postulate?
- How do you handle "disturbances"?
- What do you become aware of as a result of the TCI disturbance postulate in regard to my everyday communication, as well as your group/community leadership?

With the aid of two examples, we now propose to show how a theological process according to the TCI approach can lead to new awareness and to existential encounter among the participants.

4. Saying "Yes and Amen!" to One's Own Life

Themes connected with the TCI axioms and postulates as a rule touch the whole life of the participants. Starting from the third axiom the question arises, how can I act responsibly within my conditional freedom and how do I actually do so? For many people this question brings one's whole life into the picture. Then the following question surfaces: how do I write "my" biography with the "material" of my own life, that is, how do I interpret it at the moment and how will I definitively interpret it at the end of my life?

In so-called personality courses aimed at confronting one's own biography, even a introductory theme such as "the history of my name—let me introduce myself" may well trigger biographical narratives. Questions like the following can prove helpful to generate such discussion:

- What name do I use for myself? What do others call me?
- What am I called if I have more than one name?
- Who gave me my name(s)?
- Why was I given my name(s)?
- What does my name mean? What do I know about it?
- What has been my experience with my name during my life?
- What rephrasings (nicknames, pet names) has my name gone through?
- What do I like about my name? What don't I like?
- How do I wish to be called by you in this group?

The last question often triggers in members of the group the courage to try a forgotten or desired variant of their name.

More intensive personal interpretation of the participant's biography will be called up when the theme is, for example, "My history . . . what attracts me? What holds me back? What would I like to do here with you?" In the nontherapeutic approach to participants' life histories practiced in TCI groups, the biographical narrative[79] is particularly important. Each person is

responsible for finding his/her own middle position (cf. the chairperson postulate) between the extremes of repressing and withholding information, on
the one hand, and performing a psychological striptease, on the other. To this
end, sensitively switching the manner of working can often be helpful:

- Working individually I can express myself through texts, forms,
  colors, music, or dance, anything that is "mine."
- In the exchange within a small group (as far as possible self-
  selected) I can open up to whatever extent I choose at the moment.
  For the biographical part it is particularly important to give
  enough time and space for the small groups.
- In the group's plenary sessions, particularly in the first days with a
  new group, biographical narration focuses as a rule on "meta-
  themes" such as How did I feel during the individual work? How
  did I select "my" small group? What was I able to do in the small
  group? What could I not do? How and with what do I come back
  to you in the plenary session?

In biographically oriented TCI courses, there is one question that quickly
becomes acute, often as early as the end of the first day: How can one "spin"
a common thread for the course from so many different biographies and
interests? This question is a major stumbling block for many well-meaning
attempts to work on the participants' biography (for instance in adult education courses in theology). The threads have to be joined in such a way so
as to avoid an artificial unification in which individuals feel they have not
been taken seriously. This demands good interaction between leaders and
participants.

One useful technique to construct such a common thread out of the
diverse elements is the following. Under the theme, "Our intentions for this
course," we play a kind of "dominoes" game. Each participant, leaders
included, contributes up to three concerns written on pieces of paper. The
game now consists of laying out the papers like domino pieces in such a way
that individual concerns that belong together are "connected" to one another,
whereas those that do not belong together are set apart. In this way an initial
structure gradually takes form, showing which concerns come together and
overlap and which stand off in isolation. Now it is possible for the group,
when properly led, to revise these structures until a sort of "group plan"
emerges, which is then given over to the planning team for further work and
orientation in the days ahead.

From the biographical narratives come questions about the personal roles
that each participant plays at a given moment in different contexts. A theme
like "The roles that I play (or would like to play)" first calls for becoming
aware of and then structuring one's diverse roles. One technique is to place
coins of different sizes and weights on a piece of paper to represent the per-

son's diverse roles. Another technique is to draw a diagram showing them. The ensuing conversation about the resulting graphic representation can open the participants' eyes not only to the diversity of roles they play or would like to play but also to any lack of clarity, to overtaxing demands, and to conflicts within their individual role systems. Working together on roles in the group can thus contribute to the clarification of responsibilities taken or refused within the framework of conditional freedom. Theologians and pastoral workers are especially vulnerable to being overtaxed and burned out.

A theme that may lead in the direction of role decisions is "My roles as one trained in theology: where are the conflicts, where are the agreements?" Such a theme may be expanded further to let the participants challenge one another to lay open their understanding of themselves as theologically trained persons: "My and your conception of being trained in theology challenges each other." It is important here not to allow social and ecclesial competition to emerge in the group, that is, who best presents him-/herself, though it can never be avoided altogether. One technique is to stage an "open market," as will be described in chapter 8. In this scenario the participants and leaders enter into different roles, identifying themselves by means of labels, clothing, body language, and so on. They give one another feedback in regard to how they perceive one another in these various roles. Such role playing provides a fun element, which is desirable, given the existential character of the theme. And indeed, in such biographical and role-clarifying activities, "selective authenticity," of which we will speak later, often comes into the picture. Thus, one of our TCI groups developed in the course of a week enough trust to directly address the theme "Between the extremes of hide-and-seek and psychological striptease, am I as genuine as possible and as selective as necessary?" In this discussion the participants confronted the relationship between mutual willingness and unwillingness to open up to one another in the group.

On this basis, it becomes possible to let biographical narratives flow into theology: under the theme "God seems to have accompanied me throughout my life—was it really God?" Encounters, events, and experiences were presented, shared, and also questioned. "What makes me suspect that God has accompanied me throughout my life? What focuses my theological attention? What focuses yours?" Such a theme is introduced not only verbally but is also given ritual expression. This gives room for the working of grace in such a theological task, opening up that dimension of gratuity without which no communicative theology worthy of its name can be done.

In accordance with the dialectics of autonomy and interdependence, of exterior and interior, mysticism and politics, the intensive occupation with the participants' biographies, with the clarification of their diverse roles and their theological objects of attention should not remain locked in subjectivity. A theme should follow that goes beyond the individual and the group and addresses "the Globe" of the ecclesial and social context, thus calling attention to the participants' responsibility for the world. A theme such as "What would

I like to give, what should I give?" reflects alternative motives for decision making. On the one hand, one can act out of an external or an interiorized super-ego imperative, "I should!" On the other hand, one can act out of an ego-centered delusion of would-be grandeur, "I must." Between these extremes lies the possibility of carefully weighing the demands of inner and outer reality and listening to the voice of one's own conscience before coura- geously answering "I will!" The theme "What do I want to give?" implies standing up for one's own vocation despite the risks of failure and conflict. It means saying yes to the path that God has destined for me and that I accept with my conditional freedom. Such a path implies accepting the guilt that inevitably accompanies our imperfection.

But can I really stand up to what is and what was? "Remembered and unresolved feelings of guilt and shame are the greatest challenges for bio- graphical memories," writes Hermann P. Siller.[80] Faced with the unreconciled aspects that exist in everyone's life, two attitudes are recognizable in the (post- modern) world: some have recourse to therapy in matters that they cannot or will not cope with on their own; others try to forget or to suppress their per- sonal history. Sometimes the two possibilities are joined together: people use therapeutic procedures in order to forget everything and change nothing. Notwithstanding the utility of therapeutic approaches to one's biography with all its wounds, the decisive question remains: Must or can I transform myself and redeem myself in my multiple roles?

1. Anyone who takes account of the multiple roles in his or her life runs a risk. Can I make myself understood? Will I be acknowledged for how I am? Self-surrender and anticipatory trust must be in balance. Every person strives for acceptance: "This is what I am, please allow me to be the one that I am." As a rule, people are very sensitive to whether their diverse roles are accepted sincerely or only pro forma accepted, whether they are accepted only in terms of this or that role or are accepted only for what they are personally. Oftentimes a respectful silence following a biographical narrative signals more acceptance and recognition—even of failure—than many overblown words of assurance.

2. Taking account of one's own biography looks toward an uncondi- tional recognition and redemption. Each person hopes for the accep- tance and recognition of his or her whole life in all its colorfulness and contradictoriness, "including errors and complications, vulnerabilities and guilt."[81] In most situations of life, people must hold themselves back. As a matter of prudence, they should not give expression to everything that has happened to them in their lives or to all their latent hopes, wishes, and desires. Nevertheless, most men and women have a deep desire for transformation. This hope remains when all their suc- cesses and failures are accepted unconditionally, without moralistic

finger wagging, and when the full spectrum of their life roles, with all their contradictions, is acknowledged.[82]

Questions for Reflection

- What is the difference between your life history and your biography in the sense of your ever-new interpretation of your life?
- How do you now interpret your life or at least particular segments of your life differently than in the past?
- What parts of the described processes in a group appeal to you? What parts do not?
- What would be your themes in such a course?

5. Against the Fatal Alternative: Sacrificing Oneself or Holding Oneself Back

When it comes to the dialectic between autonomy and interdependence (first axiom), many "church people" are still afflicted with the "trauma" of sacrifice and self-sacrifice. This holds not only for those who compulsively sacrifice themselves for others and for those who proclaim self-sacrifice as a supreme Christian virtue. It holds as well for those who rebel against this ideal. Both sides refuse to enter into the dialectic of autonomy and interdependence. Why should this be so?

For generations self-sacrifice served as the hinge between what, according to prevailing ecclesiastical and moral rules, had to be done "for others" and what human beings, according to their own free will, wanted to do for themselves. The celibate life of the priest, the interaction between husband and wife in marriage, the relations between older and younger in the family and in society as a whole represented areas in which self-denial and mutual dependence were habitually regulated by the ideal of self-sacrifice. Women sacrificed themselves for "their" married or celibate men.[83] Pastors sacrificed themselves for their parishioners. Parents, especially mothers, sacrificed themselves for their children. In return, they expected gratitude and sacrifice from the ones for whom they had sacrificed themselves. Over all this kind of "trading" in sacrifice, the religions, Christianity included, spread their "sacred canopy" (Peter Berger), thus establishing an impressive sacrificial system, which, on the one hand, guaranteed a high stability in matters of role playing, but, on the other hand, deprived many people of their due freedom and happiness. In this system, everyone knew "what was due," which role he or she had to fulfill, and what they would have to risk were they to fail the expectations of the other side. Especially people in "serving" roles could not afford to get out of them.

The (post)modern emancipation and self-actualization movements, in which women especially have played a major role, and the feminist-theological critique of the patriarchal image of God have helped bring down this system of sacrifice, at least in part. Women, children, and young adults no longer accept the roles assigned to them by the system. However, the liberation from the circle of sacrifice and self-sacrifice can also be attributed to the working of the Holy Spirit. It is not right that the "elders" or church-"men" should "reign" over others in the church or in society and that those reigned over must continually sacrifice themselves. It is God alone who reigns. Among men and women, at all levels, a brotherly and sisterly relationship should be the rule. Thus, the liberation from the ecclesiastical and the social systems of sacrifice and victimization ought to be considered a prophetic inspiration. In TCI groups, such emancipation is time and again existentially experienced and carried out with liberating effect.

With regard to such communication processes, stepping out of or questioning one's ecclesiastical or social role may well be inspired by a deep, indeed prophetic insight of faith. It can mean letting oneself and others be attracted by the God of life who is relationship to a new, gift-given freedom, which allows for autonomy. At the same time, such emancipation may be achieved only at the cost of disturbing the harmony of the group, the family, the community, and so on. The bourgeois ideal of conflict-free relations is then replaced by a realistic acceptance of conflict-laden existence. Instead of the "seventh heaven" of harmonious happiness, one looks to the "open heaven" of a God-given new future. Freedom then no longer competes with self-giving; self-giving takes place in freedom, rather than in compulsive self-sacrifice.

In this respect the younger generation has developed a new awareness of the need for continually "working" on relationships, often making use of therapeutic and supervisory insights.[84] TCI groups leave room for such "role work" and initiate conscious steps toward liberation. Within the framework of TCI, a specific form of supervision has been developed. Theologically, we are justified in seeing all such initiatives, for instance, the flourishing of counseling and supervising agencies, as concrete signs and instruments of the action of the Spirit of God, who promotes relationship and liberation. The theological criterion for recognizing the Spirit-given character of such activities is their interest-free orientation and their openness, regardless of denominational allegiance or religious attitude. In calling men, women, and children out of their old asymmetrical roles of domination to new symmetrical roles of brotherhood and sisterhood, the liberating Spirit of God knows no ecclesiastical etiquette. The Spirit blows where he/she wills.

If, from the perspective of autonomy and interdependence, we describe working through relationships and clarifying roles as being works of the Spirit, the question arises, should then every conflict-laden departure from traditional roles be considered the work of the Spirit? Certainly not unequivocally! When we consider the event of Pentecost, we see how the disciples of Jesus, moved by the Spirit, left behind their role as a frightened and persecuted minority to come out fearlessly and frankly, embarking on a journey that would eventually bring them persecution and death. In this story, we see that the actions of the Spirit are by no means unambiguous. To be full of God's Spirit and step out of one's socially accepted role can be interpreted as drunkenness. And being moved by the spirit of wine should never be confused with being moved by the Spirit of God. The same holds for working through relationships in the dialectics of autonomy and interdependence. To determine which spirit is at work requires the gift of spiritual discernment. One and the same role-switching action can have quite different motives. It should be motivated by the spirit of love, freedom, and deep solidarity with the group, the parish, the partner, the children, and so forth, and can lead one courageously even to risk causing pain in opening up for one's partners an opportunity to live "in the freedom of the children of God." But it can also be the work of the evil spirit of egocentrism, of cowardice, of human narrowness, and lack of solidarity. In her variant of Fritz Perls's "Gestalt Prayer," Cohn took a clear position against self-fulfillment without relationship and solidarity.

Just how much an existentially realized dialectics of autonomy and interdependence calls for a distinction based on the Spirit of God's relationship to humanity is shown by the (post)modern arrogance with which some emancipation movements treat people who, in freedom, have devoted themselves to serving others. Such people are often "ordinary faithful," who, without calling attention to themselves, live in fidelity to themselves and to others. This kind of arrogance manifests itself also toward the churches, when they counterpoise responsible freedom to the anything-goes mentality.

The central issue of this arrogant attitude is again the idea of sacrifice discussed above. Once again it is the emancipated consciousness that claims to have liberated all victims. But, one may ask, have the emancipation movements really unmasked and eliminated all forms of sacrifice in the ecclesiastical and social orders? Can a communicative theology rest content with acknowledging the God-willed liberation they have brought? Could it not be that emancipation from traditional roles and the "normal chaos of love" (U. Beck) creates new victims in human relationships? Are not such new victims often intimately connected with efforts of other human beings to achieve liberation from their own victim roles and victimizing systems? Among such new victims we find the following:

- people who are disappointed in their hope of maintaining sustainable relationships to pastoral ministers or theologians and who then lose hope because the latter set themselves apart autonomously;
- children who suffer from their parents' separation when one or both parents depart from their parental role in search of their own autonomy;

- elderly people who suffer loneliness, because their children's careers leave no more time for them;
- single parents who have been left behind with one or more children when their partner departed in his or her quest for self-fulfillment.

Calling attention to these "new" victims is not meant to balance them off against the old ones. It is intended as a warning against the illusion of ultimate postreligious "liberation" from dependent relationships concealing the existence of new (post)modern victims. The modern, neoliberal society dominated by the market and the media produces its own victims and scapegoats who are threatened with marginalization and special treatment in therapeutic and social institutions. Along with the above-mentioned (postmodern) victims, others who disturb the smooth functioning of the system should also be acknowledged:

- unplanned and undesired children;
- so-called planned children who then fail to meet the expectations of their parents or bring the plans of their parents into disarray;
- physically and/or mentally disabled children who "disturb" the systems of "success" in the economy, education, and so forth.

As a rule people become victims in our culture when they differ from those viewed as "normal." The differences may be in language, lifestyle, clothing, social relationships, and many other things. There are numerous forgotten victims in our society: those who fall short of the modern economic and communication system because they cannot keep up, because they are unemployed, sick, disabled, or simply because somewhere they "lost the connection." To this casualty list must be added the many victims in the economically and technologically disadvantaged countries of the Southern Hemisphere.

Does an anthropology based on a dialectics of autonomy and interdependence suffice to avoid shying away from the "veiled" themes produced by the (post)modern world? It does under the condition that with due regard for the axioms and postulates it takes into thematic account the past, present, and future, thus avoiding being caught up exclusively with the here-and-now of the group experience. The thematic of victimization is well suited to show how the lack of temporal congruity between attitudes in a theological TCI group can generate mutual opportunities for learning.

In such a group there may well be people for whom the traditional theology of sacrifice has become their life-long attitude. They orient their lives according to the idea of a great "exchange" between God and humankind in which the Son of God offers himself up on the cross for sinful humankind. This exchange is then continued up to the present day by people offering themselves up for others. Józef Niewiadomski rightly describes this system with regard to the Sacrifice of the Mass in the book we wrote together on the Eucharist:

> Christ, who offers himself up on the cross in a bloody fashion and who is offered up to God in every Mass in an unbloody fashion, became—in all the ambiguity of this event—the focal point of an intensive communication process, a communication among the living (who sacrifice each other and themselves for each other), a communication between the living and the dead, and above all a communication between sinful human beings and a wrathful God, who is so appeased by the expiatory sacrifices of people that God grants unending forgiveness.[85]

Others in the group, put off by the character and the historical effects of this theological image, reject outright any notion of sacrifice and self-sacrifice because of its potential for misuse. Against the backdrop of the old and new balance sheets of victimization, such theologians see no value in the traditional image of Jesus Christ's self-sacrifice as a central theological metaphor. Should it not be totally and definitively abandoned as in fact has already happened by and large in pastoral practice?

A third group of theologians adheres neither to the traditional vision of sacrifice in popular religiosity nor to the modern trend to avoid it out of fear of misuse. These theologians realize that silencing discourse about sacrifice will not make sacrifice disappear. Faced with this reality, the awareness of Jesus' "sacrifice" can serve not only to "fix" but also to break through the great "exchange" between the human person and God (or whatever else modern persons pin their heart on). Jesus' unique self-sacrifice means that sacrificing need not be endlessly repeated, neither by therapeutic nor by ritual means. Jesus' self-sacrifice, as one onto whom the victim role has been imposed by other human beings and whom God has saved from death without making new victims of the perpetrators, breaks through the old structures of sacrifice. It tears away the veil covering the modern forms of victimization.

In the confrontation over these three positions, a new perspective can be opened, made possible by the "great God" who respects the human person's freedom and autonomy. In the group, the battle between "small gods," which generate alienation, for example, the wish for swift harmony, for efficiency at all costs, for consumption and wealth, and so on, and the "great" God of life and freedom, who generates relationships, can be existentially experienced when this battle is thematized and perhaps dramatized in a role-playing situation. Such dramatization can take place, for example, when the participants of a group call attention to the "small gods" to whom daily sacrifices are offered by representing them symbolically and then "worshiping" them by bowing down or prostrating themselves before them. Such play acting can call forth a transformation in the participants by demonstrating that it is blasphemous to give such "small gods" so much attention in one's life. It can also open the participants' eyes to see how "thin" the solidarity between human beings is when such false gods are worshiped in daily life. Such dramatized rituals reveal how we give away ourselves and how we beat up on one another with our "sacrifices" to false gods. By contrast, the sacrifice of Jesus for us represents a "compounded" solidarity; it comprises a "being for," which consistently manifests itself as a "being with"; it is no hollow activism for others but a deep experience of self-giving, which becomes relational self-fulfillment. Such an action is rooted in doing and not doing, in action and contemplation. The interpersonal and social commitment for others is spiritually rooted in the message of faith, in the practice of prayer and meditation, and in community celebration. What is here at stake is a "compounded" solidarity rooted, indeed mystically, in the love of God and human beings. In this "strong" solidarity, other persons are perceived not only as people in need of our sacrificial support and assistance but also as God-given "others" precisely in their abiding otherness and strangeness, in their own personal freedom and responsibility.

The recipients of such "dense" solidarity, be they parents or pastoral ministers, need have no fear of releasing their children or their pastoral charges into their own inner freedom, irrespective of the "crooked lines" drawn by the exercise of this freedom. To do so does not mean abandoning their charges; it means giving them over to a universal, God-given connection between all human beings that explicitly includes the poor and the marginalized. This "dense solidarity" finds its most "dense" expression in the gift of the "We" of the people of God, or the "Body of Christ" (see 1 Corinthians 12:27), especially as celebrated in the Eucharist, the center of Christian faith. In the Eucharistic celebration, which often marks the highpoint of a theological TCI week, the dialectical interplay between autonomy and interdependence, which is at the center of TCI's understanding of the human person, is dramatized. The celebration of the Eucharist thus tears away the veils cast by pseudoreligious powers over their victims. Its "gift-given We" is diametrically opposed to the pseudoreligious powers in neoliberal culture, namely, the forces of the economy and the media, which exercise so much control over the lives of (post)modern men and women. These forces reach into the most intimate spheres of human life to a degree that no religious system has hitherto managed to achieve, not only because of a lack of opportunity but also because in religious systems over the centuries the original inspiration breaks through time and again.

Questions for Reflection

- When and how have you encountered the theme of sacrifice?
- What importance does sacrifice have in your life and work—and in that of people around you?
- When and how is the sacrifice theme obscured or repressed?

- In which contexts can a discussion of victimization and sacrifice become particularly dangerous? In which contexts can it be liberating?
- What connections can you see between "Jesus as a victim" and people's solidarity against being victimized?
- How do you understand the "sacrificial character" of the Eucharist?
- What life inspirations can come from the Eucharistic celebration in terms of the theme of sacrifice?

CHAPTER 7

Keeping the Faith Tradition and Implicit "God-Talk" in Balance

Already in chapter 3 it became clear that communicative theology shows itself to be a contextual theology through and through. Its object is a critical reflection on communication against the background of religious and ideological conflicts in a knowledge-based society. This process, however, does not dissolve "God-talk" into pure anthropology. Communicative theology is an "anthropologically oriented theology": to its object belongs, on the one hand, the encounter with the communicative God of revelation in God's de facto communication in history, that is, the tradition (chapter 4), and, on the other hand, the encounter with unstable and broken human experiences of communication in groups, in parishes, in the church, and in society.

Communicative theology has furthermore shown itself to be a theology in process (chapter 1). It does not terminate in the anthropological gathering of empirical data far removed from practice; instead, it constantly takes into account the concrete "Globe" of human experience. Communicative theology is moved by people's crises of meaning and orientation, by their griefs and anxieties, their joys and hopes.[1] The vision of the human person and the ethos of the person developed by Ruth Cohn in the concept of TCI (chapter 6) open the possibility of participating consciously in socio-ecclesial communicative events. Such participation opposes a qualitative, contextually involved account to an emotionally removed, merely quantitative analysis of society and church. This method goes hand in hand with a "*kairos* consciousness," which means that theology is not mere theoretical knowledge but is rather a form of thinking and speaking immediately relevant for day-to-day living. It is a God-talk whose "transformed perspective" begins to view the world in the light of the emerging power of God. In traditional terms one can say it is a theology that views the world from the perspective of faith.

It belongs to the essence of communicative theology that it does not originate alone in isolated theoretical reflection; rather, its life relevance is experienced existentially in groups and communities. Theology "arises" in personally significant interaction and communication. In order to make possible such processes, both the TCI attitude and the TCI "technique" are of

139

decisive help. In this way, communio ecclesiology goes beyond mere insistence for a certain attitude and begins to take concrete steps to plan, carry out, and evaluate its realization.

I. The Triangle within a Sphere

For Ruth Cohn "individuality and communality have equal value"; they are "inseparably joined together."[2] Human beings do not live in isolation; they are bound up in an ongoing tradition of knowledge and wisdom, but also of inhumanity, cruelty, and indifference. Neither impotent nor omnipotent, human beings are called to decision making and taking responsibility in their communicative interaction. Not only the here-and-now experience comes into play but also the historicity reaching back into the past and the future-oriented sustainability of humanity and of creation as a whole. Human beings are co-responsible for the humanity or inhumanity of whatever topics and intentions are communicated. Thus, the respective concrete context (the "Globe" in Cohn's terminology) is involved in all interactive processes: no human beings communicate in a social void.

The very simple "TCI technique" that Cohn discovered through her long experience of working with groups requires both a high level of competence and intensive practice, reflection, and supervision. From the very beginning of this book we used this instrument to focus attention, releasing the theological perspective from an exclusive concern with explicit theological categories and symbols and directing it toward implicit but no less theologically important factors. This hermeneutical principle was developed by Cohn as a "technique" for group direction. In its light, we recall the four factors that define every group interaction:

- The "I" as the individual person. This factor is aware of itself and turns to others and to the theme in a given group situation.
- The "We" as the group. This factor represents the relationship of individuals to one another and to the theme of their interaction.
- The "It" as a task or as a theme. This factor singles out the topical concerns to be worked out in the interaction.
- The "Globe" as environment. This factor influences the group in their relationships and in their working together in both a narrower and in a broader sense.

Ruth Cohn represents the interconnection of these four factors by way of an equilateral triangle within a sphere. This figure expresses not only that the factors belong together but also that they are of equal value. The symmetry and dynamic balance of all four factors is the hallmark of TCI group direction.

For reasons discussed later in section II, we put the theme at the center of the triangle.[3] We choose this placement because we see the "triangle-within-the-sphere" figure as having greater value than simply explaining communication and group direction. In the sense of the *kairos* focus described in chapter 1, the triangle also represents a hermeneutical-analytic "instrument" to describe other significant concerns.[4]

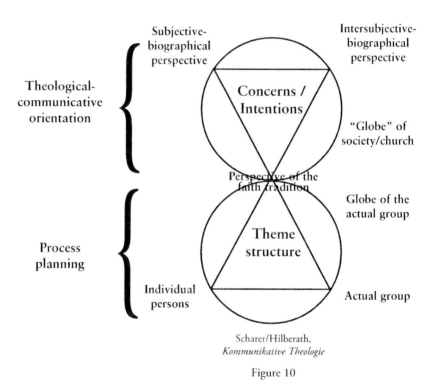

Scharer/Hilberath,
Kommunikative Theologie

Figure 10

Questions for Reflection

- Which pedagogical pattern—be it explicit or implicit—directs your approach to teaching and communicating in school, community, adult education?
- According to which pattern—be it explicit or implicit—do you "evaluate" such processes?
- What elements of the "triangle within the sphere" do you successfully hold in balance? What escapes this balance and why?
- What do you gain in matters of designing and evaluating processes by distinguishing between "theological-pedagogical objectives" and process design?

II. Using TCI in Theology and Ecclesial Practice

The way in which TCI was received into communicative theology has been dealt with in earlier sections of this book. To show how our own reception of TCI differs from other "applications" of it in theology and church we begin with a short survey of the previous models of reception.

There have been numerous attempts to make theology more vital by using TCI. In some of these approaches, the "matter" (It) is simply identified with theological themes, concepts, and notions, communicated through pedagogical processes on the individual and group levels, taking account always of the respective Globe. In this form TCI takes its place alongside other communicative-pedagogical techniques for explaining the theological process.[5]

Such an account of how theological themes, concepts, and notions can be communicated by using TCI may indeed be helpful. But it overlooks the fact that not only the "It" but also the whole theme-centered system of interaction with its attitudes and values is essential to theology. A first step in the direction of a more holistic reception of TCI was taken by Dieter Funke in his attempt to reconstruct TCI as a "pattern of thematic-symbolic orientation."[6] He calls attention to the symbolic capacity of people and to the problem of the loss of symbols in daily life since life without symbols becomes rigid routine. Thus, symbolic capacity as a matter of survival for meaning construction is closely linked to symbol construction. The topical-symbolic orientation of individual and collective symbols and their intersubjective verification, which is made possible in TCI groups by Funke's approach, prevent symbol loss. This approach, which takes account of religious psychology and religious sociology, draws attention to the ability of TCI to explain the intra- and interpersonal religious dimension, individually and collectively, as a comprehensive system.[7]

III. TCI—Theologically Spelled Out

Against the background of Dieter Funke's reception of TCI as a comprehensive system, communicative theology develops its approach in a specifically Christian theological perspective.

1. The Triangle within a Sphere from a Theological Perspective

In this approach one no longer speaks of theology as being merely the "matter" or "object of study" or as the theme (It). In theological TCI groups, the subjective and intersubjective levels are drawn explicitly into the theological context. In a communicative-theological process, alongside the content level (It), the subjective (I), the intersubjective (We), and the contextual (Globe) levels are all part of the picture—each with its own authentically theological character:

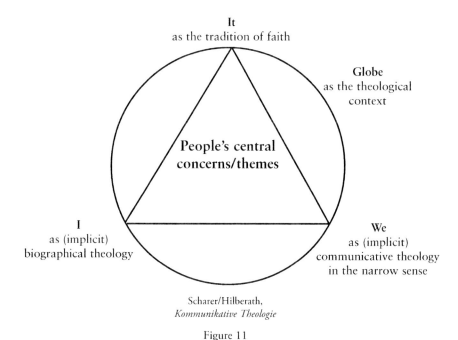

Scharer/Hilberath,
Kommunikative Theologie

Figure 11

- The I-factor is marked above all by the relationship between theology and biography in an identity-in-fragments, which is determined according to a theology of grace.[8] Modern notions of identity are pluralistic, viewing identity as coming into being on the basis of communicative situations. Such identity takes on a gratuitous character as a free gift (chapter 1). The theological level of the I-factor, that is, of the subject, is accounted for in biographical theology.

- The We-factor brings into play the permanently unstable aspect of group relationships, as well as the "gift" of communion in the community/church, which is something not created by TCI. Thus, "we as a gift"[9] emerges (chapter 5). Theologically, one can then speak, in a narrow sense, of communicative theology as being a part of ecclesiology.

- Thinking about the tradition of faith opens up an inexhaustible potential of intentions and concerns which people bring forward before themselves, before others, and before God. While biographical and communicative theology in the narrow sense have, as a rule, an implicit form, which has to be made explicit, the so-called It-factor within TCI expresses the explicit content of tradition with its system of theological symbols and categories.

- Finally, without the context (Globe factor) localizing its cultural, social, and ecclesial situation, no theology worthy of its name is possible. Communicative theology is, in fact, a contextual theology in the interplay between I, We, It, and Globe.

2. "Without Separation or Mixing" as a Criterion of Communication and Research[10]

From earliest times, Christian theology had to do with the relationship between God and human beings. This question reaches its climax in Jesus Christ, the "God-human being." Is he (only) God or is he just a special, God-filled, human being? The Council of Chalcedon (451) coined a brilliant expression for the relationship between God and the human being in Jesus Christ by saying "without separation or mixing." In him, divine and human natures are not separated in such a way that they have nothing to do with each other or that they be thought and confessed each for itself in separation. Jesus Christ is true human being and true God in the sense that the two natures do not stand alone, that is, they are not "separate." On the other hand, the divinity and humanity of Jesus do not mix in a symbiosis; they remain what they are, and, in this sense, they are "unmixed." This christological formula can be elaborated within our context in a twofold way:

1. Even though we Christians believe that the relationship between God and human being culminates in Jesus Christ, we can still find an analogy to inter-human communication as practiced in TCI groups. Wherein does such communication consist? However much we strive for nearness and relationship, each person remains an other and so a stranger in some sense. Each person is and remains a mystery. At the same time, in encounter, the other, the stranger, becomes for us a "you," a neighbor. This is not to be understood in a moral sense but rather in an existential-theological sense. "Inseparable" is the bond that links us in the encounter to the other in his or her otherness and strangeness. Yet the other remains "unmixed" with ourselves. Thus, we can speak of a borderline experience between persons, which is rich in relationships and therefore also in conflicts; without such experience, no true meeting is possible.[11] Autonomy grows and lives at the border between persons. At the same time, we recognize that inasmuch as we are interdependent and thus not isolated monads, we are "inseparable" from other people.

2. The formula "without separation or mixing" is also valid for communicative theology in another way. When, in a communicative theology, we relate TCI and theology in such a way as to structure theological processes, theology is not turned into TCI or TCI into

theology. The biographically rooted, process-oriented, and globe-conscious work of the theologian using TCI is still a theology. What sets it apart from other theologies is the fact that it co-determines the truth of its God-talk not only formally but also materially by the communicative quality of the theological process. Without seeking the "truth," interaction and communication in communicative theology cannot be genuinely pursued. A degenerated scenario of communication, in which God-talk takes an exclusively monological form, poses not just a pedagogical problem but is also related to truth. We do not mean to suggest here that the TCI approach is immune to the defects of communication. TCI is not a new god which substitutes group experience for the intrinsic truth in God-talk. It is a process of communication in permanent need of redemption with an openness—never in principle closed—to the transformation of God into the fullness of life.

This way of doing theology in the quest for truth exhibits many parallels to Latin American liberation theology. However much theology and TCI remain unmixed in communicative theology, they must not be separated in such a way as to put on the one side theological truth as the contents and on the other the process as method. In Ruth Cohn's struggle with the connections between attitude and method—a struggle that led her to change the name from TIM (Theme-Centered Interactional Method) to TCI (Theme-Centered Interaction)—we can glimpse the unmixed-and-inseparable relationship between theology and TCI in communicative theology.

3. The "I" as a Permanently Fragmented, Plural Identity in the Horizon of Identity as a Gift

The fact that human life precisely in its individual historicity is a *locus theologicus* may be traced throughout the history of theology and has come to the forefront again in recent discussions.[12] One should bear in mind that the faith of the churches that theologies reflect on is more than the sum of biographically defined theologies. The churches hand on and develop God's truth throughout history not only by means of individuals but also through communities, by living as well as by teaching. The people of God's "sense of faith" is fundamentally important for the transmission of faith, which theology is meant to serve. Where and how cooperation between the Spirit of God and the believer takes place is a mystery. In the degree to which the believer becomes aware of the connection between personal biography and "personal truth" (with all its light and shadows, its opportunities and limitations), in that measure the believer comes to recognize that he or she does not possess the whole truth and that his or her personal truth is incomplete. Even for faith and its truth the principle holds that the human person is both autonomous and inter-dependent, independent of and at the same time connected to the whole.

In a process of theme-centered interaction, theology's concern is not merely to relate theology's object to the person. Every individual is important because one's life is a venue of divine revelation; and hence, without directing one's attention to people's individual histories of life and faith, a theological discourse on God is hardly possible. This theological insight is very clear in the texts of the Latin American Episcopal Conference's Puebla document (1979) when it speaks about the "option for the poor":

> The poor deserve special attention regardless of their moral or per-sonal situation. Created in the image of God, meant to be his chil-dren, this image of God is blurred and distorted. Therefore, God takes it upon himself to defend them and he loves them. (1142)

It is not some special human qualification that makes people become "interlocutors," as the Latin Americans say—literally translated as "those who can spell out" the Gospel—but rather their God-given value, which they pre-serve even when they are marginalized, ostracized, and made victims by social systems.[13] The biographical "localization" of theology does not isolate the per-son as an autonomous subject in the Enlightenment sense. The TCI aware-ness of the link between interdependence and autonomy, which reflects Ruth Cohn's struggle with other representatives of humanistic psychology, protects against the kind of identity fantasies inherent in many religious-pedagogical projects that postulate an autonomous subject of faith as the goal of develop-ment and education.[14] As a critical theological challenge based on the inter-dependent autonomy postulated by TCI, the Christian view of the human person sees personal identity to be achieved as a fragmented identity within the world, not only transitionally but permanently:

> We are always at the same time the ruins of our past, fragments of our broken hopes, exhausted dreams, lost and wasted chances. We are ruins due to our shortcomings, failures, and guilt, due, as well, to the wounds inflicted upon us, to the losses and defeats we have suffered. This is the pain of fragmentation.[15]

Seen like this, TCI's optimistic-developmental axiom, "Respect is due to all living things and their growth," and the chairperson postulate take on wider meaning. If I understand myself as a fragmented subject—not just temporar-ily, in the sense of a necessary developmental phase of my life, but perma-nently—then the notion of growth reaches its limits; the chairperson principle requires an inner concurrence with my own fragmentation and with that of others:

> Each encounter with others, which takes them seriously as such, must lead to a serious self-questioning: "Who am I?" The ideal of ego strength and of an established identity, which does not feel insecure nor is confused when confronted with the other's otherness, leads to indifference and to a closing in of the self against the other.[16]

A theologically reconstructed biography makes it possible for people to be reconciled to themselves despite all the remembered and not-yet-resolved "stories of guilt and shame" that they might have experienced in the past.[17] On the other hand, biography looks forward to the future: "How can I tackle the fact that one day I will lose my self-mastery?"[18] In this perspective, basic religious questions and their symbolic representation receive a new urgency: "Who am I?" "Where am I going?" "What can I hope for?" "Into whose hands will I fall when at death I finally let go?"[19] The call to say "I" becomes a challenge not to split up identity but to say yes to its enduring fragments. According to Hermann Siller, this attitude is "the cause of the authority and the authenticity which come with aging."[20]

4. The We of the TCI Group as a "Gift-Given" We

The authentic *theological* places where God shows God's self to human beings in history include not only their biographies but also their interaction and communication. The Christian belief in the One and Triune God, who is personal relationship, makes every human communication a theological challenge. This challenge does not remain in the abstract realm of a theological mind game but becomes a living experience in the church—from a Catholic perspective in both the local and the universal church.[21] If the "We"-level is viewed from an ecclesiological perspective (chapter 5), communication and otherness (to the point of strangeness) become a particular challenge for TCI processes. The Christian congregation even as the celebrating community is not some kind of homogenous, charismatically enthusiastic group in which people are constantly hugging one another. The group/community is a "gifted" not a "made" We. It is a gift of the Spirit of God, in spite of and with all remaining strangeness.

In the manifold roles and relationships in the often painful transformations experienced in TCI groups the truth of the One and Triune God who is relationship in God's very self is revealed, not simply a method of interaction. In the Crucified One, God broke through once and for all the sort of fantasies of harmony and unity generated by group dynamics and opened up a new quality of encounter, a relationship that includes diversity, otherness, and strangeness. The priority of disturbances and perplexities emphasized by Cohn finds in the "Crucified Interrupter" a theological profundity that no pedagogical postulate can come close to. The stone which the builders rejected becomes the cornerstone (Matthew 21:42; Mark 12:10; Luke 20:17). This Servant of God is driven off like a scapegoat and is established by God as the redeemer. God who does not break the bruised reed or extinguish the smoldering wick (Matthew 12:20) redeems us from the all-too-harmoniously-experienced worlds of TCI. Theologically oriented TCI groups manifest a higher level of conflict competence and a particular sensitivity for the other and for the stranger. They are sensitive to the strategies of exclusion and victimization from which no group dynamics is immune. And ultimately they more deeply appreciate the entirely gratuitous character of a genuine group/community,[22] something impossible to create by any human effort.

5. The Globe as the Context for Theology

Thinking and speaking of God does not take place in a void. It is unavoidably linked to a historical, socio-cultural, and ecclesial context. While in certain periods of church history, especially in neoscholastic theology, one tried to transmit the theologically reflected faith of the church as a ready-made package, now contextuality is seen to be part and parcel of any theology worthy of the name. What and how one speaks about God is unavoidably subject to historicity and contextuality. Real theological work entails wrapping the (academic) discourse about God in a way of thinking and a language that is and remains linked to the context. At the same time, thinking and speaking of God influences the context. The "world" as "Globe" is not merely something presupposed; it is also a task to be performed.

An example of putting the Globe connection into the spotlight is provided by the Innsbruck University course in communicative theology with its modules devoted to the worldwide church. One section of this course, consisting of two week-long sessions and an excursion, always in small groups, introduces the participants to the church situation in Latin America, Africa, or some other part of the world. This "Globe expansion" transforms an otherwise European-centered theology and is thus indispensable for theological learning oriented to the universality of the church.

Questions for Reflection

- Which new perspectives do you gain by theologically assimilating the "triangle within the sphere"?
- What changes occur in your personal communication when you attend to the realities of "identity in fragment," "plural identity," and "gratuitously given identity"?
- What changes occur by attending to "We as a gift"?
- What perspectives open up when attention is given to the other, indeed to the stranger, and ultimately to the "other/stranger God"?

IV. Themes That Help Confront and Bring "Defenses" to Expression

Untill now the discussion of the "triangle within the sphere" has left out the It. As we mentioned before, Ruth Cohn identifies the "It" with the theme. The "It" is so important for her that she calls her approach "Theme-Centered Interaction." She thus takes a clear stand in favor of the contents, that is, the topical orientation of communication processes.

1. Themes That Serve Relationships

The TCI instructor Barbara Langmaack rightly calls attention to the mutual relationship between topics or themes and personal relationships:

> If people want to have something to do with one another, they must do something together, or at least think, dream, or develop some idea together. The greater their interest in the topic, the more firmly anchored will be the "relationship" connecting them. When the topical themes are exhausted, the relationship itself and its disturbance may become a theme for a while, but sooner or later this substitute theme will cease to compensate for the lack of topical content.[23]

With regard to the close ties between content, theme, and relationship, the contents/themes in religiously oriented groups and communities may come from the group's interaction or from the experience of individuals, but above all it comes from outside, that is, from the respective ecclesial or social Globe. TCI is neither a typical therapeutic approach dealing with the inner psychological problems of people, nor is it a purely group-dynamic process focusing only on what happens inside the group. Theme centering means that the "matter" of interaction is assigned the highest value. Theologically speaking, this means that the experiences of interaction between God and the human person and between people as recorded in the tradition of faith acquire central importance. Biblical texts, theological categories, central symbols of faith, such as the sacraments, enter the communication of faith not "by chance" or where it seems "acceptable" and does not disturb the self-experience and dynamics of the group. Quite the opposite: the biographically and communicatively experienced truth of faith is here and now confronted with the tradition of faith. There is no facile "reconciliation," no harmonization between "revelation and situation" or "church and world," but there is a "hermeneutics of difference" containing the potential for conflict at the content level. God, who is the "totally Other," the "Stranger," who is not identifiable with any of our wishes, longings, and aspirations, breaks up all tendencies toward a self-made religion, which might fulfill wishes but which has no place for hope.

Jesus of Nazareth—himself a victim of group-dynamic processes—"disturbs" the feelings of well-being and "we-are-all-one" themes, which many ecclesial circles tend to associate with their "patchwork religion." The "drama of the creed" in the past and the "drama of the church" in the present lead to a confrontational, conflict-laden theological encounter (chapter 8). A theologically oriented TCI relies on the fact that the texts of faith transmit a tradition of experience, which serves life in relationships.

2. Finding Concerns and Themes

But are challenging theological contents already themes in a TCI sense? Normally, one understands a "theme" to be a short summary of a certain topic. Traditional theology treats such theological topics as God, Jesus Christ, church, creation, grace, sacraments, and so forth as "themes."

What is important here is the difference between "It" and "theme," which Ruth Cohn failed to define clearly enough in her conception. Biblical texts, theological categories, or faith symbols—however challenging they may be for people today—are only the "It," the matter or the contents within the TCI triangle. They are not yet the theme in the specific sense of TCI.

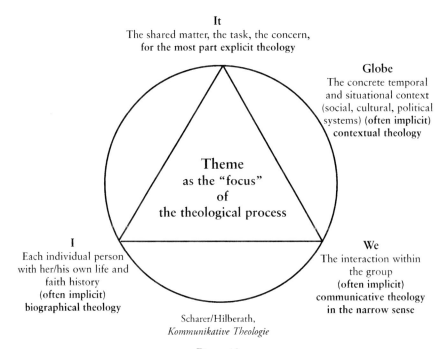

Scharer/Hilberath,
Kommunikative Theologie

Figure 12

The theme as understood by TCI links all levels of communication, the "It," the "I," the "We," and the "Globe." Therefore, along with other TCI instructors,[24] we place the theme not in one of the corners but rather in the center of the triangle. It is thus clearly distinguished from the "It." The theme results from the interplay of the "It," the "I," the "We," and the "Globe."

In order to locate themes properly in communicative-theological processes it is advisable to begin by establishing a basic theological-communicative orientation. Barbara Langmaack distinguishes between "major" and "minor" themes which provide "anchors" large and small.[25] In the sense of the existential depth and extension of themes, it helps to distinguish between general concerns and very concrete, situational themes. This distinction is particularly important when planning theological projects, courses, and so forth.

The TCI "triangle within the sphere" can help not only to formulate a specific theme with regard to a given situation. It is also helpful in developing "major concerns." It helps locate a "large anchor" for theological processes in the interplay of "biographical theology," "communicative theology in a narrow sense," "Globe," and "traditional theology." Thereby one should take into account our earlier discussion of the "theological structure" with its symbolic-sacramental-performative form and one should pay attention to the "inseparable and unmixed" connection between divine and human communication.

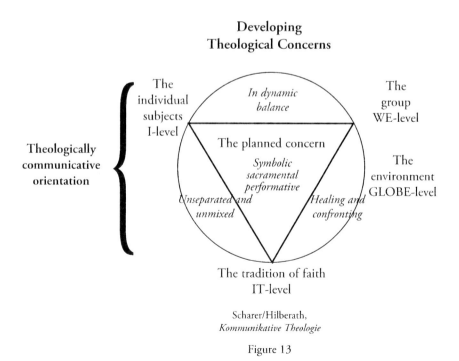

**Developing
Theological Concerns**

Scharer/Hilberath,
Kommunikative Theologie

Figure 13

The correct "major" and "minor" concerns and themes cannot be found if the corners of the triangle are connected in a merely mechanical way. Formulating concerns and themes is an art that (also) needs intuition and the "right feel" for the situation. At best, it takes place in a "creative linguistic game," which, in turn, involves the subjective identity (I-level), the group interaction (We-level), the concern with its objective aspect (It-level), and the environment (Globe). Someone who has only mastered the "method" of formulating themes without taking account of the other factors is like a musician who has learned the technique of playing an instrument but has yet to learn how to "play" real music on it.

The "virtual" game involving theological themes cannot be uncoupled from the living relationship to the tradition of faith and to concrete individuals and groups. Ultimately, "real" themes always emerge from a vital, conflict-laden mooring in a community or the church. Like a musician or a painter, one must become existentially and communicatively involved in the process of finding "real" themes. That means that the group leader:

- must enter authentically into the specific theological task and not be satisfied with the theology he or she has once "learned." Such an immersion in the situation confronts the theologically educated person with one's own experiences, resistance, and selective blindness; in short, with the pain of faith and the joy therein;
- must pay attention to his or her own "biographical theology" and to that of the other participants in the group, not in an objectifying empirical fashion but rather in an intersubjective fashion that includes internal and external expressions of empathy;
- must leave room for resistance and disruption, for affective reactions and relationships that emerge in the group process. One must enter personally into the process without thereby losing the ability to direct it;
- must pay attention, when planning the themes, to both the narrower and the wider Globes encompassing the group and take account of their social and ecclesial influence on the group's interaction.

In an authentic theological process, the theme focuses the attention of all the participants. This verbal "focus" can create space where the manifold symbolic expression of what the theological discussion is about can be dramatized anew (see chapter 8, "Credo drama"). In theologically oriented TCI groups/communities, the thematizing process can make it possible "to verbalize hitherto hidden, not yet socialized themes locked up in a speechless subconsciousness."[26] Formulating traditional theological topics as themes means, according to Matthias Kroeger, "confronting them in a language that is not reduced to the possibilities of living offered by recalling a particular lifestyle from the past."[27]

TCI, according to Cohn, is a method of "open language learning, which can be practiced. . . . This learning process thematizes the legitimacy and the strength of camouflaged defenses."[28] Theological themes, according to TCI, distinguish themselves from "trite formulas and inexpressive forms of speech by the measure of their expressive freedom, which does not demand simple dogmatic submission, but offers, instead, anticipated utopias, already lived and expressed, and a way of life attractive to the participants."[29] Such a language develops further by joining with the individual's own language to form a third language suited to the present and open to the future. The person who enters into this language game "will gradually discover the grammar of its rules of living, will learn to translate it and so will develop it further."[30] Such "differentiation" and "fusion" of horizons will give rise to a third, new horizon.[31] Openness and confrontation make living theological learning possible. Theological-communication processes thus deal with themes that serve, confront, and verbalize defensive reactions.

3. Correctly Formulating Themes

How can one "correctly" formulate themes? What are the rules of the game? Cohn gives some helpful hints. An adequately formulated theme:

- is phrased briefly and clearly so as to be constantly kept in mind;
- is not trite and therefore not boring;
- is fitted to the participants in terms of their linguistic and cognitive competencies;
- is formulated so as not to exclude anyone or offend anyone's feelings;
- is not too narrowly (concretely) formulated: it should leave room for spontaneous insights, ideas, and images;
- is not too broadly (abstractly) formulated: it should not be open for "everything" and be focused on nothing;
- has an emotionally challenging character (group jargon, lyrical or pun-like phrasing, reference to familiar events, and so forth);
- opens and favors new horizons and innovative solutions;
- is not phrased one-sidedly, leaving no room for other possibilities and so becoming manipulative;
- does not go against the axiomatic values of human rights and of TCI;
- supports the group process by fitting in, logically and psychologically, with the sequence of themes to be worked through and by maintaining the dynamic balance between the participants' concerns and concrete needs;
- takes into account the ability of group members to express themselves verbally and makes use of nonverbal means of presenting themes (images, pantomime, etc.).

For groups of children or handicapped persons, the use of pictorial material and games, occasionally also texts, may be particularly useful in other situations. Such devices recommend themselves only on a case-by-case basis. As a rule, however, the primary instrument of group work will be a verbally well-phrased theme that has been carefully prepared to correspond to the group's needs and to allow each participant to access it. Finding, phrasing, and introducing themes requires considerable time, but the effort is justified by the astonishing effectiveness of the group's interaction.[32]

4. Making Room for the "Empty Spaces"

The way themes are formulated and introduced reveals not only one's theology of faith communication but also one's understanding of the church. Phrasing themes in an abstract, noun-laden language focuses faith communication on the transmission of traditional dogmatic categories. Such formulations differ essentially from those that approach the tradition of faith with an original, creative language that reflects the subjective, intersubjective, and social aspects of faith. It is no longer a matter of "creation," or "grace" per se; neither is it a matter of transmitting such concepts in the most attractive fashion. Instead, it is a matter of thematizing adequately personal experiences of creation or grace against the rich historical background of biblical and ecclesial experiences, both positive and negative. In it the difference comes to the fore between content-oriented ecclesial transmission of faith and educational curricula, on the one hand, and pedagogical processes based on open communication, encounter, and responsibility, on the other hand. Definitive, pre-programmed answers correspond to the artificial questions of the catechisms and similar curricula, which are best learned by heart. Their language is determined exclusively by the expected assent of faith or by the transmission of relatively unimportant bits of theological or philological information. In this understanding of "learning," the knowledge of faith has to be portioned out in such a way as to command assent. According to this line of thinking, to "give assent in faith" means to say yes to what the authorized witnesses or at least the authors of the curriculum put before one as being authentic church teaching. In this view the thematic unfolding of the treasures of faith is the work of ecclesiastical authorities without any cooperation from those to whom the message is addressed. Jürgen Werbick calls this "yes/no communication." Up until now it has been the approach preferred by the church and theologians:

> In all communication processes having to do with faith, it is assumed that the authoritative interpreters of the content of faith (*fides quae*) expound upon the truths of faith as long as needed to evoke from the listener a "yes" or "no" reaction to the mysteries of faith. In this way,

the church has favored, over a long period of time, communication processes based more or less exclusively on the yes/no decision, reducing the activity of the "ordinary faithful" simply to saying yes or no and reserving to official interpreters the responsibility for formulating the teaching.[33]

Such forms fail to appreciate the crucial "empty spaces" in faith communication. These "spaces" are the places where individuals and groups can enter their own resistance, their tensions, their agreements. Such forms of communication show no appreciation for a kind of language game that does not put an end to the truth-seeking process but rather opens and maintains it.

According to Ruth Cohn, thematizing concerns means to enter into an open language game that does not block out opposition. The concerns formulated as themes do not coerce assent; they don't have to be accepted, neither wholly nor in part. "I can behave selectively with regard to them; I can live happily with them, without having to identify myself with them. If I want, I can use them as companions and mirrors, in which to discover new facets of myself."[34]

Many human and religious concerns are so repressed that they are not easily thematized. In such cases it is often helpful to address the obverse side of a theme, that is, to verbalize its "shadow," namely, the resistance the theme evokes. When, for example, the concern of the group is to reflect on its members' personal relationships to the church, phrasing the question as "how do I experience the church" will evoke little response in certain milieus and age groups. When, however, the question is formulated, "What bothers me about the church?" "What would I like to change?" there is a good chance of evoking a lively discussion and constructive proposals for action. In principle, no theme should be formulated in negative form alone but should balance criticism with positive suggestions for action.

5. What Are Themes "Good For"?

Because the theme is the focal point of the communicative process, a clearly formulated theme makes it possible to determine quickly and precisely whether the group is on target or not, whether some other theme or some point of resistance is in fact directing communication. Using methods such as the "taking-the-pulse" technique—each participant, leader included, is asked to state in one or two sentences what he/she is thinking about—it is possible to diagnose the momentary state of the communication process and to refocus it if necessary. Should it happen that a different theme than the official one proves so important that the leader believes it should direct the ongoing discussion, the process can be reoriented to take account of it. In this case, a process of clarification and replanning will be initiated involving the whole group and will be pursued until a new theme has been found and accepted by all participants.

Questions for Reflection

- What have you understood by "theme" until now? What does the word mean according to TCI?
- What are the possibilities opened up for you by attending to the theme?
- What is the difference in your practice between "concern" and "theme"?
- How do you formulate themes?
- What theological opportunities are opened up by well-formulated themes?

V. Disturbances and Perplexities as Opportunities for Theological Learning

What holds for the interpersonal, communicative level applies also with respect to the theme: "disturbances and perplexities have priority." That sounds paradoxical: how can disturbances and perplexities, which as a rule are highly emotional reactions that unbalance people, in fact provide learning opportunities in topical-thematic perspective? Are they not rather obstacles to working on a topic/theme? For the content-oriented academic, calling attention to disturbances and perplexities is a direct affront.

On the other hand, one may ask: does not the very emotionality of resistance and perplexity represent a force too little appreciated in traditional learning, teaching, and scholarship? When some thought or feeling so captivates me that I take part in a given communicative process only outwardly, then my interest is in fact occupied by the so-called disturbance. The "disturbing" concern is the real theme *for me*; it is what I am actually concerned with, and it stands in competition to the official theme. When this collision between themes is allowed to go on without it being directly addressed, as is often the case in schools and universities, it gives rise to disinterest and indifference. When, on the contrary, an atmosphere is created in which a disturbance and perplexity can be "lived out," opportunity is given for constructive resolution.

Sometimes it suffices simply to call attention to the existence of a disturbance; then the participants can return to the official theme. In other situations it is necessary to decide collectively between the official theme and the latent themes of individual group members. Paralyzed communication is often rooted in the lack of clear perception of competing themes, which, due to the unconscious rules of the game, are prevented from finding expression. Laying them out on the table gives rise then as a rule to a heated discussion not without conflict. Whether and how decisions are made by the group about competing themes depends then on the ability of the group leader to deal with conflict, an ability that is intuitively perceived by the group members.

As an aid to decision making in such conflict situations it is often helpful to recall the "official" theme as the original focal point of discussion. The more precisely the official theme and the competing themes can be formulated, the easier it will be to identify resistances and alternative themes. When the competing themes prove so intense that continued discussion of the official theme becomes impossible, it is necessary to replan the discussion.

The kind of rigid adherence to a minute plan advocated by curricular pedagogy is not what ensures communicative quality. Clear planning combined with flexible application is decisive. This means that the plan can be altered with the concurrence of the group, if need be.

VI. Structuring as "Embodied" Theology

Themes provide space for the communicative process. This open space needs to be structured. What is called for is a meaningful relationship between working modes, methods, and media. The choices made among these factors and the relationships established among them are governed by the theme and not vice-versa. Structured exercises help to keep a meaningful group process going

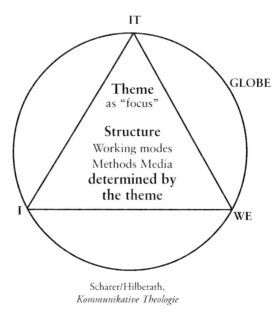

Scharer/Hilberath,
Kommunikative Theologie

Figure 14

if they are clearly formulated and flexibly managed. They strengthen trust and prevent stagnation, mistrust, and chaos. Dietrich Stollberg uses a triangle to express the mutual connections between process, structured exercise, and trust:[35]

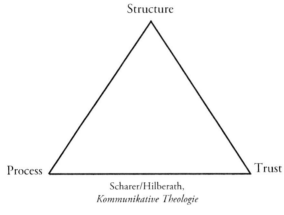

Structure

Process   Trust

Scharer/Hilberath,
Kommunikative Theologie

Figure 15

As a rule of thumb, the structure (working modes, methods, media) must be kept in balance with the ongoing process and with the degree of trust linking the participants. Structures can foster or hinder trust within the group. It stands to reason that, at the beginning of a process, when there is as yet little trust in the group, the structures must be different from those employed when the process has developed or when it nears its end. The following example from the experience of a group leader illustrates this point:

> Simon was delighted by the trust and openness that he had experienced as he discussed his "life panorama" in the small group. The simple media (paper, crayons, music), the method (painting one's "life panorama") and the social modes (working first on his own, then with the group) all fit together for him. When, in another group, he proposed using the same structured exercise, he was astonished to meet a flat refusal.

This example shows that people who are new in a group are not likely to embark on such personal processes that the "life panorama" presupposes. Resistance to the suggested structure can be taken for granted.

Many course leaders fail to realize that too tightly structured exercises (for example, too many individual or small-group stages before the larger group gets down to work) can obstruct the We of the group or prevent its emergence in the first place. Frequent use of such individual and small-group modes tends to shield the group leader from conflict-laden and troublesome confrontations in the group's plenary sessions, but it can also block the working ability of the group as a whole. Especially when it comes to ideological-religious themes, high sensitivity to correct structuring, not too tight and not too lax, is necessary.

VII. How Group Processes Might Run

From the leader's perspective we recommend the following sequence of stages as being appropriate for group processes (exceptions confirm the rule!):[36]

1. I begin by turning my mind to leading the course and make immediate preparations such as writing down the theme, preparing materials, airing the room, and so on. Before the session begins officially I try to create an open atmosphere by addressing this or that individual, for example, by making a personal remark, or by engaging in other forms of small talk.
2. After this "warm-up phase" in which not everybody need be present and in place, I make a clear beginning, calling all the participants to attention. I introduce the theme and offer a detailed overview of the planned course of discussion, including the modes of working, the methods and the media to be used. In the course of this presentation I explain what led me (or the planning group) to propose this particular theme and this mode of procedure. I also name those who contributed to the planning.
3. To help individuals to enter into the discussion I pose questions, suggest ideas, name potential resistances, and so on. I invite the participants to comment on the plan (for which I attempt to provide motivation). Together with the group, I elaborate what goals and what procedures will guide our work in this unit.
4. When it is appropriate, I provide the participants with texts, pictures, suggestions, and so forth. I may even offer them an example of how we might deal with the current problem. At this stage, however, one must be very careful not to offer too much help and so override the participants' own responsibility for contributing to the learning process. Thus, initiatives, insights, alternative suggestions, and expressions of opposition from the side of the participants should be welcomed.
5. Leaders and participants work on the theme individually, in pairs, in small groups, or in plenary sessions. These working modes must be correlated with the methods and media. The formation of small groups is a group dynamic process and requires time. It can be fostered nonverbally, for instance, with background music, or verbally in conversation.

6. When work has been done by individuals, pairs, or small groups, it should be expressly brought back to the plenary session for further development. There, for example, the theme may be addressed from another angle or expanded on; important results should be noted.

7. In a "taking-the-pulse" round, each participant should get an opportunity to comment on the discussion and to express unfulfilled expectations. In this way the group process can be brought to a (temporary) end.

VIII. Finding One's Own Expression in a Selectively Authentic Manner

For some group leaders the only thing that counts is what the whole group has dealt with. This evaluation, however, is problematic when dealing with living learning processes. Either it overestimates the degree of discretion and trust in the group, or it underestimates the personal significance of themes dealt with in an exclusively open approach. For life-relevant learning it is indispensable that the participants be given the opportunity to reflect personally on a theme, text, or image, and to develop their own form of expression without fear of having to disclose all their thoughts and feelings in the group. A selective approach to personal expression is of extreme importance in order to strengthen the participants' self-confidence and their trust in one another.

TCI advocates the notion of "selective authenticity." The rule of communication is "as authentic as possible and as selective as necessary." In communication, according to TCI, it is important to develop a feeling for authentic self-expression appropriate to a given situation. This depends on the perceptiveness of the "chairperson," listening to inner voices and paying attention to outward events. Only someone who can communicate while holding inner and outer factors in "balance" is in a position to protect him- or herself and others from an inappropriate "soul striptease" on the one hand and from a defensive distance keeping on the other.

Much more could be said about the practical work with TCI, but that is not the primary topic of this book, and we have included pertinent publications in the bibliography at the end of this work. Reading, however, should be accompanied by concrete experience in communicating with people, an experience that must include one's relationship with God. For this reason, we conclude this book with a practical example taken from a course held in Mainz some years ago.

Questions for Reflection

• How do you see the connection between process, structured exercise, and trust in your own practice?

- How do you approach working/communication forms, methods, and media? To what extent do they result from themes? To what extent is the theme/structure relationship reversed?
- Do you have certain preferred or standard structured exercises? Which ones?
- Where/how do you see the necessity of "selective authenticity" in your work?

CHAPTER 8

A Theme Takes Shape: Drama on the Eve of the Council of Nicaea and Drama in the Church Today

————————————

The Christian creed remains unfamiliar to many. And this does not merely include church outsiders. There are also church insiders who have an ambivalent relationship to this formula of faith. Even theologically educated people may have a difficult time gaining experience-based access to the creed. True experience-based access would not only shed light on the experiences that served as a backdrop for the creation of this fundamental text but could also help critically analyze issues that affect today's church. If made more accessible to and through theological experiences, the Nicene creed would be an excellent instrument to help the church better recognize and allow God's working and influence in communities and in schools.

The ecclesiastical and social conflicts that accompanied the development of the creed reflect conflicts that may still be problematic today. The living connection between the experiences of "back then" and of today allows for a set of criteria for pastoral and catechetical work that draws attention to questions about God and human beings thereby encouraging alternative *practice*. What would such a meeting of theory and *practice* from past and present look like?

I. A TCI Group Provides a Context for Church Drama

An opportunity for such an attempt to bring the creed to life within a group is provided by a Theme-Centered Interaction (TCI) seminar. In what follows we describe what happens in such a seminar. The week's theme is: "In the beginning is relationship: growing up with/without God." This was actually the third week-long course for a group from the Theological-Pastoral Institute (TPI) of the University of Mainz.

After introducing the seminar and learning about the participants' and leaders' interests, the focus turns to fears and expectations regarding the topic of God. The more we discuss the topic of God, the more urgently the group asks how people today can authentically speak about the Christian God: about

162

the trinitarian God who as Jesus Christ became a human being among humankind. What are the criteria for an adult relationship with, and for mature discourse about, God within a pluralistic and capitalistic society?

The Old Testament ban on images and "dancing around the golden calf" become provocative metaphors that define the limitations of Judeo-Christian discourse about God. The original theme reads as follows: "Between the ban on images and the golden calf: seeking criteria for an adult relationship with God." As the course goes on, the quest for criteria for an authentic discourse about God becomes increasingly important for the group. In the planning session created by the group leaders and some participants after a half-day, the idea arises that the creed could well be the basis for authentic discourse about God.

II. The Confrontation

Using the creed of the church is controversial but unavoidable for the group if the discussion of how one understands God is to move beyond personal experience. How can we approach the creed in such a way that it avoids becoming irrelevant for questions about God or that it is overlooked as a sterile, impersonal formula? The traditional Latin text reminds some of the participants of their childhood, of incense, and of pontifical Masses. For others, discussing the creed is like changing into a strange, old costume that they do not feel comfortable wearing anymore. With a balanced mix of defensiveness and curiosity the group attempts to make the historical experiences of the creed accessible today by playing out different roles in a kind of historical drama, which we come to call a "creed drama."

Focusing on the TCI model of communication helps us begin to understand the historical setting during the time of the creed's creation.

- The subjective-biographical dimension, the "I"-level, takes us to the sense of the faith of the people of God. In order to understand the faith experiences that are reflected in the creed there is an attempt to enter into the mindset of the "simple" believers, for example, letting female market vendors speak.
- The intersubjective-communicative dimension, the "We"-level, leads us to consider the synodical structure of the local episcopal churches. What moved them? What was controversial for them?
- The content-symbolic dimension, the "It"-level, is based on the Trinity itself and is expressed in the "idea of God" seen in the theology of the time. It is therefore represented by the theologians.
- The contextual dimension, the "Globe"-level, which is based on ecclesiastical and societal organization and on the significant persons and groups at that time, reminds us to consider the influence of the emperor, the philosophers, and the Jews.

After the half-day preparation for this role-playing activity, the title reads: "The Marketplace in Constantinople on the Eve of the Council of Nicaea— What is happening? Where do I belong in this scene?"

III. The World of the Creed:
The Ecclesiastical Situation during the Fourth Century

In a style similar to that of a TV show, we present the marketplace in Constantinople. We, the two leaders of the seminar, accompany each other through the scene. The practical theologian (S=*Scharer*) challenges the systematic theologian (*H=Hilberath*) with pointed questions. Chairs and posters help visually construct the marketplace scene and the characters. The group can participate in the "program" by asking questions. In addition, after this scene there is another opportunity for a group discussion about this historical scenario.

Here are the most important parts of the dramatic exchange:

S: Mr. Hilberath, we are now in the marketplace of Constantinople in 325 C.E. on the eve of the Council of Nicaea? What does the marketplace look like?

H: As you can see, the marketplace is still under construction. It wasn't long ago that Constantinople became the second capital of the Roman Empire, the "new Rome in the East." So, some buildings are not finished yet. However, one can clearly see that this square is an important and representative place.

S: Who plays an important role in this marketplace?

H: The emperor. One can see that one side of the marketplace has been expanded and remodeled. That is where Emperor Constantine resides when he visits his city, Constantinople.

S: Let him take his place, then. Emperor, what are your thoughts in 325 C.E. on the very eve of the Nicene Council?

H: "It's been thirteen years since I defeated my contender, Maxentius, at the Milvian Bridge, with the sign of the cross and with the help of the Christian God. I then gave the Christians an edict of tolerance in Milan, ensuring religious freedom for them. I myself am not so keen on becoming a Christian because this would certainly have consequences for my private life. However, I see Christianity as the new vision for unity and as a suitable ideology for my empire. Therefore, I'd like to take the initiative in putting an end to the controversies involving various Christian factions, especially those of Arius and Athanasius. What we need is one faith, one baptism, one Lord, and one emperor in this one Christian empire."

S: In addition to the emperor, there are also certain legates from the bishop of Rome who've just arrived. What are their motivations?

H: These legates have been commissioned by the community of Rome and, yes, we can now say that they are also representatives of the bishop of Rome. For, even though the Roman community was the original and shining example of faith in the Roman Empire, this role has in recent years increasingly been transferred to the bishop. And now the bishop has sent Hosius of Cordoba and others, perhaps also the abbot of St. Matthias in Trier, to represent the Roman position and Roman church politics about Christology in this Council's definition of the faith.

S: What is the Roman position and what are Rome's interests?

H: Roman theology was originally defined by Tertullian, a North African, some one hundred years before this time and by Cyprian, some decades ago. It is a theology that focuses on law and order and emphasizes the unity of God. Thus, the Son of God is at the same time the Father and the Spirit. This theology is somewhat closer to the Alexandrian or Egyptian theology, which on occasion leads to situations in which Rome and Alexandria stand over against Antioch and Constantinople.

S: What does the emperor have to do with these legates?

H: Oh, this has to do with ecclesiastical politics. First, it is interesting to note that the emperor's position concurs with the Roman one. The emperor also wants to emphasize the unity of the Father and Son because he thinks that the closer the Son is with God, the higher his position as emperor would be. The Son is a mediator between God and humankind. If the Son is equal with God himself, then the position of the emperor as Christ's representative would naturally be higher than if the Son is merely similar to God. Therefore, even though the underlying motivations are different, the theological positions of Rome and of the emperor are identical. The Romans emphasize the profession of faith and their idea of unity. The emperor has his own political agenda. Now, for the first time these two agendas come together.

S: If we look around the marketplace in Constantinople some more, we see that in addition to the emperor and the Roman legates, there are also ordinary citizens. Who is important among them?

H: Oh, this is very interesting, especially today. Early church writers report that female vendors in the markets of Ephesus, Constantinople, and other cities argued over theological issues. Some say "he is consubstantial"; others, "he is merely similar to God"; still others, "he is not even similar to God." Some say "true God from true God," while others reject this idea. And it appears that these women know what they are talking about. I would venture to say that maybe these marketplace women discuss matters more seriously than some itinerant philosophers and orators, who reportedly use the same language but only in order to add irony or cynicism to their expressions. These marketplace women obviously understand that the essential underlying question in the Arius-versus-Athanasius dispute is whether or not God, the absolutely transcendent, remote, and unmoved mover, could really become concrete, by joining humankind, by physically becoming a human being among us.

S: I believe that you also mentioned philosophers. The emperor, the conflicting factions, and the marketplace vendors are most likely not alone in the marketplace. There must be others, including Greeks and philosophers, who play a role on this eve of the Council.

H: This year, 325, is exceptional for Christianity, but it is also one that is potentially catastrophic. Athanasius, the marketplace women, and others sense that what is at stake is not a second-, third-, or fourth-tier question. It is THE primary question, the decisive question: What is at the heart of the Christian image of God? What is the core of Christian faith? Can we Christians confidently tell Jews and Greeks that God's very self can enter this world? A Greek philosopher might reason along these lines: "That is a concession made to the anthropomorphic and mythical beliefs of the people. The Divine, the One, is for eternity the unmoved Mover, and is ineffable. This One has absolutely nothing to do with the finiteness or transitoriness of matter, or otherwise could no longer be the *Theion*, the Divine, the Unchangeable. All of our efforts as philosophers, ascetics, and mystics aim to show people an intellectual, moral, or holistic way out of this earthly mess. Just as in Eastern religious movements such as Buddhism, we try to lead them out of materialism in order to become one with the "One."

S: So, the oneness of God is subject to debate. There are also certainly Jews, who arrived after the destruction of Jerusalem, at Constantinople's marketplace. What are their thoughts?

H: They think, "We won't let this Jesus be taken from us. He is a son of the Jewish people. He was a great prophet; he reminded us of important things, as all prophets do. But, he did not invent a new religion. Even though he reminded us in a radical way of important teachings, he did not say anything completely new. And to equate him with God is blasphemy. Of course, God is a living God. We also speak of the prophets and of the wisdom of God. But we never dare to hypostasize the prophets, or God's Word, or Wisdom. We never treat them as individual figures or talk about two or three gods. To speak about the living God, about the personal God is one thing. But God becoming a human being is something completely different and unacceptable for us. We believe in the closeness of God, but also in God's transcendence and intangibility. God cannot be manipulated."

S: Previously, we mentioned some conflicting opinions about the entity of God and about who Jesus Christ is in relationship with God. Who are the main players in these debates on the eve of the Council?

H: One is Arius, a priest who came from Alexandria but who studied in Antioch. Another is Athanasius, a deacon who accompanies his bishop, Alexander of Alexandria. In some ways, these two parties represent a collision between two theological schools. More specifically, we can see the conflict between the traditional, down-to-earth and liturgically based theology of Athanasius, and the highly "modern," often speculative and academic theology of Arius. To his credit, however, it can be said that Arius's theology provokes the clarification of certain issues that had been problematical for some time. Only now does the central issue become clear: what is the Christian image of God?

S: Mr. Hilberath, if you could please sit on Arius's chair for a moment and think and feel as he did. What moves this priest and theologian?

H: "We must preserve the transcendental and intangible aspects of God. No matter how much honor we associate with Jesus Christ, with the *logos*— and the *logos* concept is already known to us from Greek philosophy—he is not the Creator. He is but a creation of the Creator, albeit the first and the best. There was a time, however, when he did not exist and when the Father was alone. It was only for his other creations that God sent his *logos*, his first and best creation, into the world. Therefore, Jesus is neither God, nor is he a second God. However, he is more than a man like us because he has the special position of being God's first and best creation. He is therefore neither fully man, nor fully God. In my opinion, it is precisely because of this position that Jesus can be the intermediary, the *Deuteros Theos*, the "Second God," who comes among us humans. And because he remains morally steadfast before God, he is also adopted and exalted as the Son of God and should be recognized as such."

S: Arius's great opponent is the deacon Athanasius. What is his concern? What is his stance? What would Athanasius say?

H: "This has been the faith of our fathers and mothers for many years now. We are baptized in this faith and in this way of life. We know God through his Son, Jesus of Nazareth. This faith is not something we can give up. This is the very power of the faith: no amount of speculation can make us doubt it. We will oppose any theories that attempt to take the heart of our faith from us. This very God became a human being, lived among us, suffered, died, and rose again so that all of humankind could be accepted and redeemed. We will always defend these two beliefs, which represent the heritage and essence of our faith: Only *God* can redeem us, and it is only when God fully accepts us that we are redeemed."

S: OK, now we have the whole scene set up before us. At this marketplace we see the emperor, the Roman legates, the female vendors, the commoners, the philosophers, the Jews, and the doctrinal opponents, Arius and Athanasius, and their factions. How do these groups interact with one another?

H: Particularly interesting in church history and also in the history of dogma (which can no longer be handled as merely a history of ideas) are the entanglements between political interests, personal interests, and ecclesiastical politics between the important sees (soon to become patriarchates). The complex interactions between these groups make the whole situation exciting and lead one to raise the question today: Did the orthodox teaching really win? Or did the emperor have the last say in defining the Son as *homoousios*, or one with the Father? Who is decisive in this mix?

S: So, one could think of this as a mix of diverse theological interests or even of diverse "theologies"?

H: From the very beginning, several theologies have coexisted in the church. We can see examples of this in the New Testament. In the first few centuries, the theological schools of Alexandria and of Antioch developed. These schools are certainly comparable with some modern theological trends. One example is the exegesis from Antioch where Arius studied. It is a historical-critical or perhaps more rational form of text interpretation. Another example is the more church-oriented, canonical, or spiritual text interpretation that comes from Athanasius's hometown, Alexandria. This interpretation focuses more on the symbolic and on the universal influence of God. These examples show how two different, legitimate possibilities have coexisted for some time. A council convenes only when a ruling is needed or when the "faith of the fathers and mothers" is threatened. The councils help set limits for the Alexandrians when they go too far, and they make it clear how the creed is to be understood.

S: Thank you very much, Mr. Hilberath, for your detailed description of the marketplace in Constantinople. This helps us better identify where our own roles might be in the marketplace.

IV. Which Role Will I Take?

After the scenario of the eve of Nicaea has been played out by the participants and group leaders, the participants start the longer process of finding the role that best suits them in this scene. By silently walking or standing in the square, participants test out different roles as they decide where their place should be. Once the participants' roles and their relationships with one another are made clear, an intense learning process begins. The participants read about their roles and ask the experts about their characters. The participants enthusiastically review historical and dogmatic information about the roles and events at the time of the council. All wants to portray their part accurately.

After hours of intensive work, the reenactment begins. The whole work space is used as the stage. Choir music plays as the participants enter the room together. The play starts with lively action: The emperor's throne and the market stalls are set up. The theologians look for followers. The philosophers have discussions with the Jews. The tumult at the marketplace increases. The theologians and their followers can hardly get anyone to listen to them. Then, a female vendor takes the stand and delivers a petition containing the commoners' concerns to the emperor. The emperor responds with a hackneyed political speech. It becomes clear that on the whole, the creed drama is less about the theological question of Jesus' divine or human identity and more about the political and ecclesiastical structures. Regardless of one's role, this controversial fact cannot be ignored.

V. From Creed Drama to Church Drama

In the reflection following the reenactment, we see that it was easier for the people in the marketplace to make themselves heard than it was for the theologians. The marketplace woman identified the people's deep wish for consensus, for the liberating power of "correct" discussion of God, and made clear the inhumane complications of the political and religious power struggles. Despite the emancipating words of the newly baptized Christian woman, the emperor still had the real power. He did not hesitate to handle the situation with his own best interests in mind. As if they had just had blinders removed from their eyes, something was suddenly clear to the emotionally moved participants: The historical drama surrounding the creed had become a very relevant current church drama.

The question "How can we speak about God today in accordance with the creed's criteria?" cannot be answered by simply stating or repeating the creed's text. All who attempt to "enter" the creed will quickly find themselves in an intense controversy about "authentic" discourse about God. The fixed hierarchy and inflexible roles in the church that existed both then and today can alter theological issues to such an extent that—just as in the reenactment—other priorities overshadow the people's faith.

Before leaving their marketplace role behind, all of the participants are given the opportunity to reassess the anger, indignation, joy, excitement, and hurt that they might have felt. Logically, the next theme for this group reads, "God—power—communication: how was/am I involved?"

Questions for Reflection

- What is new for you in the creed drama? What do you find fascinating? What do you wish to question critically?
- Can you imagine using a similar practical approach to the creed in your practice? If yes, how?
- Where and how have you experienced the importance of historic-dogmatic confrontation? Where and how have you experienced the opposite?

Much Remains Open

The foundations of communicative theology sketched here in this book are only the beginning. The more we engage in and reflect on the process of communicative theology the greater becomes the need for further research and development. At the close of this book, the following questions should be noted for future investigation:

1. Theology as a process is transformed from a strategically deployable "interpretation power" to a "communicative power" in situations of powerlessness by letting those trained in theology participate in conflict-laden events of communication. This further differentiation of its "method" raises these questions:

   - How can "procedures" be developed to focus theological attention on the questions of meaning and orientation belonging to individual human beings (biographical theology)—procedures, namely, which take account of the consistent intersubjectivity and spontaneity of the theological process?

   - What tools do we need for the analysis of the theology implicit in communication processes (communicative theology in the narrow sense)?

   - How can we identify the communicative theologies at work in groups such as diocesan synods, pastoral conferences, faculty meetings, teamwork discussions, and so forth?

   - What can the critical reception of the intersubjective approaches of qualitative social-science research contribute to the development of a process-oriented communicative theology?

2. How can the communicative (in the sense of TCI) and the systematic (in the sense of prevailing notions of pastoral counseling) approaches be reconciled with each other? To answer this question, recent proposals for restructuring the church at various levels require critical discussion.

3. How can the notion of the church as communio be protected against misuse? How can we avoid establishing or maintaining in the name of communio a system that is marked by asymmetrical communication?

4. How can the role of the participating group leader, who is at once *expert for* and *member of* the group, be best lived out? What forms of intervention are permitted? What forms are desirable? What forms should be forbidden? What conclusions should be drawn from the experience of group leadership? What are the consequences for leadership in the church?

   - How can input be structured in such a way so as not to distort the communication process?

   - How much time do courses/seminars need to insure that neither the biographical concretization nor the objective theological information is minimized?

   - How can the trend toward harmonizing conflicts within the group be interrupted? How should one deal with the phenomenon of subversive "co-leaders" in the group?

5. How should we give constructive room to the potential for difference and conflict which the hermeneutic of difference according to TCI brings to the fore?

Much Is Under Way

Since the appearance of the second edition of the original publication *Kommunikative Theologie*, the ideas therein have been widely received, criticized, and further developed.

- New insights have been gained through the postgraduate master's program at Innsbruck.
- In the series Kommunikative Theologie, published by the Grünewald Verlag and edited by Bernd Jochen Hilberath and Matthias Scharer, volumes 8–10 are in preparation.
- In the series Communicative Theology—Interdisciplinary Studies, edited by Bradford Hinze, Bernd Jochen Hilberath, and Matthias Scharer, volumes 6–8 are in preparation.
- An interdisciplinary and interuniversity research group Kommunikative Theologie has been working on specific questions continuously since 2003.
- The current understanding of communicative theological work is articulated in a basic document prepared by the Communicative Theology Research Group, *Communicative Theology: Reflections on the Culture of Our Practice of Theology* (German and English), ed. B. Hinze, B. J. Hilberath, and M. Scharer (Communicative Theology—Interdisciplinary Studies 1/1; Münster/London: Lit Verlag, 2006).
- Three conferences (2002 in Innsbruck; 2005 in Stuttgart-Hohenheim; 2007–2008, a "twin conference" in New York preceded by a facilitator's conference in Roxbury, Massachusetts, and in Telfs/Innsbruck) have contributed to the proliferation and further development of the ideas of the group.
- Communicative Theology is institutionally involved in the Innsbruck Theological Faculty's research project "Religion—Violence—Communication—World Order" and the interfaculty research platform of the University of Innsbruck "World Order—Religion—Violence."

Notes

Introduction

1. Bernd Jochen Hilberath's books include the following: *Theologie zwischen Tradition und Kritik: Die philosophische Hermeneutik Hans-Georg Gadamers als Herausforderung des theologischen Selbstverständisses* (Düsseldorf, 1978); *Der Personbegriff der Trinitätstheologie in Rückfrage von Karl Rahner zu Tertullians "Adversus Praxean"* (Innsbruck, 1986); *Heiliger Geist—heilender Geist* (Mainz, 1988); *Der dreieinige Gott und die Gemeinschaft der Menschen* (Mainz, 1990); *Pneumatologie* (Düsseldorf, 1994); *Karl Rahner—Gottgeheimnis Mensch* (Düsseldorf, 1995); *Zwischen Vision und Wirklichkeit: Fragen nach dem Weg der Kirche* (Würzburg, 1999).

2. Matthias Scharer's books include the following: *Thema-Symbol-Gestalt: Religionsdidaktische Begründung eines korrelativen Religionsbuchkonzeptes auf dem Hintergrund theme-(R. C. Cohn)/symbolzentrierter Interaktion under Einbezug gestaltpädagogischer Elemente* (Graz, 1987); *Miteinander glauben lernen* (Graz, 1987); *Begegnungen Raum geben: Kommunikatives Lernen in Gemeinde, Schule und Erwachsenenbildung* (Mainz, 1995); *Sich nicht aus dem Herzen verlieren: Von der spirituellen Kraft der Beziehung* (Munich, 2003).

3. See Matthias Scharer and Józef Niewiadomski, *Faszinierendes Geheimnis: Neue Zugänge zur Eucharistie in Familie, Schule und Gemeinde* (Innsbruck, 1999).

4. For reports on their collaboration, see Karl Josef Ludwig, ed., *Im Ursprung ist Beziehung: Theologisches Lernen als themenzentrierte Interaktion* (Mainz, 1997); Bernd Jochen Hilberath and Matthias Scharer, *Firmung—wider den feierlichen Kirchenaustritt: Theologisch-praktische Orientierungshilfen* (Mainz, 1998); Bernd Jochen Hilberath, ed., *Communio—Ideal oder Zerrbild von Kommunikations?* (Freiburg im Breisgau, 1999).

5. Bernd Jochen Hilberath, Martina Kraml, Matthias Scharer, eds., *Wahrheit in Beziehung: Der dreieine Gott als Quelle und Orientierung menschlicher Kommunikation* (Mainz, 2003).

6. See the two book series on communicative theology, *Kommunikative Theologie*, vols. 1–9, ed. Bernd Jochen Hilberath and Matthias Scharer (Grünewald Verlag); *Communicative Theology—Interdisciplinary Studies*, vols. 1–8, ed. Bernd Jochen Hilberath, Matthias Scharer, and Bradford Hinze (Lit Verlag).

7. See Max Seckler, *Die schiefen Wände des Lehrhauses: Katholizität als Herausforderung* (Freiburg/Br., 1988), 79—1004; Peter Hünermann: *Dogmatische Prinzipienlehre: Glaube—Überlieferung—Theologien als Sprach- und Wahrheitsgeschehen* (Münster, 2003), 207–51.

8. A diverse range of Catholic thinkers came under the influence of the personalist ideas of Emmanuel Mounier, Jacques Maritian, Max Scheler, and Roman Ingarden, including such North Americans as Dorothy Day and Peter Maurin.

9. See, for example, Hans Urs von Balthasar, *Theo-Drama: Theological Dramatic Theory*, vol. 1, *Prolegomena* (San Francisco, Calif., 1988), 34–37, 626–48.

10. Pope Paul VI addressed the topic of dialogue in his first encyclical, *Ecclesiam Suam* (1964). For the most dramatic illustration of dialogical personalism in the writings of Pope John Paul II, see the encyclical *Ut Unum Sint* (1995).

11. Cardinal Avery Dulles, *Dialogue, Truth, and Communion* (New York, 2001).

12. Bernard Lonergan, *Method in Theology* (New York, 1972), 363.

13. On the theologian's engagement with Jürgen Habermas's theory of communicative competence, see Francis Schüssler Fiorenza and Don Browning, eds., *Habermas, Modernity, and Theology* (New York, 1992); Paul Lakeland, *Theology and Critical Theory: The Discourse of the Church* (Nashville, 1990); Edmund Arens, *Christopraxis: A Theology of Action* (Minneapolis, 1995).

14. David Tracy, *Analogical Imagination: Christian Theology and the Culture of Pluralism* (New York, 1981); and idem, *Plurality and Ambiguity: Hermeneutics, Religion, Hope* (New York, 1987).

15. Robert J. Schreiter, *Constructing Local Theologies* (Maryknoll, N.Y., 1985); and idem, *The New Catholicity: Theology between the Global and the Local* (Maryknoll, N.Y., 1997).

16. Stephen Bevans has called for the recognition of the contextual character of all theology by developing an analysis of six models in contemporary theology: translation, anthropological, praxis, synthetic, transcendental, and countercultural. Stephen B. Bevans, *Models of Contextual Theology* (Maryknoll, N.Y., 1992; revised and expanded edition, 2002).

17. See the essays by various black theologians, *Black and Catholic: The Challenge and Gift of Black Folk. Contributions of African American Experience and Thought to Catholic Theology,* ed. Jamie T. Phelps (Milwaukee, Wisc., 2002).

18. See the essays by various Hispanic theologians in *From the Heart of Our People: Latino/a Explorations of Catholic Systematic Theology,* ed. Orlando O. Espín and Miguel H. Díaz (Maryknoll, N.Y., 1999).

19. Peter Phan, *Christianity with an Asian Face: Asian American Theology in the Making* (Maryknoll, N.Y., 2003).

20. Misunderstanding can be understood as a prism that illuminates distinctive, yet often interrelated, facets in the forms of communication associated with dialogue, hermeneutics, and intercultural communication.

21. Thomas H. Groome, *Christian Religious Education: Sharing Our Story and Vision* (New York, 1980); idem., *Sharing Faith: A Comprehensive Approach to Religious Education and Pastoral Ministry, The Way of Shared Praxis* (San Francisco, 1991).

22. See the following collections of essays, Patrick Granfield, ed., *The Church and Communication* (Kansas City, Mo., 1994); Paul A. Soukup, ed., *From One Medium to Another: Communicating the Bible through Multimedia* (Kansas City, Mo., 1997); Paul A. Soukup, ed., *Fidelity and Communication: Communicating the Bible in New Media* (Kansas City, Mo., 1999). Also see Mary E. Hess, *Engaging Technology in Theological Education: All That We Can't Leave Behind* (Lanham, Md., 2005).

23. Paul A. Soukup, *Communication and Theology: Introduction and Review of the Literature* (London, 1983[1], 1991[2]); Paul A. Soukup, *Christian Communication: A Bibliographical Survey* (New York, 1989).

24. John Paul II's encyclical *Redemptoris Missio* no. 37 (December 7, 1990) and apostolic letter "The Rapid Development," no. 3 (January 24, 2005); see also Pontifical Council for Social Communication, *Communio et Progressio* (January 29, 1971).

25. Soukup, *Communication and Theology*, 75.

26. Ibid.

27. The Conference of Latin American Bishops employed the Catholic Action model of see, judge, and act, which promoted communication in the development of episcopal teaching in their deliberations at Medellín (1968) and Puebla (1979), but this method was contested at Santa Domingo (1992). The African Synod (1994) likewise fostered widespread communicative practices in the African church; see Elochukwu E. Uzukwu, *A Listening Church: Autonomy and Communion in African Churches* (Maryknoll, N.Y., 1996); and the role of "palaver" in Bénézet Bujo, *Foundations of an African Ethic: Beyond the Universal Claims of Western Morality* (New York, 2001). The Asian Bishops Conference, working closely with Asian theologians, advanced a triple dialogue with the poor, other religions, and other cultures; see, for example, Peter Phan, *In Our Own Tongues: Perspectives from Asia on Mission and Inculturation* (Maryknoll, N.Y., 2003), 3–61; Jonathan Tan, "A New Way of Being Church in Asia: The Federation of Asian Bishops' Conferences (FABC) at the Service of Life in Pluralistic Asia," *Missiology* 33 (2005): 71–94. In each of these settings the voices of women merit special attention. See María Pilar Aquino, "Doing Theology from the Perspective of Latin American Women," in *We Are a People: Initiatives in Hispanic American Theology,* ed. Roberto S. Giozueta (Minneapolis, 1992), 79–105; and idem, "Santo Domingo through the Eyes of Women," in *Santo Domingo & Beyond: Documents & Commentaries,* ed. Alfred T. Hennelly (Maryknoll, N.Y., 1993), 212–25; Bernadette Mbuy-Beya, "Women in the Churches in Africa," in *The African Synod [1994]: Documents, Reflections, Perspectives* (Maryknoll, N.Y., 1996), 175–87; Evelyn Monteiro and Antoinette Gutzler, eds., *Ecclesia of Women in Asia: Gathering the Voices of the Silenced* (Delhi, 2005).

28. See Communicative Theology Research Group, *Communicative Theology: Reflections on the Culture of Our Practice of Theology*/Forschungskreis Kommunikative Theologie, *Kommunikative Theologie: Selbstvergeisserung unserer Kultur des Theologietreibens* (Vienna, 2007).

1. Theology as Process

1. For a similar point of view, see Hans-Martin Guttman and Norbert Mette, *Orientierung Theologie* (Reinbek, 2000).

2. Praxis has been translated here as practice. The use of the term praxis in German theology, as in liberation theology, is here incorporated into a larger understanding of the term *practice.*

3. See the relevant foundational text, Jürgen Habermas, *Theorie des kommunikativen Handelns,* 2 vols. (Frankfurt am Main, 1981, [4]1987; [3]1999). English: *The Theory of Communicative Action*, 2 vols. (Boston, 1985).

4. Since the Second Vatican Council, the Latin word *communio* ("community," "communion," etc.) has come into widespread use as a technical term to express the special sacramental community that constitutes the church in its diverse forms of realization, for example, the liturgical assembly, the parish, the diocese, the particular church of a region or nation, the universal church. "Communio ecclesiology" understands the local church as the *communio fidelium* and treats the "higher levels of the church as a networked communion of churches, that is, communiones." In view of its

frequent use in this book, the term *communio* will generally not be italicized or set off in quotation marks. Communio ecclesiology will be discussed in detail in chapter 5.

5. Peter Hünermann, "Sakrament—Figur des Lebens," in *Ankunft Gottes und Handeln des Menschen,* by R. Schaeffler and P. Hünermann (Quaestiones Disputatae 77) (Freiburg i. Br., 1977), 55.

6. See the decree on the formation of priests, *Optatam totius* (OT), no. 16.

7. For an introduction see Bernd Jochen Hilberath, *Karl Rahner—Gottgeheimnis Mensch* (Mainz, 1955); Thomas Pröpper and Magnus Striet, "Transzendentaltheologie" in *Lexikon für Theologie und Kirche*[3], (2002), 10:188–90.

8. See Karl Barth, *Der Römerbrief,* 2nd ed. (Munich, 1922; Zürich, [16]1999); Jürgen Moltmann, ed., *Anfänge der Dialektischen Theologie,* vol. 1 (Munich, [6]1995).

9. See also Dogmatic Constitution on Divine Revelation *Dei Verbum,* § 2, Denziger-Hünermann 4202; cited according to the official English translation available on the Internet: http://www. vatican.va/archive/hist_councils/ii_vatican_council/documents/ vat-ii_const_19651118_dei-verbum_en.html.

10. Jürgen Werbick, *Den Glauben verantworten* (Answering for One's Faith) (Freiburg im Breisgau, 2000), 169.

11. On the relationship between Christian *communio* and communicative acts in the university, see the illuminating discussion of the fundamentals in Monika Scheidler, *Christliche Communio und kommunikatives Handeln: Eine Leitperspektive für die Schule* [Christian Communio and Communicative Acts: A Guideline for the Universities] (Altenberge, 1993).

12. See, for example, Gustavo Gutiérrez, *A Theology of Liberation: History, Politics, and Salvation* (Maryknoll, N.Y., 1988).

13. We are employing the concept of "gaze" to describe the theological hermeneutics of the communication event by analogy with Martina Kraml's investigations into the Eucharist. See Martina Kraml, "Miteinander Essen und Trinken: Prolegomena einer Eucharistiekatechese" [Eating and Drinking Together: Prolegomena to a Catechisis of the Eucharist] (Innsbruck, 2001; unpublished thesis).

2. Preliminary Observations about
the Communicative Character of Human Beings

1. See Martin Buber, *I and Thou,* trans. Walter Kaufmann (New York, 1970), 53ff.

2. Peter L. Berger and Thomas Luckmann, *The Social Construction of Reality: A Treatise in the Sociology of Knowledge* (New York, 1967), 153.

3. See Helmut Peukert, *Science, Action, and Fundamental Theology: Toward a Theology of Communicative Action,* trans. James Bohman (Cambridge, Mass., 1984), 235.

4. Paul Watzlawick, Janet H. Beavin, and Don D. Jackson, *Pragmatics of Human Communication: A Study of Interactional Patterns, Pathologies, and Paradoxes* (New York, 1967), 54.

5. See Friedmann Schulz von Thun, *Miteinander reden 1: Störungen und Klärungen. Allgemeine Psychologie der Kommunikation* (Reinbek, 1981).

6. Watzlawick et al., *Pragmatics of Human Communication,* 51.

7. See, among others, Rene A. Spitz, *The First Year of Life: A Psychoanalytic Study*

of Normal and Deviant Development of Object Relations, in collaboration with W. Godfrey Cobliner (New York, 1965).

8. See, among others, Jessica Benjamin, *The Bonds of Love: Psychoanalysis, Feminism, and the Problem of Domination* (New York, 1988).

9. Buber, *I and Thou*, 55.

10. Martin Buber, *Reden über Erziehung* (Heidelberg, 1964), 58.

11. Martin Buber, *Tales of the Hasidim,* trans. Olga Marx (New York, 1947–48), 1:200 (translation amended).

12. Emmanuel Lévinas, *Ethics and Infinity: Conversations with Philippe Nemo*, trans. Richard A. Cohen (Pittsburgh, 1985), 97 (translation amended).

13. Lévinas, *Ethics and Infinity*, 98 (translation amended).

3. The "Battle of the Gods" as a Dilemma in a Communication-Conscious Society

1. See Jürgen Werbick, *Bilder sind Wege: Eine Gotteslehre* (Munich, 1992).

2. See Paul Tillich, *Systematic Theology* (Chicago, 1951), 1:3–68. When the authors speak of the great divide they are alluding to Gottfried Lessing's "ugly ditch" between the truths of history and those of faith.

3. See Ana-Maria Rizzuto, *The Birth of a Living God* (Chicago, 1979). The author describes how each child has its childhood god under its arm when it encounters the God of the church.

4. See, among others, Edward Schillebeeckx, "Erfahrung und Glaube," in *CGG* 25, 73–116; Richard Schaeffler, *Erfahrung als Dialog mit der Wirklichkeit* (Freiburg-Munich, 1995).

5. See, among others, Rudolf Englert, "Die Korrelationsdidaktik am Ausgang ihrer Epoche: Plädoyer für einen ehrenhaften Abgang," in Rudolf Englert, *Glaubensgeschichte und Bildungsprozeß: Versuch einer religionspädagogischen Kairologie* (Munich, 1985); Matthias Scharer, "Korrelation als Verschleierung: Zur theologischen Auseinandersetzung um das Konzept des Lehrplanes für den katholischen Religionsunterricht auf der Sekundarstufe I (Lehrplan 99)," *Österreichisches Religionspädagogisches Forum* 8 (1998): 8-11.

6. See Thomas Ruster, *Der verwechselbare Gott: Theologie nach der Entflechtung von Christentum und Religion* (Quaestiones Disputatae 181; Freiburg i. Br., ³2001).

7. A more extensive discussion of this topic appears in Communicative Theology Research Group, *Communicative Theology: Reflections on the Culture of Our Practice of Theology,* ed. Bernd Jochen Hilberath, Bradford Hinze, and Matthias Scharer (Communicative Theology—Interdisciplinary Studies, vol. 1/1; Vienna, 2006).

8. See Józef Niewiadomski, "Extra media nulla salus. Zum religiösen Anspruch der Medienkultur," in Józef Niewiadomski, *Herbergsuche: Auf dem Weg zu einer christlichen Identität in der modernen Kultur* (Münster, 1999), 149–66.

9. See Patrik C. Höring, "Identität radikaler Pluralität," *Diakonia* 32 (2001): 278–84.

10. William Knoke, *Bold New World: The Essential Road Map to the Twenty-first Century* (New York, 1996).

11. Wolfgang Frühwald, "Vor uns die Cyber-Sintflut," in *Der Mensch im Netz: Kultur, Kommerz und Chaos in der digitalen Welt*, ZEIT Punkte 5/96, 12.

12. Uwe Jean Heuser, "Die fragmentierte Gesellschaft," in *Der Mensch im Netz*, ZEIT Punkte 5/96, 17.

13. Susanne Gaschke, "Frauen und Technik," in *Der Mensch im Netz*, ZEIT Punkte 5/96, 44.

14. Jerry Richardson, *The Magic of Rapport: How You Can Gain Personal Power in Any Situation* (Cupertino, Calif., 1987).

15. Richardson, *The Magic of Rapport*, 1–2.

16. Richardson, *The Magic of Rapport*, 5.

17. Richardson, *The Magic of Rapport*, 5.

18. In a discussion between professors of the Theology Department and representatives of the Diocese of Linz responsible for the training of pastoral assistants, a prominent diocesan speaker expressed the opinion prevailing in many ecclesiastical circles: "The theological faculty should offer courses in theological formation. What the future pastoral ministers need for their work in the parish should be learned in courses on communication and management training."

19. The manuscript for this book was written on a PC. Connections via Internet between the authors, with the libraries, and to diverse Web sites enabled us to obtain and exchange information with utmost rapidity. Notebook computers and mobile phones enable one to use even traveling time on train or bus for effective work.

20. The term "themes" will become a central category as we proceed.

21. Pastoral Constitution on the Church in the Modern World *Gaudium et spes*, in *Vatican Council II: The Basic Sixteen Documents,* ed. Austin Flannery (Northport, N.Y./Dublin, Ireland, 1996), no. 36.

22. Maria Elisabeth Aigner, *Dient Gott der Wissenschaft? Praktisch-theologische Perspektiven zur diakonischen Dimension von Theologie* (Münster, 2002).

23. Wolfhart Pannenberg, *Theology and the Philosophy of Science*; trans. Francis McDonagh (London/Philadelphia, 1976).

24. Raymund Schwager, Józef Niewiadomski et al., "Dramatische Theologie als Forschungsprogramm," *Zeitschrift für Katholische Theologie* 118 (1996): 322.

25. Pannenberg, *Theology and the Philosophy of Science*, 216.

26. Pannenberg, *Theology and the Philosophy of Science*, 220.

27. The German text at this point makes a distinction between "Sinntotalität," here translated as "sum total of meaning" and "Gesamtsinn," here translated as "meaningful whole." A "meaningful whole" is more than the mere sum of particular meaningful experiences.

28. See Matthias Scharer, "Wie kommen die TheologInnen zu ihrem Wissen. Die Perspektive 'Kommunikativer Theologie,'" in *Wie kommt die Wissenschaft zu ihrem Wissen,* vol. 3 (Einführung in die Methodologie der Sozial- und Kulturwissenschaften) (Hohengehren, 2001) (book and CD).

29. See Bernhard Nitsche, "Die Analogie zwischen dem trinitarischen Gottesbild und der communialen Struktur von Kirche. Desiderat eines Forschungsprogrammes zur Communio-Ekklesiologie" in Bernd Jochen Hilberath, ed., *Communio—Ideal oder Zerrbild von Kommunikation?* (Quaestiones Disputatae 176; Freiburg i. Br., 1999), 81–114.

30. See Robert J. Schreiter, *Abschied vom Gott der Europäer: Zur Entwicklung*

regionaler *Theologie* (Salzburg, 1992), here 53. The German term *Fremd* can be translated as "stranger," "alien," but also as "mystery."

31. See, among others, Matthias Scharer and Józef Niewiadomski, *Faszinierendes Geheimnis: Neue Zugänge zur Eucharistie in Familie, Schule und Gemeinde* (Innsbruck/ Mainz, 1999).

32. See Matthias Scharer, "Eucharistie und kirchliches Handeln. Ein Perspektivenwechsel," in *Im Glauben Mensch werden: Impulse für eine Pastoral, die zur Welt kommt*, ed. Franz Weber, Thomas Böhm, Anna Findl-Ludescher, and Hubert Findl (Innsbruck, 2000), 29-41.

33. See *Gaudium et spes* 1.

34. Dogmatic Constitution on the Church *Lumen gentium, Vatican Council II: The Basic Sixteen Documents*, 1.

4. The Communicative God of Christian Revelation and God's Communication in History

1. Gregory of Nanzianzen, *Ep. 101* (Patrologia graeca 37, 181f.).

2. Kurt Marti, *Die gesellige Gottheit* (Stuttgart, ²1993).

3. See Bernd Jochen Hilberath, "Der Heilige Geist—ein Privileg der Kirche?" in Walter Groß, ed., *Das Judentum—eine bleibende Herausforderung christlicher Identität* (Mainz, 2001), 174–83.

4. Vatican Council I, Dogmatic Constitution *Dei Filius* 1, in Denzinger-Hünermann, *Kompendium der Glaubensbekenntnisse and kirchlichen Lehrentscheidungen* (Freiburg i. Br., 1991), no. 3003 (subsequently cited as DH). Norman Tanner, *Decrees of the Ecumenical Councils* (Washington, D.C., 1990), vol. 2.

5. *Dei Filius*, 2 (DH 3004).

6. *Dei Filius*, 2 (DH 3005).

7. *Dei Filius*, 2 (DH 3004).

8. *Dei Filius*, 2 (DH 3004).

9. *Dei Filius*, 2 (DH 3005).

10. *Dei Filius*, 2 (DH 3006).

11. Dogmatic Constitution on Divine Revelation *Dei Verbum*, DH 4202, in *Vatican Council II: The Basic Sixteen Documents*, ed. Austin Flannery, no. 2.

12. *Dei Verbum*, 1.2 (DH 4202).

13. Max Seckler, "Der Begriff der Offenbarung," in *Handbuch der Fundamentaltheologie*, ed. Walter Kern et al., vol. 2 (Freiburg i. Br., ²2000), 47f.

14. See Jürgen Hilberath, "'Participatio actuosa.' Zum ekklesiologischen Kontext eines pastoralliturgischen Programms," in *Gottesdienst—Kirche—Gesellschaft*, ed. Hans Jakob Becker et al. (Pietas liturgica 5; St. Ottilien, 1991), 319–38.

15. *Dei Filius* (DH 3008), *Decrees of the Ecumenical Councils*, chapter 3, nos. 1, 2.

16. *Dei Filius* (DH 3011), *Decrees of the Ecumenical Councils*, chapter 3, no. 8.

17. *Dei Filius* (DH 3012/3013), *Decrees of the Ecumenical Councils*, chapter 3, nos. 10–12.

18. *Dei Verbum* Proem. (DH 4201), *Vatican Council II: The Basic Sixteen Documents*.

19. *Dei Verbum* Proem. (DH 4201), *Vatican Council II: The Basic Sixteen Documents.*

20. See Max Seckler, "*Loci theologici,*" in *Lexikon für Theologie und Kirche*[3] (1997), 6:1014–16.

5. The Church as a Community
of Communication: The "We" as Gift

1. Vilém Flusser, *Kommunikologie* (Frankfurt a.M., 1998).

2. Dogmatic Constitution on the Church *Lumen gentium, Vatican II: The Basic Sixteen Documents,* ed. Austin Flannery (Northport, N.Y./Dublin, 1996), no. 12.

3. Flusser, *Kommunikologie,* 29.

4. Flusser, *Kommunikologie,* 30.

5. Flusser, *Kommunikologie,* 30f.

6. Flusser, *Kommunikologie,* 31.

7. Flusser, *Kommunikologie,* 31f.

8. Flusser, *Kommunikologie,* 33.

9. Flusser, *Kommunikologie,* 32.

10. Flusser, *Kommunikologie,* 32f.

11. Flusser, *Kommunikologie,* 33.

12. Karl Rahner, "Kommentar zu *Lumen Gentium* 26," in *Lexikon für Theologie und Kirche*[2], Erg. I, 243f.

13. Small Christian communities are a common phenomenon in North America.

14. We describe here and use the terminology of the Roman Catholic tradition; this is not meant to exclude structures and terminology used in other traditions.

15. Cf. Bernd Jochen Hilberath, ed., *Communio—Ideal oder Zerrbild von Kommunikation?* (Quaestiones Disputatae 176; Freiburg i. Br., 1999).

16. See figure 1 on page 24.

17. *Ringmauer* is technically a city wall, and is here described in terms of the American gated suburban community.

6. Communication as a Practice
of Theological Awareness: The Perspective of TCI

1. See, among others, Ruth C. Cohn and Alfred Farau, *Gelebte Geschichte der Psychotherapie: Zwei Perspektiven* (Stuttgart, 1984), 3rd edition in the series Konzepte der Humanwissenschaften (Stuttgart, 2001); Helga Betz, Helmut Reichert, Angelika Rubner et al., *Themenzentrierte Supervision* (Mainz, 1998).

2. See, among others, Ruth C. Cohn, "Zur Humanisierung der Schulen: Vom Rivalitätsprinzip zum Kooperationsmodell mit Hilfe der Themenzentrierten Interaktion (TZI)" (1973), in Ruth C. Cohn, *Von der Psychoanalyse zur themenzentrierten Interaktion: Von der Behandlung einzelner zu einer Pädagogik für alle* (Stuttgart, [5]1981), 152–75; Ruth C. Cohn and Christina Terfurth, eds., *Lebendiges Lehren und Lernen: TZI macht Schule* (Stuttgart, 1993).

3. See, among others, Helga Belz, ed., *Auf dem Weg zur arbeitsfähigen Gruppe: Kooperationskonzept von Helga Belz—Prozeßberichte von Helga Belz—Prozeßberichte aus TZI-Gruppen* (Mainz, [2]1992).

4. Heike Hannen, *Bestandsaufnahme von wissenschaftlichen Arbeiten und Forschungsprojekten über die Themenzentierte Interaktion (TZI) in der Wirtschaft*, 2001 (http://www.tzi-wirtschaft.net/).

5. See, among others, Bernhard Honsel, *Der rote Punkt: Eine Gemeinde unterwegs* (Düsseldorf, 1983); Matthias Kroeger, *Themenzentrierte Seelsorge: Über die Kombination Klientenzentrierter und Themenzentrierter Arbeit nach Carl R. Rogers und Ruth C. Cohn in Theologie und schulischer Gruppenarbeit* (Stuttgart, ⁴1989); Matthias Scharer, "TZI in der kirchlichen Praxis," in Cornelia Löhmer and Rüdiger Standhardt, *TZI: pädagogisch-therapeutische Gruppenarbeit nach Ruth C. Cohn* (Stuttgart, 1992), 312–25.

6. See, among others, Albert Biesinger, "Lebendiges Lernen in der Katechese. Hoffnungsversuche in Schule und Gemeinde," inaugural lecture at the University of Salzburg, in *Christlich Pädagogische Blätter* 97 (1984): 6–9, 85–95, 223–26; Dieter Funke, *Verkündigung zwischen Tradition und Interaktion. Praktisch-theologische Studien zur Themenzentrierten Interaktion (TZI) nach Ruth C. Cohn* (Frankfurt/M., 1984); Matthias Scharer, *Thema-Symbol-Gestalt: Religionsdidaktische Begründung eines korrelativen Religionsbuchkonzeptes auf dem Hintergrund themen-(R. C. Cohn)/symbolzentrierter Interaktion unter Einbezug gestaltpädagogischer Elemente* (Graz, 1987); Karl Josef Ludwig, ed., *Im Ursprung ist Beziehung: Theologisches Lernen als themenzentrierte Interaktion* (Mainz, 1997).

7. In what follows there will be repeated mention of the formula "the attitude and method of TCI." Attitude translates the German word *Haltung* and implies the cultivation of a certain personal manner or frame of mind or attentiveness when responding to situations of communication.

8. See Edith Zundel, "Ruth Cohn. Themenzentrierte Interaktion," in Edith Zundel and Rolf Zundel, *Leitfiguren der Psychotherapie: Leben und Werk* (Munich, 1987), 67–82.

9. See Silvia Hagleitner, *Mit Lust an der Welt in Sorge um sie: Feministisch-politische Bildungsarbeit nach Paulo Freire und Ruth C. Cohn* (Mainz, 1996), 115.

10. Star coin is the translation of *Sterntaler*. Taler was a German coin used until 1907, and the expression *Sterntaler* is the title of a Grimm fairy tale.

11. Ruth C. Cohn, *Zu wissen dass wir zählen: Gedichte und Poems*. With cut-out silhouettes by Ann Marie Maag-Büttner (Bern, 1990).

12. This quotation and the following quotations in italics are taken from the transcript of a broadcast by the Österreichischer Rundfunk on the occasion of Ruth Cohn's reception of the honorary doctorate.

13. Compare Matthias Scharer, "Wie wird Kirchliche Bildung marktgerecht oder: Welche Bildung macht den Markt gerecht? Communiotheologische Überlegungen zum kirchlichen Bildungsgeschehen," in *Communio—Ideal oder Zerrbild von Kommunikation,* ed. Bernd Jochen Hilberath (Quaestiones Disputatae 176; Freiburg i. Br., 1999), 235–42.

14. Ruth C. Cohn, *Es geht ums Anteilnehmen: Perspektiven der Persönlichkeitsentfaltung in der Gesellschaft der Jahrtausendwende* (Freiburg i. Br., ²1993), 165.

15. Cohn, *Anteilnehmen*, 171.

16. Helga Hermann, "Ruth C. Cohn—Ein Porträt," in *TZI—Pädagogisch-therapeutische Gruppenarbeit nach Ruth C. Cohn,* ed. Cornelia Löhmer Cornelia and Rüdiger Standhart (Stuttgart, ²1993), 19–36, here 33.

17. Elmar Osswald, "Vom Sinn des Lebens und Lernens in der heutigen Zeit. Ein

Interview mit Ruth C. Cohn," *Schweizer schule: Zeitschrift für Christliche Bildung und Erziehung* 8 (1983): 389–93, here 390.

18. Cohn and Farau, *Gelebte Geschichte*, 214.

19. Cohn and Farau, *Gelebte Geschichte*, 214.

20. Cohn and Farau, *Gelebte Geschichte*, 214.

21. Cohn and Farau, *Gelebte Geschichte*, 216.

22. Cohn and Farau, *Gelebte Geschichte*, 216.

23. Cohn and Farau, *Gelebte Geschichte*, 217.

24. Paul Matzdorf, and Ruth C. Cohn, "Themenzentrierte Interaktion," in Raymond I. Corsini, *Handbuch der Psychotherapie*, ed. Gerd Weninger (Weinheim, 1983), 1277.

25. Cohn and Farau, *Gelebte Geschichte*, 218.

26. Cohn and Farau, *Gelebte Geschichte*, 331.

27. Cohn and Farau, *Gelebte Geschichte*, 332.

28. Cohn and Farau, *Gelebte Geschichte*, 327.

29. Cohn and Farau, *Gelebte Geschichte*, 327.

30. Ruth C. Cohn, "Zu wenig geben ist Diebstahl, zuviel geben ist Mord," in *Betrifft: Erziehung* 14 (1981): 23–27.

31. Matzdorf and Cohn, "Themenzentrierte Interaktion," 1272.

32. Ruth C. Cohn, *Es geht ums Anteilnehmen*, 86.

33. Ruth C. Cohn, *Von der Psychoanalyse zur themenzentrierten Interaktion: Von der Behandlung einzelner zu einer Pädagogik für alle* (Stuttgart, 1975; [11]1992), 7.

34. Compare Cohn, *Von der Psychoanalyse*, 11; Cohn and Farau, *Gelebte Geschichte*, 564.

35. Matzdorf and Cohn, "Themenzentrierte Interaktion," 1278.

36. See Karin Hahn, Marianne Schraut-Birmelin, Klaus-Volker Schütz, and Christel Wagner, eds., *Beachte die Körpersignale: Körpererfahrungen in der Gruppenarbeit* (Mainz, 1991).

37. Matzdorf and Cohn, "Themenzentrierte Interaktion," 1278.

38. See Matzdorf and Cohn, "Themenzentrierte Interaktion," 1279.

39. Frederick S. Perls, *Gestalt-Therapie in Aktion* (Stuttgart, [8]1996), 13.

40. Cohn and Farau, *Gelebte Geschichte*, 320

41. Ruth C. Cohn, "Die Selbsterfahrungsbewegung: Autismus oder Autonomie?" *Gruppendynamik* 5 (1974): 160–71, here 164.

42. We shall treat the TCI axioms in detail in section III.

43. Cohn and Farau, *Gelebte Geschichte*, 356

44. Helmut Quitmann, *Humanistische Psychologie: Zentrale Konzepte und philosophischer Hintergrund* (Göttingen, 1985), 197.

45. Cohn and Farau, *Gelebte Geschichte*, 16f.

46. Ruth C. Cohn, "Über den ganzheitlichen Ansatz der themenzentrierten Interaktion. Eine Antwort an Dr. med. Peter Petersen," *Integrative Therapie* 5 (1979): 252–58, here 253.

47. Ruth C. Cohn, "Zur Grundlage des themenzentrieten interaktionellen Systems: Axiome, Postulate, Hilfsregeln," *Gruppendynamik* 3 (1974): 150–59, here 150.

48. Matzdorf and Cohn, "Themenzentrierte Interaktion," 1272–1314; Paul Matzdorf and Ruth C. Cohn, "Das Konzept der Themenzentrierten Interaktion," *TZI—Pädagogisch-therapeutische Gruppenarbeit nach Ruth C. Cohn,* ed. Cornelia Löhmer and Rüdiger Standhardt (Stuttgart, 1992), 39–92.

49. See Karl Ernst Nipkow, *Grundfragen der Religionspädagogik*, vol. 3: *Gemeinsam leben und glauben lernen* (Gütersloh, 1982).

50. Further information about the university course in communicative theology can be found on the Internet at http://praktheol.uibk.ac.at/komtheo/lehrgang/.

51. The interviews were conducted in a study of the first university course in communicative theology: Johannes Dürlinger, "'Wie das dann stimmig wird . . .'— Theologie und Biographie. Ein Beitrag zur Evaluierung der ersten Kurswoche des Innsbrucker Universitätslehrganges 'Kommunikative Theologie'" (unpublished thesis; Innsbruck, 2002).

52. Helmut Quitmann, *Humanistische Psychologie*, 197.

53. Cohn and Farau, *Gelebte Geschichte*, 357.

54. Cohn, "Die Selbsterfahrungsbewegung," 167.

55. Cohn and Farau, *Gelebte Geschichte*, 356.

56. Cohn and Farau, *Gelebte Geschichte*, 357.

57. Matzdorf and Cohn, "Das Konzept," 62.

58. Cohn and Farau, *Gelebte Geschichte*, 467

59. Cohn and Farau, *Gelebte Geschichte*, 469f.

60. *Gaudium et spes, Vatican Council II: The Basic Sixteen Documents,* ed. Austin Flannery (Northport, N.Y.; Dublin, 1996), 16 (Denziger-Hünermann 4316).

61. Ibid.

62. Cohn, *Von der Psychoanalyse*, 120.

63. Quitmann, *Humanistische Psychologie*, 184.

64. Matzdorf and Cohn, "Themenzentrierte Interaktion," 1272.

65. Matzdorf and Cohn, "Themenzentrierte Interaktion," 1272.

66. Matzdorf and Cohn, "Das Konzept," 62.

67. Cohn and Farau, *Gelebte Geschichte*, 358.

68. Cohn and Farau, *Gelebte Geschichte*, 358.

69. Cohn, *Von der Psychoanalyse*, 164.

70. Annedore Schultze, "Das gesellschafts-politische Anliegen der TZI," in *Zur Tat befreien: Gesellschaftspolitische Perspektiven der TZI-Gruppenarbeit,* ed. Rüdiger Standhardt and Cornelia Löhmer (Mainz, 1994), 120.

71. Compare Matzdorf and Cohn, "Das Konzept," 67.

72. Cohn and Farau, *Gelebte Geschichte*, 359.

73. Matzdorf and Cohn, "Themenzentrierte Interaktion," 1293f.

74. Cohn and Farau, *Gelebte Geschichte*, 359.

75. Cohn, *Von der Psychoanalyse*, 122.

76. Matzdorf and Cohn, "Themenzentrierte Interaktion," 1294.

77. Anita Ockel and Ruth C. Cohn, "Das Konzept des Widerstands in der themenzentrierten Interaktion. Vom psychoanalytischen Konzept des Widerstandes über das TZI-Konzept der Störung zum Ansatz einer Gesellschaftstherapie," in *TZI— Pädagogisch-therapeutische Gruppenarbeit nach Ruth C. Cohn,* ed. Cornelia Löhmer Cornelia and Rüdiger Standhart (Stuttgart, 1992), 177–206, here 202.

78. Anita Ockel and Ruth C. Cohn, "Das Konzept des Widerstands," 202f.

79. See, among others, Matthias Scharer, "An Lebensgeschichten Anteil nehmen—eine Chance für Verkündigung und Gemeindekatechese?" *Diakonia* 26 (1995): 24–29.

80. Hermann P. Siller, "Die Fähigkeit eine Biographie zu haben," *Diakonia* 26 (1995): 6–16, here 6.

81. Siller, "Die Fähigkeit eine Biographie zu haben," 16.
82. Siller, "Die Fähigkeit eine Biographie zu haben," 16.
83. Compare Matthias Scharer, "Das 'geheiligte' Fragment. Annäherungen an eine Theologie der Familie," in *Gottesbeziehung in der Familie: Familienkatechetische Orientierungen von der Kindertaufe bis ins Jugendalter*, ed. Albert Biesinger and Herbert Bendel (Ostfildern, 2000), 115–36.
84. See, among others, Karin Hahn, Marianne Schraut-Birmelin, Klaus-Volker Schütz, and Christel Wagner, eds., *Themenzentrierte Supervision* (Mainz, 1997).
85. Matthias Scharer and Józef Niewiadomski, *Faszinierendes Geheimnis: Neue Zugänge zur Eucharistie in Familie, Schule und Gemeinde* (Innsbruck, 1999), 87.

7. Keeping the Faith Tradition and Implicit "God-Talk" in Balance

1. See *Gaudium et spes*, Proem. 1 (Denziger-Hünermann 4301).
2. Ruth C. Cohn and Alfred Farau, *Gelebte Geschichte der Psychotherapie: Zwei Perspektiven* (Stuttgart, 1984), 351.
3. See, among others, Barbara Langmaack, *Einführung in die Themenzentrierte Interaktion TZI: Leben rund ums Dreieck* (Weinheim, 2001).
4. Religious education applications are found, for example, in Matthias Scharer, "Erlösung 'lehren und lernen,'" in *Rhs. Religionsunterricht an höheren Schulen* 43 (2000): 103–7; idem, "Religion unterrichten lernen. Das Innsbrucker Modell," in *Bensberger Protokolle 101: Kompetenz für die Praxis? Innovative Modelle der Religionslehreraus- und -fortbildung*, ed. Isenberg Wolfgang (Bergisch Gladbach, 2000), 55–68; idem, *Leben/Glauben lernen—lebendig und persönlich bedeutsam* (Salzburg, 1988); idem, "'Erst gehen, wenn man gesandt wird?' Religionsunterricht im Umbruch der religiösen Landschaft und die Frage nach realistischen Lernaufgaben in dieser Situation," in Engelbert Groß and Klaus König, eds., *Religiöses Lernen der Kirchen im globalen Dialog* (Münster, 2000), 551–58; idem, "'Es kommt auf die Person an'— Persönlichkeitsbildung in der Aus- und Fortbildung von ReligionslehrerInnen," *Österreichisches Religionspädagogisches Forum* 7 (1997): 72–73; idem, "Integration theologischer und personalkommunikativer Kompetenz als Herausforderung religions-pädagogisch-katechetischer Aus-, Fort- und Weiterbildungspraxis: Ein Modell," *Österreichisches Religionspädagogisches Forum* 1 (1991): 1, 19-23.
5. See, among others, Sigrun Polzien and Helmut Leonhard, "Themenzentrierte Interaktion. Christliches Gemeinschaftsleben als ein Prozeß lebendigen Lernens," *Diakonia* 7 (1976): 149–57; Helga Modesto, "Theologie und Lebenshilfe," in *Wagnis Theologie: Erfahrungen mit der Theologie Karl Rahners*, ed. Herbert Vorgrimler (Freiburg i.Br., 1979), 451–63; Bernhard Honsel, *Der rote Punkt: Eine Gemeinde unterwegs* (Düsseldorf, 1983); Josef Mayer-Scheu, *Seelsorge im Krankenhaus: Entwurf einer neuen Praxis* (Mainz, [2]1981); Michael E. Frickel, "Haltung und Methode der Themenzentrierten Interaktion. Eine Anregung für das pastorale Verhalten in Gruppen," in *Das Lernen des Seelsorgers,* ed. Wilhelm Bruners and Josef Schmitz (Mainz, 1982), 111–19; Albert Biesinger, "Lebendiges Lernen in der Katechese. Hoffnungsversuche in Schule und Gemeinde," inaugural lecture at the University of Salzburg, *Christlich Pädagogische Blätter* 97 (1984): 6–9, 85–95, 223–25; Klaus-Volker Schütz, *Gruppenarbeit in der Kirche: Methoden angewandter Sozialpsychologie in*

Seelsorge, Religionspädagogik und Erwachsenenbildung (Mainz, 1989); Matthias Kroeger, *Themenzentrierte Seelsorge: Über die Kombination Klientzentrierter und Themenzentrierter Arbeit nach Carl R. Rogers and Ruth C. Cohn in Theologie und schulischer Gruppenarbeit* (Stuttgart, ⁴1989); Helga Modesto, "Miteinander geschwisterlich umgehen" *Lebendige Seelsorge* 41 (1990): 359–66; Hartmut Raguse, "Theologische Implikationen der TZI," in *Im Ursprung ist Beziehung: Theologisches Lernen als themenzentrierte Interaktion,* ed. Karl Josef Ludwig (Mainz, 1997), 29–53; Matthias Scharer, "Themenzentrierte Interaktion in der kirchlichen Erwachsenenbildung," in *Bakeb-information* 2 (1994): 19–22.

6. Dieter Funke, *Verkündigung zwischen Tradition und Interaktion: Praktisch-theologische Studien zur Themenzentrierten Interaktion (TZI) nach Ruth C. Cohn* (Frankfurt a. M., 1984); see the reception in Matthias Scharer, *Thema-Symbol-Gestalt Religionsdidaktische Begründung eines korrelativen Religionsbuchkonzeptes auf dem Hintergrund theme-(R. C. Cohn)/symbolzentrierter Interaktion unter Einbezug gestaltpädagogischer Elemente* (Graz, 1987).

7. See Matthias Scharer, "Theologie, Glaubenskommunikation und Themenzentrierte Interaktion. Zum gegenwärtigen Stand der Diskussion," in *Im Ursprung ist Beziehung: Theologisches Lernen als themenzentrierte Interaktion,* ed. Karl Ludwig and Karl Josef (Mainz, 1997), 121–27.

8. See Henning Luther, *Religion und Alltag: Bausteine zu einer Praktischen Theologie des Subjekts* (Stuttgart, 1992); Ulrike Greiner, *Der Spur des Anderen folgen? Religionspädagogische Theoriekritik aus der Perspektive des Fremden* (Thaur, 2000).

9. Matthias Scharer, "Das geschenkte Wir. Kommunikatives Lernen in der christlichen Gemeinde," in *Frischer Wind aus dem Süden: Impulse aus den Basisgemeinden,* ed. Franz Weber (Innsbruck/Vienna, 1998), 84–100.

10. See Matthias Scharer, "Die Rolle der TZI in einer 'Kommunikativen Theologie.' Konzept und Modell," *Themenzentrierte Interaktion* 15 (2001): 33–41.

11. See Matthias Scharer, *Begegnungen Raum geben: Kommunikative Lernprozesse in Gemeinde, Schule und Erwachsenenbildung* (Mainz, 1995).

12. See, among others, Detlev Dormeyer, Herbert Mölle, and Thomas Ruster, eds., *Lebenswege und Religion: Biographie in Bibel, Dogmatik und Religionspädagogik* (Religion und Biographie 1; Münster, 2000); Stephanie Klein, *Theologie und empirische Biographieforschung* (Stuttgart, 1994).

13. Matthias Scharer, "Katechese wider den Tod. Lateinamerika als Herausforderung für die Glaubensvermittlung." *Theologisch-Praktische Quartalschrift* 138 (1990): 135–43; Matthias Scharer, "Fremde Gesichter. Südlicher Einspruch gegen theoretische 'Brücken' zwischen modernem Leben und altem Glauben," in Hans-Ferdinand Angel, *Tragfähigkeit der Religionspädagogik* (Theologie im kulturellen Dialog 4; Graz, 2000), 217–26; Matthias Scharer, "Ein realistischer Blick auf die brasilianischen Basisgemeinden und die Kirche des Volkes an der Jahrtausendwende," *Christlich Pädagogische Blätter* 113 (2000): 227–31. In this connection we call attention to the section for "Intercultural Pastoral Theology" (Franz Weber) in the Innsbruck Theological Faculty, which represents the worldwide ecclesial component in our research project.

14. See, among others, Fritz Oser, *Wieviel Religion braucht der Mensch? Erziehung und Entwicklung zur religiösen Autonomie* (Gütersloh, 1988).

15. Henning Luther, *Religion und Alltag,* 168.

16. Henning Luther, *Religion und Alltag,* 169.

17. Hermann P. Siller, "Die Fähigkeit eine Biographie zu haben," *Diakonia* 26 (1995): 6.

18. Siller, "Biographie," 6.

19. Siller, "Biographie," 6f.

20. Siller, "Biographie," 7.

21. See *Lumen gentium* 13 (Denziger-Hünermann 4133).

22. See Matthias Scharer, "Gruppe," in *Lexikon der Religionspädagogik,* ed. Norbert Mette, Folkert Rickers; book and CD, vol. 1 (Neukirchen-Vluyn, 2001), cols. 773–77; Matthias Scharer, "Gruppenunterricht" in *Lexikon der Religions-pädagogik,* cols. 777–80.

23. Langmaack, *Einführung,* 107.

24. See, among others, Langmaack, *Einführung,* 73.

25. Langmaack, *Einführung,* 109-110.

26. Kroeger, *Themenzentrierte Seelsorge,* 219.

27. Kroeger, *Themenzentrierte Seelsorge,* 213.

28. Kroeger, *Themenzentrierte Seelsorge,* 214.

29. Kroeger, *Themenzentrierte Seelsorge,* 214.

30. Kroeger, *Themenzentrierte Seelsorge,* 214.

31. As to the thesis of a fusion of horizons, we follow M. Kroeger. In terms of a hermeneutic of difference, however, we explicitly develop Kroeger's ideas further. See Kroeger, *Themenzentrierte Seelsorge,* 215.

32. Cohn and Farau, *Gelebte Geschichte,* 366f.

33. Jürgen Werbick, *Glaubenlernen aus Erfahrung: Grundbegriffe einer Didaktik des Glaubens* (Munich, 1989), 222.

34. Kroeger, *Themenzentrierte Seelsorge,* 214.

35. Dietrich Stollberg, *Lernen weil es Freude macht: Eine Einführung in die Themenzentrierte Interaktion* (Munich, 1982).

36. Here we have been inspired by the conception of Jochen und Monika Grell, which we have developed (Jochen and Monika Grell, *Unterrichtsrezepte* (Weinheim, 1983).

Index

OF RELATED INTEREST

CHRISTOPHER RUDDY

THE LOCAL CHURCH
Tillard and the Future of Catholic Ecclesiology

As Christianity becomes increasingly global in its membership and its practices, how will it deal with increasing tensions between the unity of the faith and the diversity of its expressions? How should the papal ministry of unity be exercised, so that, in the words of Pope John Paul II, "while in no way renouncing what is essential to its mission, [it] is nonetheless open to a new situation"? How can the relationships between local churches and the universal church be improved? Building upon the work of leading theologians over the past two centuries, particularly the Dominican ecumenist and papal consultor Jean-Marie Tillard, Christopher Ruddy's *The Local Church* offers signposts to guide the church as it responds to these and other challenges.

Topics include

The relationship of papal primacy and episcopal collegiality • Inculturation and evangelization • The quest for Christian unity • The ecclesiology of Pope Benedict XVI and its future implications • The centrality of Christology and soteriology to ecclesiology • Baptism and Eucharist • Diverse visions of communion ecclesiology

Christopher Ruddy is an assistant professor of theology at the University of St. Thomas in St. Paul, Minnesota. His writing has appeared in *America, Christian Century, Commonweal,* and *Logos.*

Paperback, 0-8245-2347-4

———————————— ■ ————————————

Check your local bookstore for availability.
To order directly from the publisher, please call 1-800-707-0670
for Customer Service or visit our Web site at www.cpcbooks.com.
For catalog orders, please send your request to the address below.

THE CROSSROAD PUBLISHING COMPANY
16 PENN PLAZA, SUITE 1550
NEW YORK, NY 10001

crossroad

OF RELATED INTEREST

ERIN LOTHES BIVIANO

THE PARADOX OF CHRISTIAN SACRIFICE
The Loss of Self, The Gift of Self

Sacrifice is at the heart of Christian wisdom about love. Jesus' teaching that one must "lose one's life to save it" reveals a paradoxical relationship between self-sacrifice and self-realization. The invitation to imitate Jesus Christ, and to give of oneself to other, inspires great acts of love. Yet the veneration of sacrifice for its own sake can validate painful losses that are no longer life-giving. Faced with such ambiguities and struggling to discern the boundaries of giving, Christians need a new interpretation of the symbol of sacrifice.

The Paradox of Christian Sacrifice explores a revised understanding of authentic sacrifice in terms of dedication to others for the reign of God. Sacrificial self-giving becomes a means to Christian identity—a paradoxical way to find life in the fullest. Ultimately, sacrificial love is not only an imitation of the cross, but an image of the creativity of God.

"Feminist theologians have long challenged traditional Christian understandings of self-sacrifice for being embedded in patriarchal structures that demand unjust sacrifices of women. In this excellent, thought-provoking work, Erin Biviano acknowledges the importance of these criticisms and, drawing upon the work of Edward Schillebeeckx and Paul Ricoeur, explores healthy ways in which this central Christian ideal can be understood. This is an important contribution to constructive theology."
—Leo D. Lefebure, Matteo Ricci Chair, Georgetown University

"This first book on Christian sacrifice that not only faces up to its negative distortions and confusing complexity, but also begins to do justice to it as a profoundly positive and fulfilling experience. A must-read."
—Robert J. Daly, S.J., Professor Emeritus
of Theology, Boston College

Erin Lothes Biviano received her doctorate in systematic theology from Fordham University. She lives in New York City.

Paperback, 0-8245-2456-X

crossroad